Lord George Sackville at the age of forty-two, *by Sir Joshua Reynolds.*

SACKVILLE OF DRAYTON

Also by Louis Marlow :

Welsh Ambassadors: Powys Lives and Letters
Mr. Amberthwaite
The Lion Took Fright
Fool's Quarter Day
Swan's Milk
Forth, Beast !
The Devil in Crystal
&c.

SACKVILLE OF DRAYTON

(Lord George Sackville till 1770.
Lord George Germain 1770–1782.
Viscount Sackville from 1782.)

By LOUIS MARLOW

EP Publishing Limited
1973

Copyright © 1973 Kenneth Hopkins and the
Estate of Louis Wilkinson.
First published by Home and Van Thal, London,
1948

Republished by permission of the original publishers

This edition published by EP Publishing Limited
East Ardsley, Wakefield
Yorkshire, England

ISBN 0 85409 972 7

Please address all enquiries to EP Publishing Limited
(address as above)

Printed in Great Britain by
The Scolar Press Limited, Menston, Yorkshire

TO

NIGEL STOPFORD SACKVILLE

In gratitude for the great help that
he has given to this book.

CONTENTS

LIST OF ILLUSTRATIONS

Chapter I

CUT BY HIS OWN DUST

No figure of English eighteenth-century history has been less justifiably ignored than Lord George Sackville. In many works that treat of the period his name is not so much as mentioned, or is mentioned only to be curtly dismissed. Remembrance of him comes often with effort even to those who have some special interest in the eighteenth century. Those who do know something about him feel for him usually either a faint or a violent distaste. "At the mention of Lord George Sackville Mr. Balfour turned quite red. And I pointed out," Sir Arthur Conan Doyle continues, "that not only was Lord George a coward, but a most debauched man." Those public blushes of Arthur James Balfour's must have been infrequent, for Lord George's name could not have many times offended his ears. Conan Doyle was confusing Lord George with the libertine Earl of Sandwich, the famous "Jemmy Twitcher." On the same page of his *Reminiscences* he says that Martha Ray, the actress, "murdered by her true lover, the clergyman Hackman," was Sackville's mistress, whereas she was in fact the mistress of Sandwich. An unusual misjudgment of Sackville: those who know his name are as a rule content to think vaguely of him as the man who ran away at the battle of Minden and who helped to lose the American colonies.

A significant example of the general indifference to Lord George is found in Miss Victoria Sackville-West's book *Knole and the Sackvilles.* Miss Sackville-West casts a hurried glance at this particular relation only to repudiate him. She calls him "an incongruity among the Sackvilles, a departure from type," and "judges it best to leave him alone . . . and to seek neither to blacken nor to whitewash his character. I scarcely regard him as one of the Sackvilles." As for his part in the battle of Minden, in the American War, and in the complicated tangles of eighteenth-century politics, let others determine how it should be judged, she is not interested in this cuckoo in the Sackville nest. "For some reason Lord George never awakened my interest or my sense of relationship. He was a public character, not a relation."

It may be that Lord George's lack of literary distinction predisposed Miss Sackville-West to her acknowledged indifference. She quotes his words,[1] "I have not genius sufficient for works of mere imagination," and indicates that, unlike his ancestor, the great Elizabethan, or his grandfather, of Restoration fame, he was neither a dramatist nor a poet, nor even a patron of letters. He was, however, a writer and speaker of individual clarity, eloquence, irony, and power; and he was a patron of the dramatist Cumberland: though it is true that he was not a professedly literary man and it was said of him that he hardly ever, in his fine library, opened a single book.

As a character in eighteenth-century public life Lord George is pre-eminent. Before Minden, his importance as a political influence was unquestioningly recognized. "I do not conceive," writes Lord Shelburne who disliked him, "that any but the checks which stopped his military career could have prevented his being Prime Minister." During the American War he was Colonial, or "American" Secretary, and was much more valid in his direction of that war than was the lazy and witty Lord North. Nathaniel Wraxall writes that the responsibility for it "reposed principally upon his shoulders." "Not long after the commencement of the fatal American War he was suddenly hoisted to the management of it," is the phrase of Horace Walpole, who speaks also of his being "adopted to repair Lord North's indolence and inactivity." Lord North, though he had never any love for Lord George, referred to him as "a man-of-war," to himself as "an old hulk." He accepted whatever the Colonial Secretary proposed. Till Lord George took

[1] The context shows that what he somewhat ironically meant was genius sufficient to admire works of imagination to their authors' satisfaction. See p. 230.

office, there had been " no spirit or sense " in the conduct of the war.

Perhaps Lord North is remembered and Lord George forgotten because it is convenient to associate so perfunctory a Minister as the " somnolent " North with an episode so discreditable to English prestige as the unsuccessful attempt to break the resistance of colonists inspired by the greatest and oldest traditions of English freedom. Lord North and George the Third—" the two heaviest and worst sailers," as the Colonial Secretary, with his critical astringent humour,[1] dared to tell the King to his face—are exactly the right political figureheads of the inevitably losing cause that was fought for in that " unpopular and unprosperous war :" and against their names are set in vindication the great names of Pitt and Fox and Burke, champions of American rights, and the notable name of the libertarian Wilkes. Lord George, by far the ablest man on the wrong side, is almost wholly left out of count, although his rare qualities and high distinction, his " great talents of which there could not be the smallest competition," his integrity, his, for that or any age, astonishing and often embarrassing honesty, his " virtue " in the Roman sense, were recognized by all his more perceptive contemporaries. Since his death he has had no effective recognition or vindication, although few statesmen or military commanders merit them more than he does.

He was a great man *manqué*, a great man undone by accident, by his own qualities, and by his exalted birth. Like a diamond, he was " cut by his own dust." It was by accident that he incurred, at the battle of Minden, a disgrace that poisoned his whole life. The details of this controlling and determining mischance will be examined in a later chapter; it is enough now to note that both during the battle and at the consequent court-martial for disobedience to orders it was the very virtues of the man, and his unmitigated aristocratic temper, which overthrew him.

[1] Complaining to the King of the neglects and dilatoriness of the Admiralty and Ministry, and of the badness of the transports, he said : " But I must say, Sir, that the two heaviest and worst sailers are *The King* and *The Lord North.*"

After Minden, Lord George was continually the object of hatred, abuse, and persecution. Although neither at Minden nor elsewhere had he shown cowardice, and although he was not charged with it at the court-martial, he bore its enduring stigma. He never knew when the false coinage ring of "coward! coward!" might not sound in his ears. At no time could he feel himself immune from open taunts and jeers, or from bitter innuendoes, from scarcely veiled insult. These he often determined to disregard, and was sneered at afresh because he did so, however obvious it might be that silence was fitter than any reply, and that he could not be for ever using his energies and time, and suspending his pride, by a lengthening sequence of repetitive speeches in self-defence.

Singular pleasure and satisfaction have always been derived from bringing not only the charge of cowardice, but charges of any sort, against highly placed and distinguished persons who are on trial or in discredit. The names of Sackville's mistresses, who, even if all possibilities are accepted, were modestly few considering his period and his station, were canvassed grinningly in the newsprints of the day; while other ladies were invented for him, so that those who professed or pretended moral decorum might take their due offence. The most fantastic accusation of all—that of sodomy—was reserved for the author of the *Essay on Woman,* who phrased it with a grossness remarkable even for his writings. Few men of note, however, escape that charge in any age, and Wilkes, if Wilkes were the author, may have thought it a pity to omit it in Sackville's case, especially as he could find so few normal indiscretions with which to credit him. Lord George suffered from libel and slander because inferiority was compensated and envy gratified by denunciations of the fallen great, no less than it is in our own time. In the days just before the abdication of Edward the Eighth, and later, with increasing venom, vilification of the most various degrees and kinds of falsity was prompted by the malice of the envious common man. The abdication instrument had hardly been signed before the Duke of

Windsor was publicly censured for immorality and morbidity, for cowardly desertion of duty. That the great should be "guilty," that the great should "fall," must always give profound satisfaction to the little, not only because it allows release to their punitive instincts, but because it makes them think themselves finer fellows morally as well. They are compensated; and they can combine, in the face of such a spectacle, sadism with moral unction. Leading articles and sermons after Edward's abdication gave pious blackguardism what it wanted, and so did George the Second's homily after Sackville's court-martial, that the disgrace was "worse than death to a man who has any sense of honour," and that "neither high birth nor great employments can shelter offences of such a nature."

Sackville was indeed too well born for his own good. His egregiously famed and ancient family was a real handicap to him, his character and the controlling accident of his life being what they were. That an English Sackville in command of English troops should be in anything but form subordinate to a German commander whom England had consented to help must have seemed to him an unreal situation. As a soldier, he was of course well aware that he was expected to obey his titular superior, the foreigner; but he could hardly have considered himself bound to suspend his judgment when orders proved dangerously ambiguous; likely, in his view, to provoke disaster and futile waste of English lives. This course he could not take: he was too responsible, too authoritative. Authority and responsibility were in his blood, in his upbringing. That was why Prince Ferdinand of Brunswick found him so difficult, hated him, and pursued him, after Minden, with unappeasable rancour, as did a host of others, notably including George the Second.

It was this authority of Lord George's long inheritance that made for him enemies so many, so tenacious, so exultantly vindictive. It was an authority that often showed stiffly and harshly in one who had so little adaptability of demeanour and so much uncompromising honesty. Unlike most aristocrats, he could not keep his pride, his "arrogance " in order when expediency gave the hint. He had no opportunist " give," no careerist discrimination. Always he behaved like himself, often without regard for those who, because of their position, their relation to him at the moment, might obstruct his advancement or trouble his security and peace. In the face of his own danger he was all the more intransigent, all the more " haughty " and " overbearing " in the authoritative sureness of his conduct. Certainly he was not haughty, or reserved, among his intimates. But he could not, in craft, put off his pride, he could not be shaped by political necessity: he was disinterested. That was why he puzzled Horace Walpole so much, Walpole who naturally cannot at all account for him and who contradicts his own opinion of him not infrequently. If Sackville's regard for his own interest and his skill in furthering it had equalled his talents, he would now be among the most famous figures of his century.

It was not only at Minden that he overthrew himself. If he had kept quiet after Minden, if he had submitted to the deprivation of his command and offices, if he had been shrewd enough to draw back for later leaps, the Minden disgrace would have been in time forgotten. George the Second, his enemy, had only a year more to live; George the Third was his friend. It was the court-martial of 1760, the operative venom injected into it, that so deeply impressed the public mind, the army mind, the mind of Parliament; it was the court-martial that pamphleteered and lampooned and cartooned him, and the court-martial was held at his own insistent demand.

Never had Sackville believed himself guilty in any degree. It was his utter unconsciousness of guilt that made him behave, immediately after Minden, in a manner that so infuriated Prince Ferdinand. " Voilà cet homme," exclaimed the Prince, indignant and astounded, as Lord George mingled with the officers at the Prince's own table after the battle, " voilà cet homme, autant à son aise comme s'il avait fait des merveilles ! " Sackville at no time doubted that he had been unjustly condemmed on Ferdinand's representations. Every effort that he could use must be brought to defeat such injustice, not only for his own sake, but for the sake of English military prestige, and for the honour of his family.

He was too strongly indurated in his caste, he was too far isolated by it, not to lose some of the sharpness of those realistic contacts which his natural endowments would have ensured for him had he been less highly born. Himself of a courageous integrity so traditional, so taken for granted, that he was hardly more conscious of it than of the circulation of his blood, he could not be expected to understand the reluctance of other military men to acquit when there was suggestion of cowardice, their natural touchiness on that point, their fear lest, if they acquitted, they might be suspected of cowardice themselves. He could not focus either their moral cowardice or its implications, could not see that they would not dare to recognize his courage in taking a course that laid him open to the charge of poltroonery. He expected, indeed, complete rehabilitation from the court-martial. Instead, he was condemned, escaping narrowly the fate of Admiral Byng ; and was exposed to the utmost possible additional public obloquy by his sovereign, who eagerly proceeded to deliver what he thought was the *coup de grâce* to the man who was down.

But Sackville can hardly be said to have been "down," even when most disgraced. It is not easy to humiliate a man so resolute in "taking fortune's buffets and rewards with equal thanks," and one so well fortified by ironic humour. When the Secretary of War, soon after Minden, told him that he would be dismissed from the command of his regiment, and from his Generalship, and from his Lieutenant-Generalship of the Ordnance, Sackville, in reply to the Secretary's enquiry, said that he would prefer to be informed of these degradations in writing. He was told that that would be easy; "for I know but one precedent, that of the late Lord Cobham. I will send your Lordship the same." Sackville smiled, and replied: "I hope your Lordship will send me a copy of Lord Cobham's answer, too." This was the same

Lord George who, in unshadowed days, when the preacher Whitefield desired to offer his spiritual services to the soldiers at Chatham, instructed his aide-de-camp to "make my compliments to Mr. Whitefield; and tell him, from me, that he may preach any thing to my soldiers that is not contrary to the articles of war."

Yet, for all his defences of irony and equanimity and fortitude, the court-martial sentence, with its declaration that he was to be "for ever incapable of serving his Majesty in any military capacity whatsoever," gave him the severest shock. It changed him profoundly. Even, in some degree, it alienated him from himself. Thanks to the remembering malice of his enemies, it hardened and embittered him, though not in his private relationships. To his wife, to his children, he was always tender and understanding, showing his humanity unwarped. Amends for Minden might have been made to him by the high ministerial office which he held under George the Third, by the vindication implicit in his holding it. But, by mischance again, this rehabilitating promotion of Lord George[1] to the Colonial Secretaryship during the American War could give him no glory at the time, no success, even, and no fame thereafter. It was impossible that it should. He was no libertarian to "rejoice that America had resisted." He believed that the American colonies were wrongfully rebellious and must be subdued. It is useless to speculate upon what might have happened had Lord George, under an illumination of preternatural foresight, suddenly changed himself and his political convictions, and, with miracle-working will and power, scattered every article of the creed of his colleagues and wholly reversed the administration's American policy. The inevitable fact was that he took office and remained in office as the convinced upholder and promoter of the "usurpations and oppressions" which the Americans resisted, as the consistent and unswerving enemy of their "rights." He sought the success of a policy which could not possibly have succeeded. Whatever his genius,

[1] Now Lord George Germain, after his inheritance of Drayton from Lady Betty Germain in 1770.

he could not have achieved his aim. Failure, preluding and ultimate, was assured for him, as it would have been assured for any other, from the day when he took office. He was further obstructed by the corruption, by the " mercenary intrigue and treachery " of some of his colleagues : and, most importantly, by the incapacity of the British generals; though even if those generals had shown a good deal less incapacity than they did, American resistance, the new and strong American spirit, could not of course have been broken, it could only have been rather longer held at bay. But, as actually happened,

Gage nothing did, and went to pot,
Howe lost one town, another got;
Guy nothing lost, and nothing won;
Dunmore was homewards forced to run;
Clinton was beat, and got a garter,
And bouncing Burgoyne catch'd a Tartar;
Thus all we gain for millions spent,
Is to be laugh'd at, and repent.

Such generals made Lord George's task the more palpably hopeless. Horace Walpole, after suggesting that the recovery of America was unattainable when Lord George entered in office, comments on the literally unparalleled disgraces that befell British arms and declares that they were " sufficient to blast if not demolish any Minister so inauspiciously seconded by fortune."

It is clear that the twofold tragic irony of Lord George's life was shaped by his Colonial Secretaryship and by the Minden battle. At Minden he was said to have " lost, by the error or misfortune of a moment, an opportunity that would have ranked him for ever among the Marlboroughs and Brunswicks," though that opportunity was lost, not only by mischance, but by the temper of his nature. By the second accident he rose to high political place at a crisis (one out of how many that might have given him triumph and lasting fame) from which a new obloquy was for him the only issue. This was Lord George's " second chance " : thus was the disgrace of Minden compensated. Ill fortune has hardly more monstrously abused any figure of history, or worked such malign havoc by abortions and malformations of the purposes and energies of a man with so evident a capacity for greatness.

Chapter II

ANCESTRY AND EARLY LIFE

THE family name of Sackville is more widely reputed than any of its bearers. Family antiquity and might, and the fame of Knole, have overcast the distinction of individual Sackvilles; so that, while few English people have not heard of the Sackvilles in general, many know little or nothing of the three who are most notable: Thomas Sackville, first Lord Buckhurst, Lord Treasurer under Queen Elizabeth, part-author of the first English Tragedy, and, though not included in *The Oxford Book of English Verse,* author of one of the greatest of English tragic poems, *The Induction of Buckingham*; Charles Sackville, the Restoration wit and poet, less important than Thomas though better known by name, because, as Nell Gwynn's "Charles the First" and the hero of a riotous escapade, he was a livelier and a more scandalous figure; and George Sackville, the eighteenth-century soldier and statesman, of whom this is the first biography.

Lord George Sackville, born in January, 1716, was the grandson of the second Sackville poet. His ancestors were Normans who took their name from a small Normandy village and came to England with the Conqueror. "A Race of Patriots, as eminent for their Abilities as for their Quality, who have signalized themselves in almost every Reign since the Conquest, in the Service of their Country."[1] "They have never branched," said Lord George, "during more than seven hundred years." His own account of the family, as reported by Sir William Wraxall to whom he gave it, is

[1] From an address delivered to Lionel, Duke of Dorset on behalf of the Lord Mayor, Aldermen, and Sheriffs of Dublin in September, 1731.

largely concerned with the two most distinguished of his ancestors, Thomas and Charles, and with his father, Lionel, the first Duke of Dorset. He does not refer to a fact on which he surely sometimes reflected, Thomas Sackville's choice of the theme of "illustrious but unfortunate men," but he remarks on James the First's ill luck in not having Thomas Sackville for his adviser instead of those disgraceful and calamitous favourites, Carr and Villiers.

Edward, Earl of Dorset, grandson of the statesman and poet, was an interesting and distinguished man, though not a great one. He was a friend of Lord Herbert of Cherbury and a cavalier soldier during the Civil War. He fought in most of the battles, from Edgehill to Naseby. Lord George testifies to his exceptional virtues, adding that his life was shortened and the end of it embittered by the fate of Charles the First. He survived his King by only three years.

Lord George describes his grandfather, Charles Sackville, as "the patron of men of genius and the dupe of women all through his life." "Bountiful beyond measure to both," he spent most of his fortune, and his fortune was considerable since he inherited not only the Sackville estate, but, through his mother, that of the Cranfields, who were Earls of Middlesex.[1] His son, Lord George's father, was impoverished by this extravagance. Comparatively impoverished: he was eighteen at his father's death and his guardians could allow him only eight hundred pounds a year when they sent him to travel on the continent. Charles married three times, but Lord George feels that "only one of these marriages contributed either to his honour or his felicity." His first wife, the Countess of Falmouth—"a teeming widow, but a barren wife," Dryden called her—was a celebrated wanton, although as a maid of honour she is distinguished in *Grammont's Memoirs* as "the only one possessed of virtue and beauty." Charles was nearly fifty and had been for about ten years Earl of Dorset when he married his second wife, a daughter

[1] In 1675 Charles, hitherto Lord Buckhurst, was created Earl of Middlesex and Baron Cranfield. Lord George's eldest brother had the courtesy title of Earl of Middlesex.

of the Earl of Northampton. Lord George describes him as "already enfeebled by the excesses of Charles the Second's dissolute reign, in which he led the way." This second marriage, however, resulted in Lord George's father's birth. Lord George's view that it was his grandfather's only good marriage is not due merely to a natural bias, but it seems fully justified by the character of the first wife and by that of the third.

Charles, a few years before he died, "married," says Lord George, "a woman named Roche, of very obscure connections, who held him in a sort of captivity at Bath." This marriage is not recognized in the Peerages. Lord George was evidently strongly impressed by the mental and physical decline into which his grandfather fell. His own habits of temperance and self-restraint were probably inspired and confirmed by his contemplation of so warning an example. "Extenuated by pleasures and indulgences, the Earl of Dorset sunk under a premature old age, though not as early[1] as Rochester, Buckingham, and so many others of his contemporaries had done, including Charles the Second himself." During his "last illness, or rather decay," his third wife let hardly anyone near him, and she was said to have taken every advantage of his condition of "imbecility." There was talk of appointing guardians for him to prevent final depredations upon the family estate. The story of Matthew Prior, who was one of Dorset's protegés, being sent down to find out if he were in his right mind, is fairly well known. "Lord Dorset," he reported, "is certainly declined in his understanding, but he drivels so much better sense even now than any other man can talk, that you must not call me into court as a witness to prove him an idiot."

It is pleasant to think that Charles, whose wit had been so brilliant, whose gallantry so exquisite and so generous, and whose poetry had such charm, was something like himself even then. Lord George, though so well aware of his grandfather's hedonism and the harm it did his health and the family fortunes, has some good to say of him. He speaks of

[1] He was, after all, nearly seventy when he died.

his services to Queen Anne before her accession, and to William the Third. Charles, after James the Second proved himself an enemy of civil and religious liberties, was an ardent advocate of the Revolution. He escorted Anne on her memorable escape from Whitehall to Nottingham. While she was on her way from the Palace to St. James's Park where a coach awaited her, she lost one of her shoes in the mud and Charles at once took off his white glove, put it on her foot, and saw her safely to the coach. William the Third would have been very willing, it was said, to recognize his debt to him by making him a Duke, but, said Charles, " The Earldom of Dorset is quite good enough for me."

To Swift, resentful of his libertinage, his extravagance, and his notorious pranks, this Earl of Dorset was " a dull companion and the most universal villain I ever knew." " He had small learning or none." Horace Walpole is fairer : " He had as much wit as his first master, Charles the Second, as his contemporaries, Buckingham and Rochester, without the King's want of feeling, the Duke's want of principle, or the Earl's want of thought." Walpole realizes the peculiar charm of Charles when he says that " He might do anything and yet was never to blame." " The best good man with the worst-natured muse." Pope called him a holiday writer, and so he was. He could be that, and write with witty malice, too. One of his " worst-natured " poems is in manuscript at Drayton House. It is an interesting manuscript, with alternative readings :

Tell me, Dorinda, why so gay,
All (With) this embroidery, fringe and Lace,
And (The) jewells than burn night to day
The dimness of thy eyes betray,
And ruines of thy face.

So have I seen in Larder dark,
Of Veale a Lucid (rotten) Loyne (Joynte?)
Adorn'd with many a lambent (heatless) spark—
As wise Philosophers remark,
At once both stink and shine.

Lord George's father was born in 1687, and became the first Duke of Dorset in 1720, when Lord George was four years old. His mother died when he was a child, so his grandmother, the Dowager Countess of Northampton, had most to do with his upbringing. She was a friend of Queen Mary,[1] who told her always to bring the little Lord Buckhurst, as he then was, to Kensington Palace with her. Lord George recalls what must have been his father's earliest memories, of playing with a child's cart in the palace gallery. One afternoon, when Queen Mary had made tea, King William, in conference with his Cabinet, kept her waiting and she grew impatient. The four-year-old Lord Buckhurst ran along the gallery, dragging his cart after him till he reached the room where the King was and knocked at the door. "Who is there?"—"Lord Buck."—"And what does Lord Buck want with me?"—"The Queen is waiting for you, and you must come to tea at once!" The King laid down his pen, opened the door, took Lord Buck in his arms, put him in the cart, and gave him a ride down the gallery to the room where the Queen and Lady Northampton and others were waiting for their tea.

The story begins pleasantly enough, but does not go on as such stories usually do. King William was asthmatic, the effort he had made affected him disagreeably. He threw himself into a chair, could not speak for some minutes, and had the greatest difficulty in breathing. Everyone was in consternation. Lady Northampton would have punished her grandson, but the King, recovering his speech, told her she must not.

Another story told by Lord George about his father's infancy shows the amiability both of King William and Queen Mary. The Queen used to embrace and pet little Buck whenever he was brought to Kensington, and, knowing this, his nurse, whose brother had been condemned to death, gave the child a letter in which she begged her Majesty for a reprieve.

[1] Queen Mary was also a friend of Lady George Sackville's grandmother, Lady Mary Forester, to whom she wrote letters very contemporaneous, good hearty coarse ones. Quotations from them are in the Appendix, pp. 250-252.

Without saying anything to his grandmother, Buckhurst handed the letter to the Queen. She passed it on to King William, who ordered an enquiry. Again the story does not end as it should: it was decided that the man must be hanged. The Queen gave the little boy a purse of money for his nurse, asking him to tell her how sorry she was.

When he grew up, Dorset, as Earl and as Duke, was as zealous an anti-Jacobite as his father had been. When Queen Anne died, he was sent, a young man of twenty-seven, to Hanover, as one of George the First's escort to England. He was with the new King in the coach that took him from Greenwich to London. Thirteen years later[1] he was chosen to convey to George the Second the news of George the First's death. As the preparation for his suitable appearance on such an occasion took some time, he sent his wife on before him to communicate these welcome tidings at Kew, where George Augustus and Caroline, as Prince and Princess of Wales, had been living on the worst possible terms with the Sovereign. George Augustus was in bed when the Duchess arrived: he always undressed and went to bed after dinner. The Duchess insisted that she must see him, and told the Princess why. The Duke would be here very soon: not a moment must be lost: the Ministers wished the new King to come at once to London: a Privy Council must be summoned, a proclamation issued. Yes, said the Princess, she quite understood, but she could not possibly disturb her husband, he had only just gone to sleep. "Besides, he won't believe it. He'll say it's a trick."

The Duchess remonstrated. She repeated that delay would put everything awry: the Duke would expect to find George Augustus ready to start at once. So the new Queen took her shoes off, opened her husband's door as quietly as she could, and crept up to his bed, while the Duchess waited just outside the bedroom. "*Was ist das ?*" George muttered from under the bedclothes. "I am come, Sir," said his wife, "to announce to you the death of the King, in Germany."—

[1] What follows is Lord George's account. Quite different accounts have been given. See Mr. Peter Quennell's *Caroline of England*, p. 117.

"That is one damned trick," said George, "I do not believe one word of it." She assured him it was true, then threw herself on her knees to kiss her Sovereign's hand. She beckoned to the Duchess, who came in and knelt and kissed and assured also. George Augustus, convinced at last, consented to get up and dress. Dorset arrived in his coach-and-six as soon as the new King was ready and they both left then for London.

Lord George was his father's favourite son: the Duke's two elder sons, Charles, Earl of Middlesex, and the melancholy Lord John, disappointed him. That Lord George was much the ablest of the three he had never any doubt: the fact was too evident. Neither did he doubt that his youngest son was abler than himself. The Duke was a well-balanced, cultivated man, but not a strong one; he was of no more than moderate ability: and he had quite enough good sense to be aware of that. He looked with confidence and pride to Lord George to sustain and to enhance Sackville repute: to him, more tragically than to anyone, even than to Lord George, the disgrace of Minden was a disappointment and a defeat.[1] It was collapse of his dearest hopes. He was sensitive, singularly vulnerable in his affections: his portraits show it, his conduct shows it, and so do his letters. He lived on till 1765, five years after the court-martial, in unhappy retirement at the end of a life which he had spent honourably and with distinction in high office. The periods of his two Irish Lord Lieutenancies, when Lord George worked with him, or, sometimes, in control of him, are for later discussion. The Duke was always in much closer contact with his youngest son than he was with any of his other children. They were together, not only at Knole and in London and Dublin, but in Paris during Lord George's early youth. The affectionate intimacy between them is evident, year after year, from the letters that they wrote to each other.

For all the ceremonial panoply that had to invest him, the Duke's essential simplicity and lovableness, qualities

[1] "The poor old Duke went into the country some time ago and (they say) can hardly bear the sight of anybody."—Thomas Gray, in a letter.

not usual in men of rank of that age, remained apparent. He was always extremely popular and much sought after, not only because of his position as " the first nobleman in Kent." " When at Knole, he was so beloved and respected that on Sundays the front of the house was so crowded with horsemen and carriages as to give it rather the appearance of a Princely Levée than the residence of a Private Nobleman."

The Duke's letters, with their unformed childish handwriting, their unlettered style and punctuation, are engaging and naïve; as when he writes to Lord George " from ye Bath Decr ye 10th, 1757 " :

> " I must trouble you with my thanks for your letters, and particularly for that which I have this moment receiv'd, surely the King of Prussia has not his equal, we are all here in great joy, I hope Blues &c : will not hang, much longer, we are all in good health and desire our compliments to you and Lady G., Mother has had no return of her disorder, and I think grows better and better every day, we have sometimes strange news from Ireland, If you have any, I should be glad to hear it—I am, &c. &c : D,"

Reassurance about the Duchess's disorder was justified: she lived for another ten or eleven years, surviving her husband by three. She was Elizabeth Colyear, daughter of General Colyear, brother of the Earl of Portmore. She had been maid of honour to Queen Anne, and was till the last decade of her life a figure in the inner circle of the Court. When the death of Frederick, Prince of Wales, was announced to his father, George the Second, she was present with Lord George, playing cards at St. James's Palace in Lady Yarmouth's apartments, and heard the King informing their hostess, his mistress, without much feeling, that " *Fritz ist dode.*"

The Duke's many tender references to " my dear Colly "[1] show a continued affection unmistakably sincere. He was a devoted husband, though, after the fashion of his time, not a

[1] " Dear Colly," or " Little Colly," was the endearment for her also among intimates with the family. Sir Robert Walpole writes to the Duke : " I desire you will be my proxy and kiss the Queen of Ireland's hand for me, but Little Colly's—I don't presume to think of."

faithful one. Like his father, he enjoyed the solaces of women: he was well pleased by pretty low-born girls, he was as companionable to them as to all his friends and acquaintances. The famous actress Peg Woffington was one of his delights; he used to be rallied about her. Among the Drayton House papers are some bantering verses,[1] "The humble Petition of Margt. Woffington, Spinster," addressed to the Duke. They may have been written by Lord Middlesex or Lord John Sackville.

After his father, the most important figure of Lord George's boyhood was probably his maternal grandfather, now Marshal Colyear. He stayed with him, was often in his company. The Marshal had served with distinction in all the sieges and battles of the Low Countries under William the Third, and was with the Duke of Cumberland throughout the Scottish insurrections of his time. That the reminiscences and the personality of so seasoned a soldier should have fired his young grandson with military ambition is certainly probable; Lord George's bent towards a military career may have owed its origin or its determination to this early contact. But, as so often during his early period, the matter is for conjecture. Not much is known.

Lord George was born in the Haymarket, where his father then had his London house. He was named after George the First, who was his godfather and was present at his christening. One of his first memories was of being taken, when he was five, to the gate of St. James's Palace to see the great Duke of Marlborough as he came out of Court. This impressed him. Expressing his recollection of the event in the adult language of the time, he describes Marlborough as being "then in a state of caducity," but "still retaining the vestiges of a most graceful figure." "He was obliged to be supported by a servant on each side, while the tears ran down his cheeks, just as he is drawn by Johnson, who says, 'From Marlborough's eyes the tears of dotage flow.'" This was only a year or so before Marlborough's death.

Of his two brothers, Charles and John, and his three

[1] Appendix, pp. 252-254.

sisters, Anne, Elizabeth and Caroline, it was Caroline, the youngest, afterwards Lady Milton, who was Lord George's favourite. This was probably so in his boyhood as it was later. But there would seem to be no letters, no records, no anecdotes, to show that it was; and it is not intended to draw from imagination for pictures of the little George playing at hide-and-seek with his favourite sister under the historic shadow of Knole. Nor are there any available details of much interest about Lord George's schooldays. At Westminster School, when he was twelve, he was one of the boys who composed and recited verses in Latin and English on the Coronation of George the Second and Queen Caroline. This is said to be a "true copy" of his original Latin verse:

Delicium et caput Angliacae, Gulielme, juventae,
Carmine te tenui Musa coeva canit.
Spes cresce in nostras et TU, si justa benignum
Respiciant coelum vota, Glovernis eris.
Hunc rapuit Puerum mors immatura; Britannae
Tu decus esto puer gentis, et esto senex.

Such a composition is one of the more familiar, though less pleasing effects of a "thorough grounding" in the classics; and it is evident, from Lord George's style of public speaking and writing, that, like all educated men of his period, he had been well schooled in Latin and Greek. But history was at Westminster School his chief interest. His memory was remarkable when he was a boy, as it was later. He went on to Trinity College, Dublin, where he is said to have cultivated especially the study of literature; but there is little certain information about his Trinity days. One of the bedrooms at Drayton House contains a not very admirable or revealing picture of him in the Trinity College academic dress, a picture which one would willingly exchange for even the scantiest account of the nature and the effect upon him of his reading at this time. That he was interested and rewarded by his early literary studies cannot be doubted: his feeling for the use of words, his sense of their values, are, during his later life, evident again and again. For vivid, clear, and memorable expression Sackville had an inherited talent, emphatically marked. "Like a ball in the breast," he replied, when asked how Lord North took the news of the fall of Yorktown. He disliked anything in the nature of unnecessary adornment or circumlocution, this man who "would assert that fine words were not meant to be understood," and of whom it was said that "in perspicuity he has never been excelled."

It is perhaps true that most of Lord George's speeches and most of the letters written by him in his public capacities give a stronger impression of the weight and clarity which distinguish eighteenth-century prose than they do of these qualities as they distinguished Lord George himself; and many of his private letters suggest that his occupation was to express public policies. Writings of eighteenth-century public men are apt to wear the often somewhat heavy mask of that period; a mask that gives them an air of formality and even of sameness to us. Authors appear in their letters of this age, as of any other, with more flexibility and variety; the mask conceals them less, for their occupation is individual expression, they aim at it and they have the habit of it. Lord George was not an author; but in the expressions that he used the man comes out, whatever contemporary gestures he may feel bound to make. How often, by those gravely featured, conventionally balanced sentences, his own irony waits.—"Though nothing can be more expressive of your Patriotism and zeal than your generous proposal I cannot in the present moment encourage you to follow it."—"I find myself debarred the satisfaction of contributing to your Happiness and ease." A kindred humour appears sometimes in the foreground. "The people are very fond of him [the King of Denmark] and most impertinently curious, so that he has little comfort in seeing sights, since he is always made one himself."—"I shall be in town that month as I am threatened at that time with a fourth daughter."—"I have not seen the letters of the Duke of Cumberland and Lady Grosvenor, and I should be obliged to you for them, as I am curious to see the Royal manner of making love."—" Mr. Pitt spoke with great ability . . . Garrick never acted better. He was modest, humble, stout, sublime, and pathetic, all in their turns, and tho' the matter was as open to reply as possible, yet the manner and language was not to be equall'd."

In almost every letter there is something, at least, of the substance of Lord George's identity. He writes with a clear[1] direction, an honesty, a generosity, a pride, that are his own; a male tenacity is implicit.

Of his time in Paris with his father no more is known than of his time at Trinity College. To George Coventry, who was convinced that Lord George was Junius, it seemed that it must have been then that Sackville-Junius saw the burning of the Jesuitical books by the Paris hangman. He may have had that experience: that he had many new and quickening experiences in Paris and that he enjoyed their novelty with the zest of his years, is certain. To any intelligent and responsive youth a first visit to the Paris of that day must have been full of excitement and delight. With susceptibilities and energy heightened by the stimulus of the Paris scene, Lord George became rapidly much better versed in the French language. That he spoke and wrote French unusually well all his life, that his knowledge of French sharpened and pointed his English and gave perhaps some added edge to his irony, were important results of his father taking him to Paris while he still had the impressionability of early youth.

1 " Your accounts are so clear and so ably drawn that I fancy few like them come over to this country,"—Lord Bute in 1758. " The unwary frankness of the Secretary of State."—Charles James Fox, of Lord George as American Secretary.

Chapter III

DUBLIN AND IRELAND

Dublin, in the middle of the eighteenth century, was a gay, lively, and exciting city to live in, full of wit and mirth and scandalous report. " All the spirit or wit or poetry on which we subsist," wrote Horace Walpole, " comes from Dublin." His Irish years were, on the whole, the happiest, the most unclouded, of Lord George's life. He had the reputation of being " the gayest man in Ireland—except his father." This " tall man with a long face, rather strong features, clear blue eyes, a large make," had then more of the " quickness " than the " melancholy " which Lord Shelburne says were mixed in his look in later years: that " mixture . . . such as is seen in the antique statues often to accompany great beauty."

Nothing can throw into stronger relief the inhibiting and embittering effect upon him of his court-martial than a comparison between the young Lord George, so free, so debonair, at work and play in Dublin, and the Lord George of middle age, disillusioned, saddened, mortally hurt, defensive against an irreparable injustice; though he was never for long incapable of the humour, the charm in companionship, the ease and lightness of conversation that were native to him.

In Dublin, where he spent much of his earlier youth and of his later thirties, the most provocative variety of spectacles was presented, especially on such an occasion as the arrival of the Lord Lieutenant. When the Duke of Dorset, with Lord George, his Principal Secretary and Secretary of War for Ireland, returned from England in 1753, this event threw the whole city into the greatest excitement. It feverishly quickened the susceptible pulse of Dublin life : violent activities were on every side engendered by hope of gain, while normal activities were with equal violence disordered.

> "Now the L—d L—t arrives, Tradesmen gaping, Ladies of Pleasure busy, coaches, boats, and windows full. Workshops empty and Porter Houses thronged. . . . The daily Papers are stuffed with begging Petitions from Candidates for Boroughs, large promises, sinister influence, and dexterous corruption. . . . House rents in Dublin rise, Room-Keepers are ejected and shifting for new Lodgings, which are let to London Sharpers and kept Misses . . . Old Lovers are discarded, Plain Coats are hideous, Lace is in vogue . . . Now are the Fry of Poetasters and Scribblers raking the Dunghill of Flattery for Encomiums on the Viceroy. Happy the Gales that wafted him over to the bless'd Hibernian Shore ! Similes on the Prodigious Likeness between His Majesty and the Noble Representative. . . . Not a Drudge or a Curate but spurns at the Reading Desk and looks at the Episcopal Chair; while every Right Reverend squints at the Primacy . . . Members hire better Scholars than themselves to polish their Speeches and mend bad Spelling . . . The Fellows of the College prepare a most elegant speech in Ciceronian Latin for the ear of the L—d L—t . . . Emphitical Criticks with skrew'd Faces in the Pit, damning, censuring, or praising, they know neither why, what or wherefore . . . Seamstresses, Milliners, and the Train of Female Dressers, fitting out young Miss for Conquests at the Castle . . . Taylors and Barbers busy in the Creation of Beaux, Smarts, and Fribbles. . . . Women of the Town laying in their Stock of Flimsy Gowns, Gauze Shades, and Petenleres, to Bell away in. . . . *The old Tune*—Whores in Hackney Coaches, *Hum !* and Honest Women on foot. *The old Trade*—Play-houses full, and Churches empty. *The new Stile*—Eleven Days gone with Child, and the old one Barren."[1]

In this Dublin, among these "strange Wretches, these Irish," as an English Lord with an Irish pension called them,

[1] From the *Dublin Spy*, August, 1753. The Duke of Dorset's first Lord Lieutenancy was from 1730 to 1737. He was again Lord Lieutenant from 1750 to 1755.

the youngest son of the Lord Lieutenant appeared resplendent, in the pride of his youth. "Not so grand a dress," his sister Caroline writes to him in 1754, "as you had last year to make a fine figure in Dublin." He and his father were extravagantly courted and flattered. Lord George could have kept pace with his most inordinate inclinations, but the gaiety of "the gayest man in Ireland" was not of the current masculine stamp. He was never in any danger of being, in William Hickey's characteristic phrase, "a martyr to a life of excess." He did not immoderately drink or wench or gamble; he had a natural contempt for drunkenness and for paraded debauchery. In a letter to his father, written from Dublin in 1737 when the Duke of Devonshire was Lord Lieutenant, he says of the Duke: "I think as yet he does not look the worse for his drinking, he has almost killed his aide-de-camps already, and I am afraid that Gardiner will be much the worse for this winter's work." And, a fortnight later: "My Lord Lieutenant din'd yesterday at Howth, and tho' he came away at six a clock contriv'd to be as drunk as any of his predecessors have been at this place." In another letter to his father at this time Lord George vividly describes the proceedings at the Boyne Club: "The bumpers went about very fast, and those that were left grew very drunk. Cunningham stood up and in a great bumper drank the Duke of Devon's health, and said, thank God we have now a Lord Lieutenant that will keep his word and will do no jobs. Young Allen answer'd that he hoped he would at least except the last for he was sure he was incapable of doing either. He said that by God they were all alike and that the last was no better than the rest, upon which Allen told him he lyed. Then swords were drawn, and the company interpos'd and the quarrel was made up . . . Cunningham . . . excus'd himself by saying he was drunk and knew nothing that he had said or done."

Unlike his famous grandfather, Lord George kept silence about his love-affairs. He was out of sympathy with the contemporary goodfellowship which led a man to treat his own gallantries as a topic for amusement of friends and acquaintances, as a savour for polite casual conversation, a goad for drawing-roon and dining-room wit. But, though impressing strangers and inferiors—often unfavourably—by his aloof dignity or hauteur,[1] he was, in youth as in age, seldom inapt for lively entertainment of or by those whom he knew and liked. From his earliest years he had learned to accept wit, suppleness and adroitness of spoken phrases, good sense and spirit in good talk, as natural accomplishments. He had listened to Lady Betty Germain[2] in racy intimacy with his father, the " iron pelt of words " of the great Dean Swift was familiar to him; he had been often diverted by the brightly glancing flippancies of Lord Holderness, who talked as he wrote, and by Bubb Dodington's forthright expletive chatter—" God, no body keeps any treaties with us, why should we keep any with them, faith, hey ?" Lord George had, though with a difference that his nature gave it, the relish of his period for pungent small-talk, for that scandalous and barbed chit-chat or tattle which in that age reached the last limit of its development, its extremity of *leger-de-main,* and exhausted, perhaps, all its possibilities as a *genre.* Prudes and romantics may look back with distaste to the conversational cut-and-thrust, the persiflage and repartee, the unshamed levities of a libidinous and heartless century, agreeing with Hannah More's denunciation of that " cold compound of irony, irreligion, selfishness, and sneer," but, with our machine-made pleasantries, what have we to-day in its place? Their wit, however cold and malicious, had, at its least and lowest, the organic energy of life.

During the Duke of Dorset's second Lord Lieutenancy, intrigues and scandals in London were, it seems, under eclipse. There was nothing to talk about. " Nothing is stirring," wrote Lord Holderness from London in 1752, " which would afford your grace the least amusement. Point de petites intrigues, point de galanteries. Vos belles

[1] The Primate, in 1754, wrote denying that Irish dissensions were due, as asserted, either to " Lord George Sackville's haughtiness of behaviour " or to his own ambition: not a surprising denial.

[2] This lady used to write with characteristic spirit to Dean Swift. " Let me see you in England again, if you dare . . . I defy you in all shapes ; be it dean of St. Patrick's governing England or Ireland, or politician Drapier. But my choice should be the parson in Lady Betty's chamber."

compatriotes les Gunnings font toujours l'admiration de tout le monde, mais gardent toujours, peut-être malgré eux, la même condition et le même nom." The Miss Gunnings were not the only beautiful Irishwomen who went over to England at this time. "I ought to prepare you," Lord Hardwicke wrote to the Duke, "for one ugly hampering business before you return. It is an application from the English ladies to prohibit the importation of beauties from Ireland. It is thought that your fair subjects are making reprisals upon ours for the many draughts the latter have made of fine gentlemen from that kingdom."

In Dublin much was stirring, all the time: amusements, gallantries, intrigues. There the imported wealthy English aristocracy might mingle in social delights and in debauch with the native impoverished artistocracy, whose passion for show and for all kinds of extravagance was inexhaustible. From the Castle to Parliament House, from Parliament House to the theatre, the coaches rumbled through the dilapidated streets, carrying their immaculate passengers, bewigged and scented, adorned with laces and bulrush fribbles, fashionably inhaling snuff through delicately contracted nostrils. Gaming was prominent among the diversions imported by the English caste. In Lord Carteret's time this proclivity of English rulers inspired a poem on the erection of a groom-porter's house to adjoin the Castle chapel, where

A wall only hinders union
Between the Dice and the Communion,
And but a thin Partition guards
The Common Prayer Book from the Cards.

"Pious Boulter" was adjured to behave like Christ with the money-changers, and

Drive out this unbelieving Crew,
The Fop, the Soldier, and the Beau,
In Pieces crush this damn'd Device,
Burn all their Cards and break their Dice;
Desist, o F—d, for none believes
That House to be a Den of Thieves.

The gamesters drank; everyone drank. "After the D. of Dorset's health, your lordship's was the toast, and with great zeal in the drinking. This, you know, is the way of judging in Ireland."[1] "More Burgundy is drunk in Dublin in a week than in London in a month." Not only more, but probably better. Claret in Ireland was certainly better and more easily obtainable, if the account given by an Irish clergyman in 1761 may be trusted. In London, at *The George*, he "call'd for a Bottle of Claret, but as they had none in the House we were contented w*th* Humble port. W*t* strange vicissitude was this to me who had just Left ye Best Claret to Drink ye Worst Port."

All Ireland was notorious not only for its hard drinking but also for its illicit wine and spirit trade. When cargoes of spirits were landed at Dublin Quay, the Commissioners, due notice having been given them, looked the other way.

The English in Ireland, unlike the Irish natives, ate as copiously and as richly as they drank. "They keep always a good Table," writes "Hibernicus" in 1727, "and that is one of the first things they establish. After the Table comes the Mistress, whom they entertain at an extraordinary Expense." Morals, a generation later, were unchanged. "The love of the sexes is much indulged this winter," the *Dublin Spy* announces in 1753, recounting contemporary Dublin phenomena. "Sharpers at the Tavern with my lord and men of Sense with his Butler in the Cellar. Q. Which keeps the best company?" "Actors drinking Burgundy for the good of their Creditors; and Actresses intriguing for the good of their Health." "Every Woman has her own Amours, though she looks as cold as a Vestal. . . . Horns sprouting abundantly . . . the Charity of Women tending to their favourite Passion, the Cause of Propagation, Bravo! my Girls!" "The Women themselves have thrown aside all Veils as superfluous things; they laugh at Queen Bess and her Muff. They strip their breasts even down to their Mid Waste and Beauty prostitutes her Mysteries to the Eye of the Common People." It is surprising, after this, to learn

[1] The Primate to Lord George: February, 1753.

that "Imaginary intrigues and fancy'd Joys are boasted of by every Petit Maitre in Town." The ambitions of some of the younger ladies, however, passed beyond the scope of mere pleasure: "Now young Beauties form sanguine Hopes of sharing the happy Fate of the Miss Gunnings; dream of Coronets; Titles and Equipages."

But the incursion of the English nobility, though inspiring the more venal with expectation of release from that poverty which so irked the Irish few and degraded the Irish many, was viewed with distaste, and even with abhorrence, by all Irish patriots. No reader of the *Dublin Spy* could fail to be aware of that. "The Kingdom is full of Bugs and English Locusts, they infect our very Bedposts. Come, Drapier!—Dean! Gulliver! or what Title thou delight in, help my Song, inspire my Breast with some of thy Humour, thy darling Irony to conquer these Brobdignags, these Houhynyms which infest thy native City."

The great Swift knew, indeed, in what state Dublin and Ireland really were. Among the multitudes of Irish poor the standard of living was the lowest imaginable: the conditions of decivilization throughout Ireland were disorderly, savage, and brutish. Dr. Hotham, afterwards Bishop of Ossory and then Bishop of Clogher, wrote graphically to his "warmest and steadiest friend," Lord George, about the poverty, the physical and moral degradation of Ireland in the 1770's, giving him perhaps some clearer pictures than he had ever had the opportunity of seeing for himself. Writing from Dublin Castle in the summer of 1777, this postulant for a bishopric cannot accustom himself to the "inveterate sloth and shocking poverty of the lower classes of natives." In the winter of the same year he writes:

> "Though I am now full ten months gone in Ireland, it is rather difficult for me to give an account of the country. The very little of it which I have hitherto had an opportunity of seeing, I must frankly confess does not enchant me. The mud fences and rough stone walls, both of them unfinished at best, if not ruinous, as they generally appear to be, and the next to total absence of wood, hurt my English eye

very much; nor can I reconcile myself as yet either to the excessive dirt and poverty of the natives, or the universal dejection of mind visible in the countenances of the lower sort. They are certainly cruel also and savage in their nature, and as ignorant of all law, and indeed averse from all wholesome restraint of it, as the wildest Indians. They are slothful, gloomy, obstinate, and ungrateful; and neither improved by benefits, nor sensible of kindness.

"This must be understood of the peasantry, and most inferior ranks. If we consider those who stand a step higher, who have votes for members, who serve on juries, and in short are reputed of some sort of consequence . . . I fear an account of them, if truly given, will not be very favourable. They are absurd, shortsighted, tumultuous, and corrupt; and such friends to perjury on almost all occasions, that though no people go more to law than the Irish, I believe there is no country in the world where real justice is so seldom done by the determination of a jury.

"With regard to the lowest orders of gentry, I mean those who calling themselves esquires, and being called so by their neighbours, live by their dog, their gun, and fishing net, or by retailing the land which they rent in the wholesale, a practice which is the bane of this Island—I can say but little of them, not having hitherto fallen in their way; but as far as I can hear or discover, they are not a race of beings from whom much information, or advantage of any kind is to be extracted, by any human chemistry.

"As to the Nobility and Gentry of landed property, they are of two kinds; foreigners and natives. The first are such as possess considerable property in Ireland, and enjoy it elsewhere. To these lovers of their country, I have nothing to say. The last, that is the natives, live indeed in Ireland, and enjoy their possessions so thoroughly and in a manner so truly Irish, that they generally become beggars in a few years' time, by dint of hospitality and inadvertence. From distress of circumstances to modern Patriotism, the transition is not uncommon, but daily;

indeed the one is the certain consequence of the other. Accordingly they all turn Patriots, and vociferate in Parliament; where, if nature do not admit of their being able, custom I am sure does not prevent their being abusive, to an astonishing degree; and scurrility we all know is the forerunner of places, pensions, sinecures, &c., &c., &c., which in this country have the singular property of gathering like snowballs, and multiplying themselves and one another, *ad infinitum*. In short, either from the want of public virtue, or superabundance of it, in people here, (I will not pretend to decide which,) Ireland seems an unfortunate country. Its size, situation, soil and climate, make no part of its misfortune; for it is peculiarly happy in them all. It suffers only by the conduct of its principals. Would but the chief people of the Island open their eyes to its real interest, and therein their own, Ireland would be a favoured spot; but I have long said, and do maintain, that its first and greatest enemies are the men of the greatest rank, property, and popularity in the country; and so long as they continue their present line of conduct, so long will Ireland infallibly continue in the state it is; namely . . . growing every day worse and worse."

No wonder that, things being as they were, Sir John Irwin should, two years later, be fearful of Irish rebellion. The "volunteers," ancestors of the Irish Republican Army, might be capable, Irwin thought, of "forcing England to consent to all the demands of this country. What can we do? We disapprove of all these violences, but we have the bayonets at our throats and must submit." After a few more months General Irwin was writing again to Lord George in the same vein, telling him that British authority "is more than shaken, for I think it is gone." The only thing that gives him any comfort at this time is that "the House of Commons is now shut, thank God, for six months." But, whether the House were shut or open, the "democratick and enthusiastick" spirit of Ireland, of which the then Archbishop of Dublin so bitterly complained, was equally "ready to burst out at any moment."

Some friends of English Government were not, however, oblivious of Irish wrongs or ills. The Primate, Dr. Stone, in 1753, wrote Lord George a forcible reminder of the calamitous state of the Irish roads, which "all over the country are gone to ruin. The tolls are mortgaged so as to leave nothing for the repairs, and the tax upon the people still continues without any benefit to them. This affects every person in the nation. That grievance has arisen from mismanagement, but it is a grievance . . . If the government were to take the lead it would be a very extraordinary mark of the King's attention to the internal affairs of this country . . . The roads are almost impassable and there are no funds for repairing them." The Bishop of Derry,[1] some twenty years later, was profoundly convinced both of the justice and the necessity of a "seasonable indulgence" to Roman Catholics and Presbyterians. "Whilst Benjamin's mess is distributed only to a few Episcopalians you cannot wonder that the rest of the brethren should do something more than murmur. 'Tis unreasonable to expect equal loyalty where there has not been shown equal favour; the crop will ever correspond to the culture, and woe betide that farm where one spot is cherish'd and the rest neglected. One happy, masterly stroke may save Ireland for ages; its ruin shall not lie at my door."

The same inequities prevailed year after year. The English Parliament, with corruption and bribery, continued to introduce English "creatures" into positions of authority, creatures who "were obliged to oblige those who created them." Venality spread and became general. It was in a natural dependence upon general disregard of law, and against law "the entire nation, high and low, was enlisted in an organised confederacy." "Distinctions of creed were obliterated, and resistance to law became a bond of union between Catholic and Protestant, Irish Celt and English colonist." "There are several Protestant gentlemen in the county of Kerry," wrote the Duke of Devonshire in 1740, "yet for one odd reason or another there is little prospect of doing good by their means."

[1] His letter, undated, is to Lord George *Germain*.

Blame for Irish conditions has been thrown, with violence, not only upon English oppression but upon Roman Catholic influence. Disciples of Froude will protest that the roots of Ireland were mortally sapped by a degenerate faith which, unfailingly co-operative with the forces of disease, accumulates rot and poison in itself and infects its victims with them more rapidly and more surely than any other faith in the Western world. They will urge that, under cover and protection of the Papists, horrors were perpetrated which stand out in hideous relief even against the general barbarity of that age and which even to-day are hardly surpassed by the cruel abominations current in Europe. It is not proposed here to enter upon a field of battle that has for so long so loudly resounded.

With Irish problems and Irish idiosyncrasies Lord George Sackville came into close contact during important periods of his life: early in youth during his father's first Lord Lieutenancy, when he finished his education at Dublin University; after the Duke of Devonshire had succeeded his father, when he stayed on in Dublin as Clerk to the Council, and at the same time held his first military commission as Captain of Guards in a regiment on the Irish Establishment; from the age of thirty-five to thirty-nine when he was Principal Secretary to his father and Secretary of War for Ireland,[1] and sat for the borough of Portarlington in the Irish House of Commons; and in 1765, at the age of forty-nine, immediately after his father's death, when he was for a year Vice-Treasurer of Ireland. At the end of his life, as a member of the House of Lords, he showed his continued concern for Irish affairs.

It will have appeared that the position of the King's representatives in Ireland was difficult and unenviable, that administration of English injustice was not only an inglorious task but one which it was impossible to execute efficiently, and that the Irish were no more amenable then to alien domination than they have ever been. Horace Walpole, in one of those frequent attacks upon Lord George with which

[1] Lord Chesterfield, in 1751, described him as " the Duke of Cumberland's military man of confidence in Ireland."

he redresses his hardly less frequent encomiums of him, declares that "the insolent petty tyranny of Lord George Sackville during his father's Lord Lieutenancy first taught Ireland to think"; but Ireland had thought, and thought disturbingly, long before the Duke of Dorset took office.

English destruction of the Irish cattle and shipping trade in the 1660's, of the woollen trade in 1699; the consequent heavy drain of money from Ireland, and the attempt to deal with this by the patent to coin half-pence, granted in 1720 to George the First's mistress and sold by her to the iron-master, Wood, were all events calculated to provoke Irish reflection. Swift, as is well enough known, gave a great deal of envenomed thought to Wood's half-pence in the *Drapier Letters,* and not only to the half-pence. His indictment of the whole recent course of English rule in Ireland is still the most memorable ever made.

From a condition in the middle of the seventeenth century of at least moderate prosperity in some branches of manufacture, trade, and commerce, Ireland had been brought, by the beginning of the reign of George the Second, to ruin. Not only Irish trade, but Irish political independence, had been killed, and Irish religion penalized to the extreme. In 1719, eleven years before Dorset's first Lord Lieutenancy, was passed the Act, "the Sixth of George the First," that gave the English Parliament the right to legislate for Ireland, and deprived the Irish House of Lords of their rights to hear appeals. The period of the penal laws, with their ruthless persecution of Roman Catholics, had begun a generation earlier. Protestant ascendancy, after the Treaty of Limerick, was complete, because the English Parliament, to the extreme chagrin of honest King William, at once broke that treaty, in faith of which Limerick had surrendered at the end of the war of the Revolution. All Ireland was now to be governed and almost all Ireland possessed by its Protestant minority. Law after law subjected the crushed and beggared Catholics[1] to

[1] The Bishop of Derry had good cause to assure Lord George that "the Romish clergy and the people of that persuasion hold everything cheap in comparison of their religion."

exclusions, to forfeitures, to prohibitions. They could hold no civil or military office, could not sit in Parliament, could not possess arms or carry swords, could not be lawyers or doctors, could not teach, could not buy land. "A Protestant Ireland for the English" was the unswerving policy of the Lord Lieutenant and all his imported officials, a policy obstinately continued throughout the eighteenth century, long after it had been proved and proved again that Irish subjection and Irish ruin could not make English profit.

Recent excesses of English policy towards Ireland made the Lord Lieutenancy a peculiarly invidious and unpopular office for the Duke of Dorset when he first assumed it, nor was it any less so when he was re-appointed twenty years later, with Lord George Sackville as his active adjutant. Both he and his youngest son, as representatives of British rule, acted of course invariably in what they thought were British interests, which must, in the very nature of the case, be Irish[1] interests as well, just as their interests at Knole were also the interests of their tenants. Ireland, to the Duke and Lord George, was an English estate, and a very difficult one to manage. They took England with them to Ireland, they took Knole with them, acting for their king and country as they acted at home for themselves and for the Sackville posterity. They were not more rigorous than they thought they had to be. The Duke, indeed, was often kindly and considerate, as when he allowed the Irish Catholic gentlemen to wear their swords again.

Whatever either of them had done, no good could have come of it. Compromise, severity, abdication, would alike have tended to the same inevitable though distant end: complete Irish independence. All Lords Lieutenant, or Viceroys, of earlier Irish times and later, had the same sterile and vexatious task. Lord Buckingham's numerous letters to Lord George in the 1770's show plainly enough that Ireland under his Lord Lieutenancy was exactly the same Ireland,

[1] "The Duke of Dorset, whose zeal for his Majesty's service and regard for the true interests and happiness of Ireland long since endeared him to the kingdom, and have formed the unvaried rule of his Grace's present administration."—The Lord Chancellor of Ireland to Lord Holderness, July, 1753.

giving exactly the same sort of trouble, as when Lord George was there. " I can answer for nothing," said Lord Buckingham, and much more. No wonder that by 1755, when he had had so much of it, the Duke of Dorset asked Lord George to write that he " neither desired nor declined continuing in his office." He knew by then, and indeed long before, that the English in Ireland were always being called upon to " stop the ocean with a hurdle." Lord Buckingham expressed later, in this phrase, what the Duke, Lord George, and Dr. Stone had felt long since. " I have no opinion of their acquiescing," the Primate wrote to Lord George in 1753, " till they see that the alternatives must be their ruin." And often, he must have known, not even then. What could be done with a people so blind to their own interests ? This tedious and wearing recalcitrance was always cropping up, always making fresh difficulties.

Attempt to survey these varying and recurrent difficulties in the detail that they presented during Dorset's Lord Lieutenancies would be unprofitable here. The Duke's concern, and the concern of Lord George, who was more closely and more laboriously involved than his father with Irish administration, bore mainly upon Irish money matters and the intractabilities of the Irish Speaker and the Irish Parliament. Former Lords Lieutenant had aimed at keeping the Irish House of Commons in order through the Speaker, whom they courted with that end in view. So he had come to have too much power; and Lord George and Dr. Stone successfully urged Dorset to get the English Government to remove him in 1754. Lord George had tried kindness first. He offered the Speaker a peerage and £1,500 a year. The reply was a blunt one, full of pride. " If I had a peerage, I should not think myself greater than now that I am Mr. Boyle: for t'other thing, I despise it as much as the person who offers it." To Henry Boyle, as to other Irish patriots, Lord George was " the known enemy of this country."

In the previous year the Earl of Kildare's[1] famous " Memorial " had protested to George the Second that

[1] Afterwards first Duke of Leinster, and Lord Edward Fitzgerald's father.

> the Duke of Dorset's son, Lord George, though in high and lucrative employment already, not satisfied therewith, has restlessly grasped at power, insatiable in his acquisitions. That the Primate, who is now on the pinnacle of honour, connected with the said noble Lord, has made use of his influence to invest himself of temporal power, and like a greedy churchman, affects to be a second Wolsey in the senate. That influences being so predominant, corruption is so formidable, and election so controlled by the mighty power of these two statesmen, your loyal kingdom of Ireland feels the sad effects of it, and dreads the Duumvirate, as much as England did that of the Earl of Strafford and Archbishop Laud.

This Archbishop Stone, with whom Sackville acted in such close collusion, certainly was a wordly and most politically minded ecclesiastic, who did not for long have to "squint at the Primacy." An Englishman, son of a Lombard street broker, he came to Ireland with the Duke of Dorset as his chaplain in 1731. After having been hurried through two or three Irish bishoprics, he was still "unwarrantably young" when he became Primate in 1748 at the age of forty. He wrote a great many long letters to Sackville about Irish politics. These, and the letters of Sackville himself, show how always exacting and how frequently dull the Principal Secretary's official life in Dublin must have been. But it was a useful political training, and Lord George[1] made his reputation as an exceptionally able and reasonable man of affairs. He had not much chance of doing more than that. He was no more fortunate in the opportunities which Ireland gave him than he was in those of his later life; and it was with relief that he left Ireland, after four years of service, to take up again the military career which was what he had always really wanted.

[1] "Whatever trouble you have had," Pelham wrote to him, "it has only served to set off your character of ability and integrity. May you be as useful to the King and your friends here as you have proved to your father and his servants in Ireland." In another letter Pelham "heartily rejoices at the great success of the King's affairs in Ireland" under Dorset's Government and Sackville's Ministry. But he knew how harassing those affairs were. "One more bill, I conclude, will finish your sessions, at which time I presume your Lordship will not be the most unhappy in Ireland."

Yet he must have been glad to remember much of those Irish years. It was the time when his abilities were first tested and realized. He was in full vigour, his savour for life and his gaiety unabated; he was young, not rich,[1] as he was later, but without family cares: and no disaster had come upon him. When he gave up his Secretaryship and left Ireland for an English command as major-general in 1755, the year after his marriage, he was not yet forty, and he had still four years before Minden. In Ireland he had known bitter opposition and enmities, but they had not scarred him: they were expected and received as the natural incidents to his position. He had his friends, his companions, with whom he could forget political vexations and clamours. Dr. Stone, for all his intriguing careerism, must, with his lack of "learning or sanctimony," have been an agreeable man to spend a few hours with when he was off duty. To Sackville he was not merely a clerical Lord Justice, a prelatical adventurer, for ever writing lengthy dispatches about pensions and Spanish pistoles and the linen premiums. They were good friends. The Primate is one of the very few who writes to Sackville as " My Dearest Lord "; and during his last illness in 1764 Lord George's continued sympathy with him is evident. " I doubt much of his having strength to get over it after all that he has suffer'd." " Cuninghame says he bears his illness with great firmness of mind."

Lord George would have remembered then all the more amiable idiosyncrasies of this busy archbishop; his pleasant appreciation, his sound understanding of the amenities, his engaging zest. Dr. Stone had a palate for wine; so discriminating a wine-drinker as he was must have had much good in him. The letter—unfortunately the only one of its kind—in which he records his disgusted disappointment with the atrocious wines palmed off on the Lord Lieutenant, throws his better nature into bright relief. Vastly refreshed, the reader of his other letters, packed with politics,

[1] Sir Robert Wilmot wrote to him a few months before his marriage, advising a trifling legal expedient "which would save your lordship some guineas, which, as you are a poor younger brother, and likely to have an increasing family soon, may as well be laid out on a coral for your first child."

sighs with regret that this prelate should not have been content to live his life as a retired connoisseur, a mute Herrick, immune from vulgar ambition. Perceptive of wine, he could not have lacked perception of other values, and what rich and generous years they would have afforded him, if only he had allowed himself due leisure and not been led astray by the itch for authority. Even as it was, he did his best, and he hoped. "I promised myself last year the pleasantest winter that could be. Notwithstanding all that happened I had infinitely more pleasure than pain. I will make no more promises to myself, but in all probability we shall repay ourselves for former troubles and have time to enjoy all the season of leisure without anxiety." The Primate's disappointment of some two years earlier about the Duke of Dorset's wine had been, however, less tempered.

"I have tasted" (he writes in May, 1751) "all the different wines sent for the Lord Lieutenant and find to my great concern that there is nothing but the claret which can be made to answer any purpose. Of the two sorts of champagne that sealed with wax might go off at balls, if there were a better kind for select meetings. The red wax is too bad for an election dinner at Dover. The four parcels of Burgundy are almost equally bad. If there is any difference that sealed with black wax and falsely and impudently called Vin de Beaune is the worst, and is indeed as bad as the worst tavern could afford; but I am sure that no person will ever drink a second glass of either. I know how unhappy his Grace and you [Lord George] would be to see the tables so provided. What can be done I know not. You have been most scandalously abused, but I doubt his Grace will not think that a sufficient excuse for bad entertainment through a whole winter. The claret called Chateau Margaux is exceedingly good; the La Tour very good; but the smallness of the bottles (though a trifling circumstance compared with the others) is so remarkable that I am very apt to conclude the whole business has been dishonestly transacted, and I am confident that not a drop of the wine so called was ever in the province of Burgundy.

"The melancholy operation of tasting was performed at my house yesterday. General Bragge, and eight or nine more . . . were present and agree to this sentence in the utmost extent. To prevent as far as I could any fancy or prejudice I slipt in a bottle of my own Burgundy, and they all cried out 'This will do.' I would not have you persuaded that the fault is from want of keeping or from having been disturbed in the passage. If I have any knowledge, the wine is fundamentally bad. It is a vile infamous mixture and never can be better. The only security against its going worse is that there is hardly room for it."

It was no such wines as these that made glad the hearts of the Primate and his guests at those "pontifical repasts" which lasted till early morning, amid the "Popish magnificence of Archbishop Stone," which "nothing seen in England could rival."

Five years later, almost to the day, Dr. Stone was writing a very different letter to Lord George, who had by then left Ireland. Fallen now, he wrote of why he had been disgraced, and of the indignities put upon him. "Considering that I am looked upon as a man abandoned and left without a single friend to lean upon in England and that all power there is to be exerted to break and crush me, and that it is a point determined from thence by the present administration both there and here that I am not to be taken up in any public way of business or confidence . . . I am surprised that so many people are ready to persevere in avowing their regard for me." Lord George is the man he is most anxious to see in his distress, he is the one friend upon whom he knows he can lean in assurance of the sympathy which can now be his only help or solace; and he will come to England immediately, on hearing when he is to come. It was about this time that Dr. Stone declared that, although his legs had been cut off, he would make a good fight on his stumps.

To Lord George the picture of himself and the Irish Primate as wielders of a usurped and oppressive authority over a resentful, suffering people was not one that could have presented itself. He knew, of course, that Ireland was ill at ease and very difficult to deal with; he must have realized, before he left office, the "Herculean labour of recovering English influence over Ireland": but that it was his duty to govern the country as a loyal supporter of the Royal prerogative he never questioned. In his position it was not easy to gauge realities, not easy to appreciate "the little awe in which Ireland stands of the mother-country." To Lord George in Dublin there were evidences of awe, and of good feeling too. Though the English wool might be burnt there and the mob groan at the houses of the Lord Justices, and his father and himself be lampooned,[1] and attacked by Lord Kildare, there was much, so it seemed, to be set against such unpleasant incidents as these. The Duke of Dorset was personally popular, and shown to be so. In the *Kit Cat Club Memoirs* it is noted that he "did his duty as became a loyal subject to his prince, yet managed to keep on good terms with the rabble; and to have effected this . . . must have required no inconsiderable generalship." "It is agreed on all hands," so Lord George was assured,[2] "that no Lord Lieutenant has ever been so attended as his Grace was, and among the prodigious number of people who assembled to see him pass there was no sign of ill humour, but all the decency and respect imaginable. It may perhaps be accounted for how it happened that nothing like an insult was attempted on the streets or upon the North Wall, but I am sure nothing could have prevented any indecent indications of disrespect from the windows of the houses . . . This behaviour of the people in general must have proceeded from good will, and it may certainly be concluded from it that the attempts to poison and enflame them have by no means had the desired effect."

[1] When to the King it is complain'd
What base advantages they gain'd
And how the Packets were detain'd
That they may tell their Story,
His honest Heart will take it amiss,
His Viceroy, too, perchance dismiss,
And for Lord G—ge we've a Rod in P-ss
Will make him dance a Boree.

From the Patriot Club song, 1755. It was about the Money Bill.

[2] In a letter from Alexander Bisset, who writes from Dublin in May, 1754, describing the recent departure of the Duke of Dorset for England.

Such an account must have confirmed Lord George. The praise of his own work, the tributes of his friends, were also constantly reassuring. The jolly letters of his intimate friend Captain Cunningham, as well as his company, must often have cheered him. " I am just now come from drinking your health at the Solicitor General's. Stannard dined with us. He says nothing is wanting but resolution to make everything go well. His toast was 'Resolution to our friends and let the Lords Justices take care of themselves.' "

But towards the end of Lord George's time in Ireland there were deepening shadows of intrigue against the Duke of Dorset and of his loss of favour at Court. Cunningham's letters did not always make agreeable reading. Dorset was liked, even beloved by many, but not by all of those who had the ear of George the Second. " The hopes of your ennemies," Cunningham wrote to Lord George in August, 1754, " seem to be founded upon the supposition of his Grace being out of favour with his Majestie." A week later Lord George heard from Thomas Waite of a report that " the King has rump'd the Duke of Dorset lately three or four times and did not speak to his Grace at the levée." The Irish patriots rejoiced at a rumour that Lord Chesterfield was shortly to replace the Duke, " to quiet the minds of the people." The policy of the Duke, a moderate man, was not acceptable to either side. Dr. Stone, in the same August, was complaining to Lord George that the Lord Lieutenant refused to support his own and the royal authority and was thus losing credit both for himself and for those attached to him. Dorset stood too firm to please the patriots, and not firm enough to please Dr. Stone. Everything, during that last year of Lord George's in Ireland, was going worse. " The spirit of patriotism," wrote Cunningham, " is higher than ever and Government more abused." One difficulty followed another, and nothing could be at all satisfactorily settled. At length, early in 1755, Dorset was dismissed. Walpole says that he " bore the notification ill," but, only the month before, he had disclaimed any desire to stay on. He did point out that a recent meeting of the

Opposition had been less violently offensive than usual. Lord George, however, discounted this, and characteristically observed that one temperate meeting could not justify a belief that "animosities were composed." He agreed that it would be better that his father and himself should not return to Ireland.

After Dorset's dismissal the Irish popular party triumphed. The new Lord Lieutenant was Lord Kildare's intimate friend; Henry Boyle was made Earl of Shannon; and in the following year Lord Kildare was appointed one of the Lords Justices. It was Lord George Sackville's first defeat, a grave one. It was also, ironically in view of later events, a defeat for George the Second, who most unwillingly consented to these significant changes in Irish rule.

Those years of Dorset's first Lord Lieutenancy, when Dean Swift was living and Lord George was at Trinity College, and the time when he was Clerk of Council, had pleasanter memories. Swift, greatest champion of Irish rights, had never treated Dorset as an oppressor. He liked him well and knew how to treat him; he was an old friend of the family, proud of it, and very ready to take all the advantage he could from it. He was very friendly, too, with the Duke's close friend, Lady Betty Germain.[1] To her, and to the Duke, he wrote long and intimate letters, from which it is clear enough that his regard and affection for them both were not at all affected by political disagreements. The Duke, during his second Lord Lieutenancy, must often have wished that Swift were still alive. But it is not likely that Lord George did. For Swift he had the natural intolerance of early youth; to him the great Dean was a wrong-headed, irritating, trouble-making old man, a rather ridiculous one, too, and not quite right in his head. When he was twenty-one he wrote from Dublin to his father: "The coinage has made a great rout here and the Dean has shewn himself more mad and absurd than ever." Lord George's sympathies were all with the "poor Primate" who had been "greatly threatened by anonymous letters, so that he has been oblig'd to have a

[1] Appendix, pp. 262-264.

corporal and six men lye in his house every night for this month past to secure him from any insult. The other day at the Lord Mayor's feast the Dean before all the company talked against lowring the gold, and told the Primate that had it not been for him he would have been torn to pieces by the mob, and that if he held up his finger he could make them do it that instant."

It was after all to be expected that Swift's obsessive mania for power, so strikingly exemplified in the incident which Lord George records, should have sometimes exasperated his contemporaries, both young and old; and that neither Lord George, nor the Duke, placed as they were, should have recognized Swift's extraordinary genius or realized how high a privilege they enjoyed in their contact with one of the most original men who has ever lived.

Swift's letters[1] to the Duke are largely taken up with requests for favours; sometimes for favours which others had asked him to ask, "desiring my poor good offices to your Grace because they believed you thought me an honest man and because they heard I had the honour to be known to you from your early youth." Sometimes he wrote on behalf of a protegé of his own, as when he solicits preferment for a Mr. Marmaduke Philips, "a loyal subject of K. George." He writes always with a certain formality,[2] and with deference, but with dignity; and his compliments seem to derive from a perfectly sincere regard for the Duke's qualities. He wrote of the Duke: "I do not know a more agreeable person in conversation; one more easy or of better taste; with a greater variety of knowledge." Writing to him, no doubt he sometimes said more than he really meant, conforming to courtier's convention so as to make sure of getting what he wanted. "I humbly beg your Grace, out of the high veneration I bear your person and virtues . . ." "I humbly

[1] Appendix, pp. 254-262.

[2] The duration of his official visits was exactly timed. "I should have waited on your Grace, and should have taken the priviledge of staying my usuall thirteen minutes if I had not been prevented by the return of an old disorder in my head, for which I have been forced to confine myself to the precepts of my physicians."—December 30th, 1735.

entreat your Grace to pardon this long trouble I have given you, wherein I have no sort of interest except that which proceeds from an earnest desire that you may continue as you began from your youth without incurring the least censure from the world or giving the least cause of discontent to any deserving person."

But there are other letters, less formal, with a note of friendly banter as in a letter of the spring of 1735,[1] when Swift recalls a dinner in the Duke's company, and humorously, but with no sort of satirical venom, implies his variance with the Duke on Irish politics:

> " Your Grace must remember that some days before you left us I commanded you to attend me to Doctr. Delany's[2] house, about a mile out of this town, where you were to find Doctr. Helsham the physician. I told you they were the two worthyest gentlemen in this kingdom in their severall facultyes. You were pleased to comply with me, called at the Deanery and carryed me thither, where you dined with apparent satisfaction. Now, this same Dr. Helshamm hath ordered me to write to your Grace on behalf of one Alderman Aldrich who is Master of the Dublin Barrack, and is as high a Whig and more at your devotion than I could perhaps wish him to be. And yet he is a very honest gentleman, and, what is more important, a near relation of the Grattans who in your Grace's absence are Governors of all Ireland and your Vicegerents when you are here, as I have often told you. They consist of an Alderman whom you are to find Lord Mayor at Michaelmas next; of a Doctr who kills or cures half the city; of two parsons, my subjects as prebendaryes, who rule the other half, and of a vagrant brother who governs the North. They are all brethren and your army of twelve thousand soldiers are not able to stand against them.
>
> " Now your Grace is to understand that these Grattans

[1] Another letter in something of the same vein is on p. 259 of the Appendix.

[2] Doctor Delaney was a Fellow of Trinity, Dublin, and a fine scholar and wit. He was intimate with the Sackville family. In 1743 he married Mary Granville, who wrote her Autobiography and Correspondence in six volumes. She was a niece of Lord Lansdowne.

will stickle to death for all their cousins to the five and fiftieth degree; and consequently this same Alderman Aldrich being onely removed two degrees of kindred, and having a son as great a Whig as the father, hath prevayled with Dr. Helsham to make me write to your Grace, that the son of such a father may have the Mastership of a barrack at Kinsale which is just vacant. His name is Michael Aldrich. Both your Grace and I love the name for the sake of Dr. Aldrich, Dean of Christ-Church, although I am afraid he was a piece of a tory. You will have severall requests this post, with the same request, perhaps for different persons, but you are to observe onely mine because it will come three minutes before any other. I think this is the third request I have made to your Grace. You have granted the two first and therefore must grant the third. For when I knew Courts those who had received a dozen favors were utterly disobliged if they were denyed the thirteenth. Besides if this be not granted the Grattans will rise in rebellion, which I tremble to think of.

"My Lady Eliz. Germain uses me very ill in her letters. I want a present from her, and desire you will please to order that it may be a seal. Mine are too small for the fashion, and I would have a large one worth fourty shillings at least. I had a letter from her two days ago, and design to acknowledge it soon; but business must first be dispatched. I mean the request I have made to your Grace, that the young Whig may have the barrack of Kinsale worth 60l. or 70l. a year. I should be very angry as well as sorry if your Grace would think I am capable of deceiving you in any circumstance.

"I hope and pray that my Lady Dutchess may recover health at the Bath, and that we may see her Grace perfectly recovered when you come over. And pray God preserve you and your most noble family in health and happiness."

Swift's memory was failing, for he writes about eight months later making a request that he says is the second one he has ever made directly, and he seems to forget that any of his requests have been granted. That he had expected more compliance than he had found from the Duke is evident. He chides him, tactfully. " I cannot but think that your Grace, to whom God hath given every amiable as well as usefull talent, and in so great a measure, is bound when you have satisfyed all the expectations of those who have most favor in your *club* [the Irish Parliament], to do something at the request of others who love you better and meerly upon your own account without expecting anything for themselves. I have ventured once or twice (at most) to drop hints in favor of some very deserving gentlemen . . . But I easily found by your generall answers that, although I have been an old courtier, you knew how to silence me by changing the subject, which made me reflect that courtiers resemble gamesters, the latter finding new arts unknown to the older."

A letter of May, 1736, again shows some bitterness and resentment, with irony, and refers more directly and more seriously to differences of opinion. Swift was a sick man, conscious of approaching death. The Duke was about to leave Ireland, and " considering my years and infirmities, I cannot reasonably expect ever to see you again." " My lord," he continues, " I am very sensible of my unhappiness in thinking differently from your Grace both as to person and affairs, and at what distance you thought to keep me whenever I offered to speak in favor of any one who I thought deserved well. But whether I am to be believed or no, I protest in the presence of God, that I never moved anything to your Grace which I did not think would be for your service and acceptable to those whom you appear most to value and who have the greatest veneration for you . . . I hope I have not been too importunate or too frequent a sollicitor. To put a great man in mind of rewarding virtue and merit is indeed not often after the usual course of proceeding; and perhaps by the violence of factions is less practiced at present than it hath been for many years past. For I much doubt whether one representation of persons in a thousand to a Prince, a Viceroy, or a Prime Minister be not more to serve a scheme than to reward virtue, learning or good sense."

In one of his letters Swift writes about Trinity College, Dublin, and Lord George's education there, assuring the Duke that " not onely the University but even the whole kingdom are full of acknowledgements for the honor your Grace hath done them in trusting the care of educating one of your sons to Dublin Colledge, which hopes to continue always under your Grace's favor and protection." Swift professed a higher opinion of Trinity academic and moral standards than was generally held at that time. " A Fellowship in this University differs much in some very important circumstances from most of those in Oxford and Cambridge. My Lord George will tell your Grace that a Fellowship here is got with much difficulty, by the strict examination they undergo in almost every branch of learning, to which must be added the reputation of regularity in their conduct. It is also disposed of with much solemnity."

Solemnity, learning, strictness, and regularity were not, however, distinguishing features of undergraduate life at Trinity in Lord George's time. Other characteristics must have impressed him more. Trinity College, half bear-garden and half brothel, as Sheridan's father[1] called it, had an extremer tone than Oxford or Cambridge had, either then or later. Life was wilder there. Students were always at pistol-practice in their rooms and elsewhere in the College. They carried their great keys in the tails or sleeves of their gowns and used them as " devilish good weapons on a dark night in a street wrangle or a gutter fray." One of the Fellows was murdered in 1734, the year when Sackville, at eighteen, took his Master of Arts degree. It was some dozen years afterwards that Oliver Goldsmith was beaten and knocked down by his tutor, Dr. Wilder. Later in the century a snow-balling boy was shot in the Library. Lesser violences were practised in the College Commons, where on occasion geese were thrown about, trenchers smashed, and " everything tore and broke." Lord George, as the son of the Lord Lieutenant, his noble birth proclaimed by the gold and silver trimmings of his gown, may have been more or less outside all this rough-and-tumble,

[1] He graduated five years later than Lord George.

or he may not have been. No evidence either way seems available. But this was how most of his fellow-undergraduates behaved, and he must have felt that he was a good deal further out in the world than he had been at Westminster School.

Ireland, from his Trinity College days to the end of his life, was an important part of Sackville's experience. His correspondence shows that his interest in and concern with Irish questions never abated, not even during the American War. In later life he had new and intimate personal connections with the country when his daughter Diana married Viscount Crosbie, afterwards Earl of Glandore, of Ardfert Abbey, and when his daughter Elizabeth married Mr. Herbert of Muckross. During the last year of his life he was in Ireland to see them; and his last speech, the speech that he felt he had to make though he knew he was so ill that the effort would kill him, was on the "Irish Propositions" in the House of Lords.

During his whole life-time there had been no real change in Anglo-Irish affairs, nothing of good augury for the future. Sackville's hope, just before his death, was that soon there would be. He realized that he had taken his part in what was, as his friend Dr. Hotham wrote to him, no more than a prologue. "We have as yet spoken the prologue only. The play is still to come; I hope it will not prove a tragedy; a comedy I am very sure it cannot."

Chapter IV

FAMILY AND PRIVATE AFFAIRS

OF Lord George's children his eldest daughter Diana was, from all we know of her and of them, the most spirited, the most vivid, the strongest in character, the most like her father. He was, when young, one of the gayest men in Ireland; and she, some four decades later, one of the gayest women. In November, 1778, when she was twenty-two and married to Lord Crosbie, she wrote to her father from Dublin one of the

Diana Sackville, afterwards Countess of Glandore, *by N. Dance.*

many letters which show how little constricted Lord George was in his intimate relationships. She is free to divert him with her gossip, her jests, her vanity, she knows he will enjoy it. The girl who can write in this vein is no more afraid of her father than is any daughter of to-day:

> My dear Father,
>
> I have spent a week with a friend of yours, Mr. Pery, at Edmunsbery, and been very much entertained there.
>
> Ld. and Ly. Buckingham have been obliging enough to give a Ball on purpose for me at St. Woolstan's, where I danced in great spirits, with Sir Nathaniel Barry's full consent, being now mighty well, and able to enjoy, as usual, all Amusements. We had a good deal of Company at Edmunsbery and dear Whist flourished every evening. I had the long wished for happiness of driving a little Cabriolet myself every morning and am grown an excellent coachman.
>
> I must inform you that your friend the Speaker, with all his outward gravity and demureness, is a jolly Buck at bottom, and does not dislike the sight of a pretty woman, for such, *entre nous*, am I universally thought here, whatever I may be reckoned in England, but no Prophet is a Prophet in his own country. I was much surprised as I was quietly seated one evening to feel myself pulled back in my Chair by the shoulders, and, looking up, perceived it was the frisky Speaker's doing, who vowed he had such an inclination to kiss me he could hardly withstand the longing he felt; instead of looking grave, I really burst out a laughing, and indeed well I might, when I saw that demure old face extended into a tender simper. He afterwards confessed he repented not having gratified his kissing inclination, and assured me if I gave him any encouragement he should certainly do it in spite of me. Mr. Pery was half inclined to look grave, and I to be much entertained.
>
> Poor Sir John Irwin's head is quite turned with his Mrs. Squib, he gets himself abused everywhere for his behaviour with her, he escorts her to all Publick places, sits with her in a side Box at the Play, and what is worse carried her

down to the Camp, which as he was there the first object, was thought particularly indecent, as he was continually appearing with her; she went to a charity Consert, where all the Ladies who were at Camp, had promised to assemble, but she no sooner appeared, than every woman left the room and all are exceedingly angry at his permitting her to attempt mixing with them.

We talk of returning to England in a very short time. I confess if it were not for seeing you all, I should feel sorry at leaving a Place where I have been so well received, and am so well amused. Adieu, My dear Father, I shall direct this to Richmond as my sisters do not mention your leaving that place yet.

Dutifully yrs.
D. Crosbie.

Lord Crosbie will not let me seal my letter till I make you his respects so as I have filled up all my Paper must add them here.

The Duke of Leinster told somebody the other day I was a dear charming Girl and danced like an angel.

The letter is addressed to her father at " Kew Lane, Surry."

Diana's way of writing suggests her looks. All her portraits show a young woman of individual quality, one who will have her own way[1] and whose fashion of having it would be singularly attractive. Humour, roguery, satirical flair, are in her eyes and in the beguiling catch of her lip. Without doubt she inherited her father's irony and authority, though she was never schooled to his patience.

Boiling with rage [she writes in 1790, when she had passed her first youth] against that impertinent Archbishop of Dublin I sit down my dear Sir to write to you in order to

[1] But you,
Whom we cannot command, we most fervently sue,
Let them talk of Killarney its *lovely fine* shades,
Its woods and its wilds, and its dreadful cascades,
Its mountains, its monsters—my passions are human,
Give me to contemplate a *lovely fine* woman.
—Contemporary lines addressed to Diana Glandore.

vent myself. I enclose you a Letter I received from him which I do think exceeds anything I ever read, think of his talking of my father's being so wonderfully obliged to him for a paltry living. I send you my answer under a flying seal which I beg you to read and to send to him for I do not know where the Beast lives . . . Pray send that Letter immediately as the odious wretch will have left town otherwise. God bless you, you are a dear good natured Creature and I am

Very sincerely and affect.
yrs. &c.,
D. Glandore[1]

Send me back this letter by return of the Post if you please as I wish to keep it as a sample of *gratitude*.

The letter is to "Charles Sackville, Esq.," the family adviser, the man of affairs, partner in the banking house of Sir Robert Herries & Co. in St. James's Street. He was a natural son of Lord George's brother Charles, the second Duke of Dorset.

Nearly all Diana's surviving letters are to Mr. Gladwell, who was for many years a confidential steward at Drayton House. He was banker, commissionaire, and friend to the family, who gave him affection as well as trust. Diana found him continually useful when, in consequence of her marriage, she was living at Ardfert, in Ireland. She was always writing to ask him to get her something—a flute or a frame or some foil, or money: or—most importantly and most frequently—provision of beer. In demands for beer her letters to him abound: "I cannot drink the beer at my own house and it is quite a misfortune to me." "It is a long time since you have thought of replenishing this old Mansion with comfortable strong Beer, you know my brother always allows me a large cask to be sent to me yearly, and I cannot suffer you to forget it, pray send it off as [soon] as you can, for we have not one single drop left." "My brother tells me he sent 4 Hogsheads of strong beer to Ardfert . . . pray let me know

[1] Viscount Crosbie had become the Earl of Glandore.

the name of the ship it was put on board of." " Ld. G. requests you would send him the promised strong & small Beer he says that it is a farce to imagine that good strong brewing won't keep . . . he requests he may not be disappointed as he really rejoices in a draught of good English Beer, the only luxury we cannot get in this Country." — " I want to consult with you [she writes from Lord George's house in Pall Mall] upon the possibility of taking over with us to Ardfert some Northamptonshire Man or boy who you think understands Brewing well . . . We would give him whatever wages you thought reasonable but then he must really understand it—and you would much oblige me by bustling yourself a little about it . . . You must be expeditious about this business . . . " " Now pray exert yourself on this occasion & we shall be really obliged to you." Beer, when read of in Diana's letters, achieves an almost human personality. " Let me know whether it actually set out and on board what ship it was put and let me know immediately its name & that of the Captain, that we may know where to apply for intelligence of the Vessel." One of the ships carrying the beer seems to have sunk: "It is a serious loss to Ld. G: as at Ardfert we cannot compass getting good beer . . . Pray write soon and tell me the fate of the Beer."

This matter of Beer never fails to provoke Diana's *élan vital:* but, indeed, everything provoked it. Whatever she writes about, she is always interested, impatient, eager, lively, vigorous, and often entertaining. Sometimes she writes with telegraphic urgency ; she is never guilty of *longueurs,* or of such unnecessary repetitions as those for which she joins her sister in chiding Mr. Gladwell: " My sister desired me to advise you to be a better oeconomist of your time and paper by only repeating the word *Ladyship* twice in the course of your letters instead of two dozen times, which you generally do." Lord George's daughters were evidently as " direct and to the point " in dealing with their own affairs as he was in the House of Commons. Diana frequently reminds us of her father's imperative clarity and dispatch.

To Mr. Gladwell she often writes familiarly. " Give my

love to your wife she is a good creature, & you a faithful swain, tell her I don't doubt she has added a few yards of pink ribband to her Cap for she was always famous for that colour." "Mrs. Love (I beg pardon) Mrs. Gladwell . . ." she writes; and "I beg to be kindly remembered to your old woman (I recollect the time when she would have been highly offended at such an appellation.)" "You cannot imagine Gladwell how much pleased I was with your Letter where you express so much anxiety for my health & happiness." "I write now Gladwell to inform you that we have received the busts very safe, only Ld G: bids me tell you that you are a *shaby dog* . . . for getting them in black instead of gilt frame & that he must now send them to Dublin to repair that oeconomy of yours, so you see you have a good scold by the bargain."

It was rather as a favourite dog that Diana seems to have treated Gladwell, one whom she could treat pretty well as she chose, but whom she was really fond of and liked being kind to so long as she could always bring him to heel when necessary. He was, however, much more useful than any dog. "Finding on my departure from this place [Cheltenham] that my money run short, I have very saucily drawn on you for 20 Pds." "I must begg the favour of you," she writes later on the same matter, "not to draw for your 20 Pds till you come next to town . . . as I know you are as *rich as a Jew* I shall make no apology about the matter, therefore you must needs make the best of it."

In Ireland, too, she found it hard to economize. "As in Dublin one is apt to be short of money let me know whether . . . I may not draw on you for my half year." She was often preoccupied by money difficulties. "I had flattered myself with the idea of a jaunt to England this autumn, but I fear our Finances, which are none of the best, will not allow us to stir, so I must make the best of it." Debts were sometimes a trouble. Diana, while still in her twenties, had resolutions for economy which are at some odds with her later conduct. In a letter to Gladwell of 1785, five years before her "saucy" draft, she tells him that "I was as extravagant a fine Lady as any in the world, but now being grown a good domectic [*sic*] wife I wish to clear my debts and never to run out again." All bills were to be paid " before I allow myself to touch a farthing of the annuity, so now my good Gladwell here is more trouble for you." She gives him a list " of those that are most distressed for their money & who have wrote me the most pressing letters." Twenty-seven pounds eight shillings and ninepence is owed to Mrs. Beauvais, Milliner in Jermyn Street, twenty-six pounds to Mr. Diemichien, Habit Maker, no: 12 Rathbone Place, Oxford Street, twenty pounds to Mrs. Shinglair, Mantua maker. But "my difficulties end not here."

She encloses a much more formidable account, " an overgrown bill from Butler, by the by, I think the interest he charges monstrous, would you have the goodness to write to him & promise him from me £50 next March in part Payment & the remainder as soon as I can get it ? try to satisfy him by this assurance & do not delay writing to him." Twenty pounds were to be paid " to Robinson our fine hairdresser, & if I can, a little bill of 3d. owing to Barrow Powell & Brace, Milliners in St. James's Street." She asks Gladwell to " be so good as to deduct for yourself the two Guineas a year my poor Mother used to give you."

Bills, none the less, continued to be overdue. A year and a half later she asks Gladwell to pay the whole of her last year's annuity to Messrs. Butler & Crook. " Of all my Creditors they alone have charged Interest & most exorbitant Interest it is." In 1800 she asks that a tradesman should be told " how much ashamed I am of having so long neglected settling his account." Gladwell, on one occasion at least, had to buy for her in his own name: " I beg of you to advance the Money & send it for as I have a bill there which I cannot as yet pay I should not chuse to have my name mentioned." In 1794 she tells Gladwell that " in compliance with Ld. G's wishes I have disposed of that annuity, but I beg you would not mention it." Lord Glandore's appointment, five years earlier, to an office " worth about fifteen Hundred a year which is no small addition to our finances," does not seem to have made so much difference as his wife expected.

Diana Glandore, there is no doubt, went on being an

" extravagant fine lady," and a careless one. Of her carelessness she is well aware, and writes of it often in holiday humour. " You may conclude that, carelesslike, it is lost." " I am not sure whether I am right as I have according to custom lost your last letter. I hope I have not overdrawn but if I have as it cannot be more than 1 Pd. you will be so good as to make it up." " Like a stupid fool as I am," she writes in another letter to Gladwell, " I have forgot the street that Lackington lives in." And again: " I am ashamed to tell you that I fear I have mislaid the stamped paper . . . so that I cannot enclose the receipts till you get me more of it. I am sure you have known me anywhere by that intolerable carelessness."

But she was not a fool about money: it is evident that she had, again like her father, a head for business. She was always well aware of the facts of her economic case, and had sense enough to regard them when it was really necessary: " Ld G. talks of taking a house in London, but I am frightened at the account I have heard of the taxes & the expence of residing there, however I suppose we must attempt it, tho' he is so much attached to Ardfert, & is doing so much to the place, that he will certainly not give up Ireland, & we shall have a pretty constant expence in journies backwards & forwards." And, careless though she might be, she was not careless enough to pay a bill twice: " I should also be much obliged to you if you would call at Miss Howells, for tho' her bill was paid last spring, her Clerk wrote last post to Ld. G: again for it." Diana was quick also to take occasion for a sarcastic fling: " I suppose she is too fine a Lady to inform when her draughts are answered, but I think she might as well have done so, & so I beg you will tell her."

Diana's letters give a singularly clear and complete picture of her. How barren in comparison is the only account of her that seems to exist, written by John Hotham to her father at almost exactly the same time as she was writing about the " frisky Speaker." Hotham writes from Dublin Castle :

> . . . Lord and Lady Crosbie I have the pleasure to assure your Lordship are in perfect health. He seems a most good

humoured and well-behaved young man; and She is not only the same as ever in that respect, but in full bloom and spirits. She appears much pleased with her reception in this country; and by her affability of behaviour and propriety of conduct is very deservedly an universal favourite among us Irish.

This can hardly be called an evocative account of her. But her letters bring her to full life. They reveal her every detail. In their light she is not only quick-tempered, importunate, impatient, pleasure-loving, authoritative, sarcastic, but generous, sympathetic, compassionate, and of warm affections. "We have all here been much affected," she writes from Ardfert in 1794, "by a duel that took place between Mr. Herbert's opponent, & Sir Barry Denny, a great friend of Lord Glandore's, which ended fatally to the latter . . . Such are sometimes the sad effects of contested Elections. I have taken the Widow home to my house, poor thing, she is not yet eighteen, this subject has so engrossed my thoughts that I can hardly write or think of any thing else." But Diana was no sentimentalist. After giving practical expression to a real sympathy, she could think and write of a familiar matter of concern. She continued forthwith: "So much of the strong beer has been quaffed down at this Election that we should be much obliged to you if you would have the goodness to ask my brother to allow you to send us the yearly supply he has always indulged us with, I beg you will have it shipped immediately."

She cherished memories of her life as a girl at Drayton House. "Tell her *her child* wishes much to see her," is a message that she sends to Gladwell's wife, with affectionate greeting. "I seized the opportunity," she writes in another letter, "of once more beholding dear Drayton." "How do you all go on at Drayton? Let me hear something about you." "I beg my love to your wife [Mrs. Gladwell] & pray remember me to my old friend Molly Thomas. Tell her I saw Nurse Porter at Ld Grandison's, that she enquired a great deal about her & is as happy as the day is long, dresses fine, gets everything she likes, her eldest son is bound Apprentice to Ld

Grandison's Cook, & the youngest is settled near her, so that she has everything she can wish for, & Lady Grandison doats on her." "Remember me kindly to all the good people at Drayton to whom I believe I shall be tempted to make a visit next year . . . Wont you all be glad to see me?"

Diana writes with pride, loyalty, and fondness of her husband. "I am very vain of Ld. G. who has distinguished himself greatly in the House of Lords, you cannot imagine the applause he has met with, but his speeches have been so murdered in the English Papers, & even things diametrically opposite to what he said put into his mouth, that nobody of your side the water can judge by such an account of his abilities, which however have here gained him the greatest credit." "Lord Glandore has played truant a great while. I am very impatient for his return." "Yesterday Ld Glandore was sworn into his new Office, an Office he has reason to be vain of, as he owes it entirely to his own abilities, never having met with any assistance from my family or his own."

How keenly Diana felt the one great lack in her life is evident from a letter that she wrote when she was thirty-one, during her nephew's visit. The boy's mother, her sister Elizabeth, Mrs. Herbert of Muckross, was six years younger than she.[1] Her other sister, Caroline, who did not marry, was eight years younger. "Mrs. Herbert," she writes, "is very well and her eldest son who has been with me for some months the most lovely child I ever saw, would to God I was blessed with such a one."

She herself had three children, but they all died soon after birth. On June 22nd, 1782—Diana was then twenty-six—her father wrote to General Irwin: "Lady Glandore is as well as, I may say better than, I expected, for she has been so ill with the influenza that I despaired of her going out her time. Hitherto no accident has happened and she reckons the very beginning of August." Less than a month later he wrote: "I am sorry to tell you that Lady Glandore was delivered of

[1] "Before five, the young lady was making an uproar in the family, and Di was pacifying it in French, whilst the nurse kept talking nonsense to it. A more ridiculous scene you never saw."—Lord George to General Irwin, from Pall Mall, July, 1762.

a son which lived but a few hours, but she is perfectly well. Mrs. Herbert is at Muckross and promises to behave better than Lady Glandore has done.'' On the birth of Diana herself Lord George had written to the same correspondent that her mother was "as well as possible,'' and he adds: "I always was an excellent physician in other branches. I pretend now to some knowledge in midwifery, and I offer my advice gratis whenever Mrs. Irwin pleases to consult me.''

Some six years after Lord George's death Mrs. Herbert, who was then twenty-nine, became "unfortunate.'' "I hear my unfortunate sister is in town,'' writes Diana, "and that she was seen the other night at the Play. I wish I knew something certain about her.'' She was unfortunate both in her sister's eyes and in those of her husband because she had run away. In January, 1792, Mr. Herbert wrote from Dublin to his brother-in-law, now Viscount Sackville:

> My dear Lord,
>
> I had hoped long before this time to have met you and your brother in England, & to have consulted with You on several points relative to my unfortunate Wife, & my Children now deserted by their Mother. When I heard you were to be at Shobdon last summer I had determined to meet you there, but the strong dissuasion of my Lawyers prevented my going as they were all of opinion I should not for at least ten months enter the same Kingdom with your unhappy sister: they still wish me to postpone quitting this Country . . .When I left Muckross last week your Nephews were both perfectly well. They are fine Boys: the eldest remarkably handsome, & I trust, thank God his constitution has surmounted every danger . . . ''

The scandal must have made a considerable stir, but it does not seem to have had any features of distinguishing interest, nor is much known of Mrs. Herbert except that she had character enough to be the heroine of it. There is, however, another recorded and certainly unfortunate occurrence in her family life which may have been a contributing cause of her disaffection from her husband and children. In the autumn of

1789 her little boy, writes his aunt Diana, " met with a dreadful accident, he was burnt almost to death, but thank God after being in the greatest danger he has recovered." The recovery, however, was extremely slow, for his great-aunt, Lady Bateman, writes to Mrs. Gladwell in March of the following year that " though it was near four months since the accident happen'd I can scarcely imagine anything so dreadful as the wounds in his arm and side, they were almost as large as at first, he is placed in the House of the Physician who attends him, I believe you would have cured him sooner." This was a horrifying calamity; and the horror of it may well have had a dislocating effect upon the boy's mother. She left her husband and her children about two years after the accident. Her impulse to escape from its reminders and associations may, later, when aided by other circumstances, have become uncontrollable. Or perhaps Mr. Herbert's addiction to fishing and his lack of humour were too much for her. " Herbert is upon a fishing party," Sackville writes to his son Charles in the Summer of '85, "and Bess attends; what a bout for her."—" The Herberts had the happiness of catching and eating several pike. I told them their equipage and attendance were the subject of conversation at Oxford. Bess laughed, but Herbert thought I had invented the story and rather looked grave."

One letter of the youngest of Lord George's daughters, Caroline, survives. Unfortunately only one, for it has much of the same spirit and force that animate Diana's letters. Evidently Lord George's qualities descended to his daughters rather than to his sons. The letter is to Mrs. Gladwell and is mainly about Diana: it shows that her name was abbreviated, in what some think of as a modern fashion, in the family circle to which Mrs. Gladwell, like her husband, evidently belonged.

> Charles says you are grown a prodigious Buck in your Dress, that you have got quite a youthful bloom in your Cheeks after the many years of misery which you drudged on in those horrid Rooms in Pall Mall, and, if you feel like me, you will never wish to see them, or anything else in that *cursed* Town of London as long as you live.

I heard from Di lately who has been at Ly Grandison's and seen Nurse Porter who she says has not a wish ungratified but that of seeing Betty Love whom she quite raves about. Di is to return to Ld. Grandison's at Christmas where she is to meet all the best company from Dublin and to live in a continual train of amusement. She is so popular in Kerry that when she goes to a Play which is acted by strolling Players at Tralee, the whole House rings with applause at her entrance, and she is obliged to curtsy her thanks like a Queen.

Remember me to Gladwell, and believe me dear Mrs. Gladwell,

Yr. sincere Friend
C. Sackville

The letter is undated, but the reference to Diana seeing Nurse Porter at Lady Grandison's indicates the autumn of 1787. Diana is shown in her " full bloom "; but even then, when she was only thirty-one, she had begun to suffer ill health. There is a letter of the year before in which she speaks of " some medecines which are absolutely necessary for me to get, particularly a bottle of powdered Bark which I am very anxious to get from Apothecary's Hall." At thirty-four she was taking the Bath waters; and her aunt, Lady Bateman, writes of her as having at that time, on her way to Bath, " suffered cruelly from pains in her Stomach from which she gets no relief but being put into a warm Bath, however it is only at times she has these attacks being some days as well as ever, I really do suppose by this account that she has the Stone like her father . . ."

This unlucky inheritance may have been abetted by the strain of Diana's nervous energy upon her physical resources. Energy and haste mark the style of her letters, which she wrote in the midst of varied activities, often with part of her mind on something else : " I am writing on my knee whilst my hair is dressing, having always so much business on my hands that I have not a moment to spare." She may have been sometimes as careless of her health as she was of much else;

exceeding liberal resources because they were liberal. " She had a very severe illness last year," her husband writes in 1807 when she was fifty-one. But " She is very well," he adds, " & has been so throughout this year." She was physically resilient as well as resilient in spirit. She lived till 1814.

It is a pity that no letter of Diana to her father, except the one already quoted, should have been preserved: for no doubt she wrote him better letters than she did to Gladwell. That single letter, and her letters to Gladwell[1] which he so faithfully kept, are almost all that seem to be left. But they are enough; they fulfil all expectations of the subject of those admirable portraits by George Knapton and Nathaniel Dance, and of the inheritor of her father's brains, zest for life, power of command, irony, and will. She, the most brilliant and the most attractive of his children, drew most from him. In her the happy, the well omened reflection of Lord George can be seen, in contrast most unhappy with his reflection as it stands in the mirror of those ominous realities of his fortunes, of " the course of my unprosperous life," as he called it when he came to die.

Of Lady George not much is known. She was Diana Sambrooke, second daughter and co-heiress of John Sambrooke who was the only brother of Sir Jeremy Sambrooke, Baronet, of Gibbons, Hertfordshire. Her great-grandfather was the Earl of Salisbury. She married Lord George in September, 1754, when he was thirty-eight and she twenty-four. " She'll but ill deserve you," wrote Lord George's close friend, Captain Cunningham, just before the marriage, " if she cannot make you happy ": and there is good reason to suppose that she did. The Captain himself was newly married—" Matrimony agrees vastly with Cunningham, for he is as fat as ever "—so he writes on this occasion with especial raciness and verve. The letter shows close contact with his friend's realism and honesty and humanity, and with that good gross stout humour that never

[1] For some of her letters to Gladwell, not quoted in this chapter, see Appendix pp. 265-267.

matches with pretence or meanness or with any of the lurking vices.

My dearest Lord,

Before you receive this Letter I do suppose your Nuptials are consummated . . . We can both easily imagine how you will be employed next tuesday night, and shall certainly do what we can to imitate your example. I shall persuade Betty that what you have in size I have in vigour, that our wives, when they meet, may not dispute who are best served. . . . Adieu, my dearest Lord, I expect to hear from you when the hurry of your wedding is over.

On the third of September, 1754, Captain Cunningham writes again :

We shall not be unmindful that this [is] your wedding day. Betty and I shall celebrate it before we sleep, with all the sprites we can command, but it is not to be supposed that we are as well provided with ammunition as you and your Bride must be. May this be the happiest day of your life is the most sincere prayer of your ever faithful R.C.

" We expect you are now in entire possession," he writes nine days later.

The continual expressions of affection and gratitude, without hint of servility but always warmed by the sense of friendship on equal terms, in Cunningham's letters, prove that Sackville, so sinister by general repute, so harsh, so full of forbidding hauteur, had the qualities and the impulses that win love.

My Dearest Lord [Captain Cunningham wrote from Dublin, thanking Lord George for ear-rings, probably a wedding present], Lady Blayney and Bess do believe, and I cannot help joining with them, that you have at least added £150 to my father's hundred, else you cd. not have afforded a pair so fine. Lady Arabella Denney is just gone, and thinks them the Genteelest she ever saw. In short my Dear Lord we all have a tolerable share of vanity (tho I must say yours bears no proportion) and we are very proud of the finery of them, as well as of the attention and real kindness from a person of your rank and reputation in the world. . . . Your present situation is not the pleasantest. I have heard so much of late of the Ladies temper of disposition that I do not doubt of her making you very happy. . . . Widdow Madder lives now very publikely at Loftes Hume's house. Tho it is suspected they are married, neither of them chuse yet to own it.

Mr. Pery, the " friend of yours " at whose house Diana Glandore was to be " very much entertained " twenty-four years later, wrote with affectionate wishes for Lord George's approaching marriage; and Thomas Le Hunte asks " leave to felicitate my Lady Sackville [*sic*] on her certainty of happiness." " I know you," he adds, " and therefore say certainty of her Ladyship's, and I may say your Lordship's too, since she is your own choice."

Another letter of congratulation on the same occasion is Lord Lauderdale's. The marriage seems to have affected him as it affected Cunningham, for he writes that it " gives me new relish for matrimony." This letter is full of the bluff and naïve egoism of the writer. " I lost my only son last week, I would rather have seen ten Regts. of foot cut off . . . I wish you'd give me an Irish Regt. I understand yt. trade well."—" You are always doing me good and I am very sensible of it," writes Lord Lauderdale in another letter.

These letters and many such others show that those who knew Sackville well enough to understand him responded warmly; that they were neither intimidated nor embarrassed; that it was said truly of him that few could be at greater ease with their intimates or put their intimates at greater ease with them; and that though " on first acquaintance his Manner and Air impressed those who approached him with an idea of proud Reserve," yet " no man, in private Society, unbent himself more or manifested less Self-importance." " I began to take much to him," Lord Sheffield wrote to Mr. Eden soon after Sackville's death. " Began " is indicative that those " very good points " which Lord Sheffield mentions—" he was fair and downright: he had a right understanding"—were not instantly displayed. Lord Sheffield was beginning to know something of the man; he was beginning to know something of what Sackville's closer friends knew, though certainly not everything. The integrity of Lord George's nature, his utter lack of sham, were, for his intimates, involved with other qualities that roused affection: affection that gave material token when General Bragg, under whom he had served, left him the residue of his estate, about four thousand pounds. Sackville's correspondence proves that real friendship with him banished diffidence or fear of giving offence. Even in that franker period such observations as Cunningham's on his marriage could not have been made to a man who had any taint in him of touchiness or squeamishness or sentimentalism or false reserve. Captain Sharman wrote in something of the same vein on the same occasion: "I do most heartily wish your mornings may be good, your Noons better, your evenings and Nights best of all."

Sackville and his friends had not that modern "delicacy," that modern "taste" that has of late exercised itself in tampering improvingly with the language and the thought of our Marriage Service, purifying them for the approval of the semi-impotent or the dishonestly-minded. In the eighteenth century there was little of the shame that is now felt in speaking openly the truth about marriage as a physical relationship, physical essentially, since its motive-in-chief is the appeasement and solace of the flesh and the consequent enrichment by children; children who cannot be begotten, cannot continue in their early hidden life, cannot be born, except by a succession of physical processes entirely animal and very "indelicate" indeed. That an excluding emphasis should be laid on the companionship of marriage, on its day-time domesticity, on keeping house comfortably and on having a partner whom it is nice to talk to—all matters to which Nature is indifferent, though they are well—signifies nothing but a morbid incapacity for truth. It shows a focus which is false. For "if all be well in the bedroom, all is well through the house."

From Lady Mary Coke comes most of such information as there is about Lord George's wife, and Lady Mary's references are few and brief. In her account Lady George appears as a lady of fashion—rather too much so for Lady Mary's entire approval—an attractive woman, a lavish entertainer, fond of gaiety and fond of cards. Lady Mary Coke was frequently at her house to play at Lu, while Parliament was sitting. "I was engaged," she writes in 1769, "to Lady George Sackville where I found a great deal of company. I observed Lady Gower, the Dutchess of Hamilton, etc., much enlivened by the praises which Mr. Wedderburn's fine oratory had procured him in the House of Lords." A month or so later there was a ball given by Lady George who "scolded me for coming in a hoop, but as I don't dance nor ever stay supper at those places, I could not see why I was to be without. I did not go into the dancing room, and wish'd myself at home till Lady Powis and two or three of my acquaintances sat down in a corner to Lu." Lady Sarah Lennox writes of playing at quadrille at Lady George's. "It was vastly pleasant, I assure you." This was some two years after Minden, when Lady George was thirty.

During Lord George's court-martial, his wife kept a firm front; she would not retire, abashed or disheartened. We hear of her walking at this time in Leicester Gardens with that most elegantly and resplendently dressed lady of the day, the Duchess of Devonshire, who, on the occasion of a birthday party of the Queen's, appeared in "a blossom-coloured full suit of cloaths with rich spangles and white ermine." Lady George lived to see her husband's rehabilitation, his return to prominence in public life. She died at forty-seven, about two years after his appointment as American Secretary. Horace Walpole records her death, with a curious faint innuendo: "Lord George Germain lost his wife, who died of the measles. As she was a good wife and mother and a sensible woman, her death was a great blow to him at this moment."

The announcement in the *Morning Chronicle* is a perfect example of the obituary formality of the time; a eulogy without any personal indication, indeed without any meaning at all :

> After a severe illness which she bore with uncommon patience and resignation, died, yesterday morning, Lady George Germain. She was distinguished and admired for every amiable and excellent quality. She was the delight of her husband and of her family and the ornament of her sex. She was beloved by all who knew her and no lady of our time has died more deeply and more justly lamented. Her Ladyship has left two sons and four [*sic*] daughters, the eldest of whom was lately married to Lord Viscount Crosby.

The few surviving letters from his wife to Lord George show that she was sensitive, capable of strong emotion; that she sincerely and, indeed, passionately loved him. Parted from him because of his military duties, she wrote to him while she was carrying her first child :

> My Sister is just gone, My Dearest Man, which is a very great mortification to me, tho' less so at this time than at any other, as my heart & soul is so taken up by one thought that I can scarcely feel pleasure or pain about anything which does not relate to it; and I feel a kind of insensibility both with regard to my self and all the world besides, excepting thee, thou dearest everlasting object of all my care and tenderness. Lord James Manners made me very happy on Tuesday by telling me that he left you well at Chatham that Morning, which I hope to have confirm'd to me by a Letter today. I don't much like your new operations with Ball, but hope in this respect and in every other that providence will take care of you & restore you to me. I have just received your Letter. My Dearest Man; I should have been miserable if I had not had one today, as I always expect to hear three times a week from you, and particularly upon this occasion. I need not tell you how overjoy'd I am that you have heard nothing since, & begin to feel a dawn of happiness to which I have been an utter stranger for sometime. I hope in God I shall not be disappointed, & plung'd again into that excess of misery which no body can have an idea of that has not been in my shocking situation . . .
>
> I have just had a letter from the Lady Tuftons [?] to let

me know they will come to me on Sunday se'ennight, which I am very sorry for, as I am sure I should be quite incapable of seeing them or any body else, if you shou'd be sent away from me; as it has been with the utmost difficulty that I have been able to walk about (a spectacle of misery) only upon the uncertainty of it, and if this misfortune shou'd not happen, fear it will prevent your making me a visit, tho' hope you will not mind that, if you don't come to me before, for I take for granted they will not come till night, and as you must go away on Monday morning, you will be troubled with very little of their company.

Another early letter, written when she was not afflicted or disturbed, shows that she was by no means as "stupid" as she professed to be, and that she had some humour:

I hope, My dearest Love, that you got safe to Chatham on Monday, and that I shall receive an account of it to morrow, great were the lamentations here at your departure, and the solemnity of my countenance betray'd my sorrow upon the occasion, however next week I hope to be enliven'd again with the pleasing hopes of yr. return. My sister has just been inform'd that Lord Bateman proposes staying three weeks at Windsor, therefore is now writing to ask leave to stay here during that time; I own I doubt his granting her request, but if he don't shall keep her two or three days longer by that means, as she can't receive an answer till Saturday. Our Balls began yesterday which perhaps you will hardly believe considering how few Men you left here, and that there are not above one or two more arrived since you went, but such as it was, it will serve for a puff in the Newspaper. Adieu, my dear Man, I am very stupid and won't detain you any longer from yr. more weighty warlike affairs, to hear my nonsense. I hope you have recover'd the King of Prussia's defeat.

The last sentence but one is not only disarming and engaging; there may be irony in it, and perhaps in the last sentence as well. With or without irony Lady George evidently regarded herself as a background figure, apart from her position in the fashionable world. That she had a strong sense of responsibility towards her children is evident from the letter she wrote to the daughter of Madame de Beaumont who was educating her daughter Diana. The letter throws a curious light upon the very conscious and active Protestantism which English people in general have been losing only within the last fifty years or so; its occasional flashes of what must surely here be unconscious irony are entertaining, but it does not reveal Lady George as a woman of any particular distinction of mind or spirit. The most that can be said is that she shows some commonsense. But not tact, for she is dictatorial, she is somewhat overbearing. Her humour, too, seems to be suspended; she seems indeed sometimes comically humourless, and the reader of Madame de Beaumont's letter is glad when Madame gets the best of it, glad that "Providence had given her a fortune sufficing her ambition," so that she could answer back and answer to effect. Lady George's letter is in French, but it reads more naturally when translated. She refers to her correspondent's mother as "Mme Beaumont," not recognizing the "de."

> I have always understood that Mme Beaumont had promised never to speak to the children on the subject of religion. I avow that I would never have resolved to send my daughter to her if I had not reckoned on her observing an inviolable silence on that point, and even though several of my friends laughed at my credulity. There are very few persons of the Protestant religion whom I should permit to speak to my daughter on so important an article . . . There are people who take their Religion with their Nurses' milk, without ever giving themselves the trouble to reflect on what they should believe, and I know well that by the feebleness of some and the *fourberie* of others, superstition has slipped into all the churches of the world, and that in all countries human institutions are too much mixed up with divine laws: but one cannot err with the Gospel for rule and reason for guide and I am sure that my

daughter will never find in the one anything repugnant to the other, and I would assuredly not consent to her faith being represented to her as an unintelligible jargon or her religion (the only real subject of joy and consolation to a Christian) being painted in a manner so lugubrious as to make her sad and make her weep. *Enfin* I demand from Mme Beaumont a profound silence on the subject of Religion and of Piety . . . I request that Mme Beaumont will tell me the days on which she will speak to the other children about Religion, for I would never consent that my daughter should go *chez elle* when she touches *sur ces sortes de sujets*.

I prefer to send you to Mme Beaumont than to go myself, for I do not care to enter with her into disputes which would lead to nothing, my above resolution being absolutely *inébranlable*.

After again emphasizing her determination that Mme. Beaumont shall not " mix herself up with my child's religion," Lady George concludes :

I cannot consent that she return to Mme Beaumont's school unless Mme Beaumont gives me her word never to speak before her of God, Jesus Christ, or the Holy Ghost. I will teach her myself, I repeat then again that I exact her word of honour from Mme Beaumont to keep profound silence.

I should be much obliged if she cultivates her *esprit* and helps me to cure her faults but beg her not to go at all beyond the bounds which I prescribe her.

The letter is, at least, a perfect " period piece," with its religious " feeling," its well guarded recognition of " reason " as religion's ally, its dislike of any tragic element in religion, its sense of caste, and the elegant, delectable artificiality of that " *Nurses*' milk."

Any reply to the letter seems to have been lost; for Madame de Beaumont's letter which follows here refers to secular subjects of instruction and must be in reply to a lost letter of Lady George. Madame probably had religious differences in her mind, but does not refer to them directly. Her position was difficult; she loved Diana, and no wonder, but she had to put up with much more from Lady George than she would have put up with if the little girl had not been so attractive, so intelligent, so high spirited, and with such abundance of character. " En un mot, j'aime l'enfant, cet amour m'a soutenue contre mille difficultés qui m'auraient fait tout abandonner." Madame de Beaumont complains to " My Lady Sacqvill " that my Lady's daughter has been given to believe that

> je la charge mal à propos de sciences inutiles. Quand les autres enfans parlent de ces choses [geography] Mademoiselle ouvre de grands yeux et s'ennuye. . . . Rien n'est plus propre à degoûter Mademoiselle de ses Leçons que de voir sa Maman désaprouver ce que sa maîtresse approuve . . . Je ne puis lui être utile qu'autant qu'elle aura confiance en moi, elle n'aura de confiance en moi qu'autant qu'elle ne trouvera jamais la maman en contradiction avec moi; si en perdant Sa confiance je me trouve hor d'etat de lui être utile, rien ne m'engage plus à la garder, puisque la providence m'a donné une fortune suffisante à mon ambition, et que je ne travaille plus que pour former des sujets estimables dans la société.

It is a letter full of spirit and point; a model, to-day and to-morrow, for all independent teachers who want to keep parents in their proper places.

The surviving indications of Lady George are not such as to rouse much curiosity for a detailed portrait of her. It seems clear that she made Lord George a thoroughly adequate wife and gave him no trouble. She " looked after him." Convinced that " nobody understands lace so well as General Irwin," she asked the General to " lay out 50 Pds. at Paris on new ruffles for Lord George." If she lost at Lu she would have been sensible enough to lose less than could have embarrassed either her husband or herself.

The company of his sister Caroline, of his daughters, of his men friends, and, perhaps, of his mistresses, may have been on the whole more rewarding to Lord George than that of his wife.

During the Minden uproar there was some tattle about mistresses. How much or how little truth there was in it cannot be known. Sackville had no doubt an eye for a pretty woman. Writing, when he was thirty, to Major Younge, he mentions Captain Cunningham, and adds, discreetly changing to French : " il a une sœur au Chateau de Stirling qui n'est pas laide." But he could not have been much addicted to amours or the inquisitive and unscrupulous newspaper gossips of the day would have found more material and, with it, more stimulus to invention. *Town and Court* does what it can, informing us that " His l———p before his marriage with Miss S———k had several amourettes on his hands. Miss Juliet D———y was a lady of Guernsey, who then resided in Soho, an elegant creature, and, having travelled through most parts of Europe, she spoke many languages with great fluency." She helped, perhaps, in the perfection of her lover's excellent French. Unhappily this accomplished girl died young, for "Soon after the death of this lady he engaged in correspondence with a Miss P. H., well known in the circle of the demireps of that time." This correspondence would have interest, but it may never have existed. The " gossip-column writer " —how much freer than those of to-day!—goes on to pay a charitable tribute to Miss P. H.'s comparative chastity. She was faithful, we learn, to his l———p during the period of his intimacy with her, and then she went to the West Indies. There is a brief reference to Miss Polly P———ll, a tenant's daughter in the neighbourhood of Lord George's seat in Sussex. He left her to go to Germany.

A particularly spiteful piece of scandal which reads as though it were sheer invention is that " L— G—— S———, escaped from the plains of Minden, was first found in the arms of Mrs. Wh-t-e, a lady from Ireland, but the application of his l——p's business required to clear his character, gave her so much leisure for other conquests, that the number of her admirers during the *trial*-summer, can scarce be enumerated."

The most likely story seems to be the one about Mrs. W——ft, whose husband was an officer under Sackville and served at Minden. Sackville dined with him when they were back in London and was said to take great pleasure in his wife's company. But, while her husband lived, he was not her lover, even by news-sheet repute. After her husband's death he became her secret benefactor, and, at last, in the same secrecy, he was her lover. Then, the tale continues, she became pregnant and there was scandal which caused her retirement to the country.

Between Lord George and his sister Caroline, who married Lord Milton of Milton Abbey in Dorset, the bonds were close. At Milton Abbey Lord George was often a guest. Caroline's letters to him, though they have the formality and reserve of her period, give an unmistakable impression of real affection. Such references as that to the " grand dress " which Lord George has got " to make a fine figure in Dublin," shows her special interest in her brother, as do her letters written just before his marriage. Lord George named his youngest daughter after her. Her son, George Damer (named after Lord George), later Earl of Dorchester, wrote long letters to his uncle, by whose confidence he is " much flattered," giving detailed accounts of naval engagements in which he had fought against the French (as in 1780 when he was on board the *Intrepid* off Martinique); and accounts equally detailed of incidents of the American War.

To his brothers Lord George was less happily related than he was to his sister Caroline and her family. Lord Middlesex and Lord John Sackville were a disappointment to their father and they were unlikely to inspire anyone with enthusiasm. Wraxall writes of their accompanying Prince Frederick, George the Third's father, on his " vulgar and puerile " expeditions to fortune-tellers or bull-baitings, which the Prince attended in disguise. Lord Middlesex was a typical minor poet of his time, imitative, dull as only Pope's devotees can be; with what might be called a talent, but a very small one. At Drayton House there are manuscripts of his verse and of verses which he copied: it is fairly easy to tell which is which, in spite of lack of indication. Some discriminating member of the family has marked one of the manuscript-books: " Poetry—bad." He wrote a lot.

So fast from S———e's mouth the verses fly,
You'd swear he had a Gleet of Poetry.
But Gleets the Back of strength and moisture drain,
And pray, do Verses fortifie the Brain ?

The epigram is pertinent to Lord Middlesex. "The meanest of the muses' throng," he called himself, with a modesty which carried him a little too far. He occasionally provoked verse from his friends. These lines, addressed to him by Dr. Stone, Lord George's colleague in Ireland, show that he was fond of being abroad :

Still, my Dear Lord, do fair Italia shores,
Florence proud gates, & Venice sea-girt Towrs,
Still do the ruins of Imperial Rome
Please more than Parks or Palaces at home?
Or say, if ne'er one wish unbidden stole
From Tiber's banks, to poor forsaken Knole?

And, were it not for a confounded Ferry,
Your Lordship might be happy ev'n at Derry.

Scurrilous and comic anonymous lampoons surviving at Drayton House,[1] sometimes concerned with the liaison between the Duke of Dorset and Peg Woffington, may be the work of Lord Middlesex; perhaps not, or perhaps someone collaborated with him in guying his father. These examples of ribald verse are far more readable and entertaining than any of the compositions which may certainly be attributed to Lord Middlesex, such as his Pastorals and the lines, written when he was only eighteen,[2] "To Mr. Pope, Occasioned by reading Mr. Addison's account of the greatest English Poets." The bawdy verse, in various styles and of various periods, copied by Lord Middlesex, is also for the most part entertaining, sometimes highly so. The selection shows some judgment.

It may have been that his brother's poetry helped to deter Lord George from literary pursuits and accounted for that

[1] See p. 18.
[2] Appendix, pp. 267-268.

undercurrent of irony in his remark that he had not genius sufficient for works of mere imagination. What is certain is that between these two there was long continued dissension. "I am sorry to say," wrote Lord George to Lady Middlesex, "that my Ld. Middlesex's behaviour towards me for a Considerable time past has been such, as makes it impracticable for me to concern myself in his affairs." The marked dissimilarity of Lord George's character to his brother's was no doubt the chief cause of this alienation. Money matters also played an important part. Lord Middlesex considered that he had been mulcted by the family man of affairs to the extent of over eleven thousand pounds. He compiled "A Full and True Account of the Horrid, Barbarous & Unnatural Murther committed upon the Credit, Quiet, & Estate of the Earl of Middlesex by Charles Sackville, Esqr." "Spare my Life," he added, after this preliminary, "& take *All* I have."

When Lord Middlesex became head of the family, at the end of 1765, Lord George felt that it was time for some sort of reconciliation. If only for his sons' sakes, he could not be on such bad terms with the new Duke of Dorset. He wrote to him in the third person, still addressing him as Lord Middlesex; he is anxious that there should be no operative disharmony between them now, but equally anxious, it would seem, that a distance between them should be kept. The letter is strictly impersonal in tone, and strictly practical:

> Lord George has nothing more at heart than to preserve that union in the family which he flatters himself now happily subsists, and he is sensible that any disagreement between Lord Middlesex and him will lessen the credit and consideration of them both. Lord George is resolved on his part to take every step that may prevent even the appearance of any misunderstanding, and trusts that he shall find the same friendly disposition in Lord Middlesex.

He goes on to the matter of the representation in Parliament of the family borough of East Grinstead, mentioning three suitable candidates. One of these was elected on the recommendation of the new Duke, who in this way gave Lord George the " satisfaction " which he requests of " proving himself united with the head of his family."

This brother of Lord George was Duke for only a little more than three years. He died at fifty-eight, in 1769, " having worn out his constitution," says Walpole, " and almost his estate. He has not left a tree standing in the venerable old park at Knole. However, the family think themselves very happy that he did not marry a girl he kept, as he had a mind to do, if the state of his understanding had not empowered his relations to prevent it."

Lady Mary Coke's remarks on the same occasion have the same tenor :

> The Duke of Dorset is dead, and happy had it been if he had dyed three months ago, for since that time he has cut down all the wood in the Park at Knowle, even the trees of his father's planting. How bad a use did he make of a very lively understanding—ruined himself without doing good to a single mortal! . . . H.R.H. was surprised to hear of Lord George Sackville being at the Drawing-room on Tuesday. His brother the Duke of Dorset dyed only on Friday and could not then be buried. There is certainly very little Affection and still less decency practised in this Country.

Not only Sackville's honesty, but his strong resentment of the mutilation of Knole, may have accounted for this lack of " decency " after his brother's death.

" A proud, disgusted, melancholy, solitary man, whose conduct savoured strongly of madness," is a description of this second Duke of Dorset, but it seems, in part, at least, more pertinent to his brother, Lord John, who, though less " lively " in mind and less sensible to humour, is the more sympathetic character of the two. He suffered cruelly from a melancholia which was, at its worst, a melancholy-madness of the most afflicting kind. At Drayton House there is a very moving " Prayer "[1] in his handwriting : " Lord John Sackville's Prayer," giving a detailed account of his sufferings, made " en sortant de sa melancholie, le 26 Juillet, 1759." " Je suis plongé

[1] Appendix, pp. 268-269.

périodiquement dans une tristesse accablante." He seems to have found some relief in his cricket, his name appears in various records of matches. In one of these an eleven was captained by the head gardener of Knole. Lord John's wife, a sister of the Duchess of Bedford, quarrelled with Lord George, who was thus alienated from this brother as well.

The first Duke of Dorset was disappointed in his sons, and so might Lord George have been in his if he had lived to see them grow up. Wraxall, writing after Lord George's elder son,[1] Charles, had in 1815 inherited the dukedom, materially qualifies his already somewhat qualified commendation of Charles and his brother as "men by no means wanting talents" by adding that they "have nevertheless hitherto remained in a sort of political obscurity, better known at Newmarket or on Ascot Heath than at Westminster, on the turf or at the cockpit than in Parliament." But this was more than thirty years after their father's death. Lord George knew them only as boys; and that his "*tendresse pour mes enfants,*" which would not, he wrote, permit him "*s'éloigner*" from them for "*une education etrangère,*" together with his solicitude, persisted, is evident from the letters he wrote to Charles at Oxford and from a letter written five years before his death to the then Duke of Dorset. "My son," he writes, "will look up to you for Protection as a father when he loses me; but your successor will be but his distant relation and he cannot claim the same attention and affection from him as I am persuaded he will receive from you." Lord George hopes, therefore, that "he may have that interest in your Borough [East Grinstead] which may make him a useful if not a necessary ally to the head of his family."

Lord George's letters to Charles are pleasant, easy, kindly, and communicative, written in the leisure and peace of his last years. Two months before his death he was writing to him about cricket and about politics:

[1] He was the fifth and last Duke of Dorset, succeeding after his cousin's only son had been killed in an Irish fox-hunt. Colonel N. V. Stopford Sackville, in his *Drayton,* notes the "unusual chain of relationship" connecting Lord George with all the Dukes of Dorset. "He was son to the first, brother to the second, uncle to the third, great uncle to the fourth, and father to the fifth."

The Red Monk [?] is at last gone to Withyam. G. Damer [his nephew] went to the cricket match at Peckham, and was much entertained with seeing old Cumberland [the dramatist] directing all the players, and Charles acting first part in the game but unfortunately Tunbridge lost the match, and the only comfort the father had was that his boy had done his duty. We have had a little rioting about taxing of shops and maid servants, Mr. Pitt was hiss'd and pursued in going to and from the House of Commons, and in the evening the Guards were sent to disperse the mob collected about his house. Even Mr. Pitt must share the fate of all ministers in this country, and submit to be for a time unpopular.

The P. of Wales has given a magnificent ball, and is now wise enough to go to Court and behave with seeming propriety to his father.

Another letter, in very shaky handwriting, signed "Adieu most affectionately yours, Sackville," is of a month or so earlier, and it has the best begining that any son could wish: "You do very right in acquainting me when you want money, when I can spare it you shall not be distressed for it; I send you a Bank note of twenty pounds, which I hope will do for the present." Family news follows: "We are going on here [Pall Mall] as usual, Caroline is nursing a sore throat which is not the better for having been last night at Le Picque's [?] benefit. Bess is almost well, but she keeps Herbert constantly at Fulham. I have bought several things for Lord Waldegrave for the House at Whitehall, and I hope soon to begin cleaning it for your reception next year."

During the previous year Sackville was writing to Charles at Oxford from Stoneland Lodge. There is a letter of June, 1784, which shows him still active at an age when many men of that century were decrepit. His interest in his family, in his friends and acquaintances, strikes strong and lively notes:

My dear Charles,

I am happy in hearing that you like Oxford better than you expected, I was sure you would meet many of your old friends who would be civil and attentive to you, but I am particularly pleased with your approving so much of Mr. Pett [?], for had you disliked him you would have had no satisfaction in reading what he recommended, or receiving any instruction from him, as you begin so well with the Dean I have no doubt you will preserve his good opinion.

I continue in the resolution of being with you at Oxford on the 15th of July in my way to Ireland, I hope to dine with you at the Star on that day and staying there that night, I trust that you will entertain us well and that you will take Caroline and me under your Protection, I suppose you dine at four o'clock. Here we are, Miss Leighton[1] still coughing but rather better than she was at first, we are now expecting Lord Milton and Miss Damer, who stay only one night with us, and Baron Seckenfeldt [?] announced his intention of being here *les premiers jours de la semaine* . . . ; Miss Jane Pery honours us to-morrow with her company, so that with the help of the Cumberlands from the Wells we have not been very solitary. Dick Cumberland enters into Possession of Miss Hobart this evening, and he is to be at his father's on Saturday, so that we may flatter ourselves with the pleasure of seeing the Bride and Bridegroom.

My horse continues [MS. illegible here], your Col. [?] is rode every day by Mark, and goes very quickly and looks like a Gentleman. I am sorry as yet he can hear of no hunter in this Country that will suit you, but Mark promises to do his best in looking for one but he by no means speaks confidently of success, he intends making the most of Madam, he has turn'd her to grass that he may take her up at the proper time and prepare her hunting . . . This is all the news at Stoneland, Mr. Bale is very well and looks agreeably at Miss Leighton.

George seems happy at Westminster, he bears the loss of you with great fortitude, and I daresay he looks forward with pleasure for the Holydays when he will be his own

[1] Of this lady Sackville wrote to Charles a year later that "She honours Caroline with her company to Stoneland when we settle there. In the meanwhile, she lives in Berkeley Square at Mrs. Corbett's, her sister in one apartment, and she in the other. They only meet at dinner to quarrel."

Master in this place. Caroline is so alert that she rides before breakfast that she may attend Miss Leighton at eleven in the Buggy.

Adieu most affectionately
yours Sackville.

George, when he grew older, was not disposed to bear the loss of Charles with " fortitude ": between the two brothers there was a strong attachment in later life. " Should you decide, " George wrote to Charles in 1828, " to leave England or withdraw yourself elsewhere, I promise you you shall not go alone, and I am determined to follow you where ever you are. You have adhered to me in sickness and in health, in joy and sorrow, and I should feel ashamed of myself if I hesitated one moment in deciding to follow your fortunes under all circumstances . . . " Their sister Diana writes also with marked affection for Charles. She gives some idea of him as he was a year or two after he left Oxford. " You have no idea how stonished I was at the sight of my dear Charles when he arrived at Castle Ward after having rode a post horse all night . . . he knew he could not get there before we left unless he posted all night, which he did, without even taking a servant or knowing the way. It was very good of him to be so anxious to see us. He travelled with Ld G: & me to Kerry & is now here well & happy but will I fear be obliged to leave us soon to my very great regret. He is universally liked & I feel quite vain of him." A little later Diana entrusted Charles with a commission about Beer, but " as he is a little giddy he may very likely have forgot it." " I cannot tell you how much I long to see him," she writes, again to Gladwell, in 1788, " & poor George who must be grown out of my memory." " Pray give my Love to George," she wrote in an earlier letter, " who, I hear, has entirely forgot me." The health of both brothers sometimes gives her anxiety: " Pray let me know exactly the state of George's health, for I have been alarmed of late by hearing but an indifferent account of him." " I am sorry to tell you that Sackville [Charles] looks very ill, & what is worse, feels so, I hope he will take care of himself for really it is necessary." References to Charles, of various kinds, occur frequently in Diana's letters. "If Charles is at Drayton tell him that I am much hurt at his not having written to me for some months. He never was so unkind before." "I am again this year disappointed of going to England which as I long more than I can express to see my dear Charles is a great mortification to me." George is mentioned in a rather different tone; he is generally "poor," not "dear." We both long to see poor George," Diana writes in 1787. "I cannot but think he might as well make us a Visit as idle away his time elsewhere, I should be obliged if you would mention to him our wishes on that subject."

George, less gay and "giddy" than Charles, lived at Drayton House after his father's death, managing the estate for his more or less absentee elder brother. Caroline, their unmarried sister, who had consumptive tendencies,[1] lived with her aunt, Lady Bateman. Charles did not inherit Knole or the Sackville estates in Kent and Sussex, as these had been settled on the fourth Duke's sisters. The importance of Drayton to Lord George's branch of the family was therefore augmented. It was on account of the legacy to him by Lady Betty Germain of this famous Northamptonshire seat that Lord George Sackville changed his name to Germain in 1770. Colonel N. V. Stopford Sackville, in his *Drayton,* has given a full account of the various ownerships of this "most venerable heap of ugliness, with many curious bits," as Walpole so stupidly and tastelessly described a house that is one of the most beautiful and interesting in England; and has quoted the request made to Lady Betty by her husband as he lay dying in 1718. After expressing the hope that she would re-marry and have children to inherit Drayton, which he had left her, Sir John Germain added that "if events should determine otherwise, it would give me great pleasure to think that Drayton descended after your death to a younger son of my friend the Duchess of Dor-

[1] "I am very uneasy about Car as all the accounts I receive from her seem to be very bad. I earnestly wish she would go abroad, a warm climate being the best remedy for Lungs."—Diana Glandore to Gladwell, August, 1789. "Caroline has a bad cold, made worse by her going to Ranelagh," her father wrote four years earlier.

set." Lady Betty, a brilliant figure of her day,[1] friend and correspondent of Pope and Swift, liberal in politics and a lover of art and letters, survived her husband for fifty-two years. But she did not re-marry, and she bequeathed Drayton in accordance with her husband's last wishes. Sir John had inherited Drayton from his first wife, the Duchess of Norfolk,[2] whom the Duke divorced on account of her notorious liaison with this handsome Dutchman, this soldier of fortune, "always a distinguished favourite of the other sex," as Lord George described him. Drayton, to Sir John Germain, was therefore a reward for adultery.

To Lord George's children and descendants it was a well loved home. Even his son Charles, who loved London life, seems to have visited Drayton at fairly regular intervals to see how George and the house and estate were doing. In one particular Charles was unexpectedly businesslike: he used to arrive in Northamptonshire with remarkable punctuality. "I will go and meet him," George would say, looking at his watch. "I am sure to find him at such and such a milestone." And he always did.

Charles was a fashionable figure of the Regency. He was Master of the Horse, a Knight of the Garter, and a friend of the Regent. A life-long bachelor, he was a lover of the turf, and of women. "A little smart looking man, and a favourite with the ladies," he is described in *Raikes Journal*. Expensively a favourite, not rewarded as was Sir John Germain, for Colonel Powlett, in his divorce case, got three thousand pounds damages against him. The celebrated Harriette Wilson was not so demanding as the Colonel: she asked and received only two hundred pounds as the price of her promise to omit from her Memoirs "any anecdotes personally offensive to your

[1] See pp. 25 and 42 : and Appendix, pp. 269-278.

[2] She had been Lady Mary Mordaunt, daughter of the pro-Stuart Earl of Peterborough. "Evelyn, the diarist . . . tells us how Lady Mary had taken part at a court performance of a Masque, entitled 'Calisto, or the Chaste Nymph.' The title, as it proved, was hardly appropriate to Lady Mary herself, for more than half of the Duke's married life was spent in attempting to get a divorce from her for very adequate reasons."—From Colonel Stopford Sackville's *Drayton*, p. 11. Colonel Sackville refers to the general belief that Sir John was a natural son of William the Second of Orange, and thus a brother of King William the Third.

Grace, or to the individuals in whom you take an interest."

Charles, surviving his brother George, was in a sense the last of the Sackvilles. "The very name of Sackville," writes Wraxall, "appears to be near extinction . . . the present Duke of Dorset being unmarried, and Mr. Germain [George][1] without male issue, though both have long passed the zenith of life . . . Even the dukedom itself seems to be already deprived of its greatest ornament, and to be half extinguished by the loss of Knole, a mansion which was to the Sackvilles all which Blenheim is to the Churchills or Penshurst to the Sydneys . . . That venerable pile, where the Earls and Dukes of Dorset had resided in uninterrupted succession for more than two centuries . . . it is highly probable will be transferred to the Earls of Delawar, in consequence of a will which, whatever legal validity it may possess, militates against every feeling of justice and propriety."

On the death of the last Duke of Dorset in 1843, his brother George's daughter, Caroline Harriet, inherited Drayton. She was already married to William Bruce Stopford, grandson of the Earl of Courtown. The name of Sackville was not extinguished, for Caroline Harriet later assumed it by royal licence, together with the Sackville arms. And Queen Victoria created the owner of Knole, Mortimer Sackville West, Baron Sackville, the title borne by the present owner. The eldest son of William Bruce Stopford and Caroline Harriet succeeded to Drayton, and he was succeeded in 1926 by his nephew, Lord George's great-great-grandson.

[1] He was known as Sackville Germain.

Chapter V

MILITARY SERVICE

FROM the age of twenty-one, when he had his first commission as Captain of Guards in Ireland, until the age of forty-three, when his military career was cut short after Minden, Lord George Sackville was a soldier. During this period only the four years of his Irish Secretaryship, which began when he was thirty-five and ended when he was thirty-nine, were engrossed by politics. He served in Flanders against the French and in Scotland against the Jacobites. When he was twenty-nine he fought and was badly wounded in the battle of Fontenoy: three years later, after his return from Scotland, the Duke of Cumberland sent him on a critical mission from the English lines to Marshal Saxe. These are the two most interesting events, before Minden, of his military life.

In 1740, five years before Fontenoy, Sackville had been appointed Lieutenant-Colonel of the 28th Foot (now the First Gloucester) under Major-General Bragg. By 1742 England was, yet again, at war in Europe. George the Second, before he himself joined his forces abroad as commander, was reviewing British troops at home. His sons, the Prince of Wales and the Duke of Cumberland, accompanied him on these occasions, which were gala-days for the citizenry. Uniforms then to be seen at military reviews were indeed gala-dress : Sackville, with his fine commanding figure, must have looked both gaily picturesque and impressively martial. A scarlet frock was worn, closed by two or three loops across the breast, folded back in broad lapels to show the white shirt. The skirts reached to the knees and were caught up at the corners to show the bright lining. Under full breeches legs were gaitered, and a cocked hat with gold lace was worn in and out of action. The sword hung at the side from a broad military belt. The lively, gaudy dress of the officers was at ironic odds with the dull, sordid miseries, the hardships and sickness suffered generally by the forces during the ensuing march into Germany.

After Dettingen Lord George's merits as officer during his first experience of active service were recognized by his being made one of the King's aides-de-camp. He wrote descriptive letters to his father at this time of the War of the Austrian Succession,[1] in 1743 and 1744, from Biebrick, Worms, Spire, Ostend, Bruges, Ghent and Berlingnen. Many passages of these letters are of considerable interest, but chiefly so for students of military history and technique. They show how well Sackville understood his profession. The narrative is often very characteristic in its point of view and its expression:

> "Sir Thomas Wynne," (he writes from Biebrick in August, 1743) "keeps a magnificent table; he complains of the expence, indeed it must be prodigious. He would gladly make it less, but does not know how to contrive it. He thought the number of dishes at the Green Cloth so great that if the King knew it he would order it to be lessen'd, so Sr. Thos very cunningly gave him the bill of the Green Cloth dinner instead of his own, but the plot did not take, and Lord Dalawar told Sr. Thomas that the King thought it was a shame there should be so little. In short it is a joke with the Duke of Richmond, &c. to make everybody drink as much wine as they can on purpose to work Sir Thomas Wynne, and he is fool enough to show that it hurts him. A ribbon was never better bestow'd than upon General Honeywood. It is impossible to conceive how ridiculously fond he is of his new honour. Lord Rothes is very ill of the bloody flux. It is what vast numbers of people have had, and the camp in general is more sickly at present than it has been yet, and chiefly of that disorder. It got first among them by their being obliged to lye out in

[1] England's entrance into this war on the side of Austria and her allies was of course dictated by the "traditional enmity" between France and England. France had allied herself with Prussia against Austria in 1741. Our alliance with Prussia during the Seven Years' War (1756-1763) seemed no less natural, because it was in alliance with France as well as with Russia and the German princes that Austria attacked Prussia.

the rain after the battle of Dettingen, and they have never been able to get rid of it since. And what is more extraordinary it is catching, so that in one hospital no less than thirty-seven nurses have died of it. We have at this time upwards of 2,200 English sick, and as many Hanoverians . . . The Duke [of Cumberland] is still lame; he says he shall soon be well, but I do not believe it, for the leg that was wounded is considerably shrunk up, but as it is the fashion to say that he is almost well I ought not to say otherwise . . ."

" . . . I suppose by our stopping so long here it is not yet determin'd what is to be done next . . . The Elector was yesterday at the King's quarters and was very graciously receiv'd. As he came in his Majesty moved towards the door to meet him, and when he came close to him it was something between a bow and an embrace . . . The Elector is a very good looking man, not unlike my Lord Orford."

A letter from Spire in October shows how much dependence was placed, in warfare at that time, on information from deserters as to the enemy's movements and dispositions; also how difficult it was to restrain soldiers from bad behaviour. " Since we have been in the Palatinate the soldiers will not be persuaded but that they are in an enemy's country, and they have plunder'd and committed all sorts of disorders." This led to the King ordering that anyone found half a league from camp should be " immediately hang'd up without any trial." " The Provost goes his rounds with a strong guard and an officer of each nation to put this order in execution. It had a very good effect, for tho' the Provost was out all day yesterday I do not hear that any body has suffer'd." The order was comprehensive. " It not only extends to soldiers but to officers' servants and to the women that fill the camp."

The soldiers were as predatory and rough as they were brave and enduring. Baulked of pillage, they found other means of self-expression. " The Blues have shown their desire of fighting this campaign by picking quarrel with Ligonier's regiment. It began with boxing, but ended in drawing their broadswords, and four or five of the Blues are so hurt that I am afraid they will be able to give no further marks of their courage this year . . . It is really very lucky it ended in the disabling only of four or five men.''

Relations between the English and the Hanoverian soldiery were more harmonious. ''I cannot help every day looking with surprise on the good agreement of the English and Hanoverians. They get drunk very comfortably together, and talk and sing a vast deal without understanding one syllable of what they say to one another.'' The contrasting unpopularity of the English with the natives is emphasized by Lord George in the same letter. ''If we think to make them our well wishers by good usage we shall only when it is too late find that we are mistaken, for they hate and detest us for a parcel of damn'd heretics, and for their own sakes would be willing to-morrow to put themselves under the protection of the French.''

On this campaign there were not only difficulties, sickness, and hardship, there was danger enough for all. Sackville writes on arrival at Ghent in June, 1744: ''The garrison here was in great pain for us, and General Campbell march'd out to our relief the day we had like to have been demolish'd.'' The month before he had written from Bruges : ''To our great disappointment we were yesterday obliged to return to this place after we had march'd about twelve miles in our way to Ghent, and by very good luck we retreated without any loss. Had we reach'd the half-way house where we intended to have halted (and we were within a quarter of a mile of it), I think we must have all been cut to pieces or taken prisoners.''

It was at Fontenoy that Sackville came nearest to losing his life. Of that hazard he has apparently left no record. He was shot in the breast by a musket-ball while leading his regiment, which was at that time so advanced, so near to enemy headquarters, that Sackville, after being thrown upon a waggon with many other wounded men, was taken to the French King's tent to have his wounds dressed. It was a terrible battle. ''The soldiery,'' James Wolfe wrote at the time from Ghent, ''behaved with the utmost bravery and courage during the whole affair, but rather rash and impetuous." British dead covered the field. According to one contemporary rhymer, the gallantry of the British was not matched by that of the better fed Hanoverians :

Our men almost starv'd, yet in Heart were full stout,
They repuls'd, they attack'd, and the French put to rout;
The Hanoverians, tho' cramm'd to the eyes with good food,
Faced about to the Right and sneaked into the wood.
Their bellies so full, too unwieldy to Fight,
For decency they step'd aside for to sh-te,
Tho' some have affirmed that as sure as a Gun,
'Twas Fear made them sh-te, 'twas Fear made them run.

Sackville preserved his Fontenoy uniform, tattered by bullet-holes in the skirt of the coat and marked by the musket-ball that nearly killed him. When he said that Lord North received the news of the fall of Yorktown " like a ball in the breast," he knew what he meant.

Major-General Bragg's regiment was ordered home for the Rebellion of '45, but, before the Pretender, Charles Edward, set sail for Scotland in the summer of that year, Sackville had returned to England to recover from his wounds. He was at his house in Whitehall when the Rebellion broke out. His letters of this period to his close friend, Captain, afterwards Major Younge, who was stationed in the north, are of some importance. They show Lord George's interest in the politics of the day, noting such matters as the support given by Pitt, Lyttleton, and the Grenvilles to the Ministry when it was expected that they would join the Opposition. When he did not think it likely that the rebels would give any serious trouble, Sackville was not anxious to go north. "I am obliged to you for wishing me at the head of the regiment in your neighbourhood [Berwick-on-Tweed]. I cannot say I am solicitous about it; if the king pleases to give it to me, I must accept of it with thankfulness, but as I have already the rank of colonel, *il me fera plus d'honneur que de plaisir* . . . Our fears of an invasion are almost entirely laid aside, and as we are apt to go from one extreme to another, we are already thinking what regiments are to be sent abroad; there is not the least doubt of ten thousand men going, if the rebels in the north do not grow more formidable than they are at present."

"It is generally believed," he wrote in another letter to Younge, "that they [the rebels] will soon disperse, though the French have a mind, I suppose, to keep up their spirits, by ordering the embarkation made at Ostend, of about fifteen hundred of the Irish brigade, to sail at all events." He enters into some present details of the war in the Low Countries, anticipating the surrender of Brussels to the French. "If the Hessians had but staid in Flanders, it would have been of the greatest advantage, and surely they will only be troublesome to you in Scotland. We remain still in the same uncertainty about the part we are to take upon the Continent. If we receive good news from Brussels, I dare say we should do something immediately, but if that garrison, consisting of the best part of the Dutch army, should be lost, I know not what submissions and conditions the French would impose upon the Dutch that they would not, with thankfulness, receive." Believers in Sackville's identity with Junius note with satisfaction that in this letter Lord George shows the same intimate knowledge of the circumstances of Lord Ligonier's removal from his command as is shown by Junius when he wrote replying to Sir William Draper.

Lord George was soon well enough to be able to relish the pleasures of London life. He went to a ball at Lady Rochford's, "one of the best I ever saw." He writes of those who were wounded with him at Fontenoy and were evidently a good deal worse for it than he was, less apt for enjoyment of ball-room exercise and display. "Recté is now Captain Lieutenant, and upon crutches; he was shot through the foot at Fontenoi, and though he has saved his leg, he has not yet much use of it. . .Captain Sailly is just arrived from captivity; his wounds are well, but his beauty rather decreased."

When the Scottish Rebellion had become a serious matter,

"The attention of every body (Sackville writes) is entirely upon the North, and we wait with great impatience to see the effect the arrival of Marshal Wade in that country will have upon the rebels. By their not yet having marched southward, it seems as if they had laid the thoughts of it aside. Some go so far as to imagine that they will retire towards the Highlands upon his approach, without venturing a battle, but I think as their force is now equal to whatever they can hope hereafter to draw together, that they will engage him at all events; and if they should have success, God knows what the consequences would be. France would not then delay a moment the making a decision in some part of England,—their coast is crowded with troops, and there are now above forty sail of small vessels at Dunkirk, which may be designed for an embarkation.

"The House of Commons sat yesterday till seven o'clock; Mr. Hume Campbell and Mr. Pitt moved for enquiring immediately into the causes of the progress of the rebels, but the motion was thought a little premature, as the truth of those affairs was not so easily come at during the rebellion; so that upon the division the motion was rejected by 124 to 112."

About six weeks before this letter was written George the Second, with the Duke of Cumberland, had returned from Germany. As the Jacobites were more and more successful in the north, it was decided that the Duke of Cumberland should take command against them. Sackville was with him. In February, 1746, Cumberland's forces reached the neighbourhood of Edinburgh, which they soon recaptured. They then pushed on to Stirling Castle, Falkirk, and Inverness; and, after exhausting marches, the famous engagement at Culloden followed. The Rebellion was virtually over. Sackville's services at Culloden were recognized by his appointment as Colonel of the 20th Foot, now the 1st Lancashire Fusiliers. In early June he was at Fort Augustus in command of a detachment, and bringing with him "eight prisoners and upwards of 2,400 black cattle besides a great number of goats and sheep." To set against this, the narrative in *Scott's Magazine* continues: "Lord George Sackville's baggage was taken by a party of about a dozen, a very little way behind the detachment.

They took all his horses, bedding linen, provisions; and, after plundering his servants, released them."

At Fort Augustus the barracks had been destroyed, and the Duke of Cumberland had to sleep in a tent. But whatever inconvenience or discomfort he suffered did not abate that Prince's hearty Hanoverian sense of fun. "The brave Duke makes all about him as jovial as the place will admit of. Last Wednesday he gave two prizes to the soldiers to run bare-backed galloways taken from the rebels. These galloways are little larger than a good tup and there was excellent sport. Yesterday H.R.H. gave a fine holland smock to the soldiers' wives, to be run for on these galloways, also bare-backed, and riding with their limbs on each side the horse like men. Eight started, and there were three of the finest heats ever seen."

Sackville proceeded to Perth as commander-in-chief of the British forces there during Major-General Skelton's absence. At this time he was barely thirty years old. With a touch of his usual irony he writes to Major Younge of his being "in the great and elevated situation of Commander of his Majesty's forces in Perth. Major-General Skelton having, or pretending to have, business in England, so that till his return I have the honour to supply his place. *Haud equidem tali me dignor honore.* I should not have made use of Latin words but in compliment to *socios habuisse dolores.* I take for granted you have recourse to any other language rather than French, thinking my criticisms extend to no other, et il faut avouer que Monsieur ait raison." "A stupid letter," Sackville calls this one, perhaps because it is particularly light; a long idle letter written because he was in the mood to write it, though he had nothing much to say. It is a letter written at ease and in good humour, just the kind of letter that is of especial value to those whose interest is in the writer. Lord George did not like being at Perth, but he could make himself reasonably happy, somewhat after the fashion of Epictetus.

"I must confess, that although I should not receive with the least reluctance an order to repair to London, yet I am not fashionable enough to be miserable in my present situation, remote as it is from those I am used to live with, and different as the country and the climate are from those I might expect to be in. I do not pretend to much philosophy but the maxim I have laid down, and have hitherto constantly pursued, is to compare my situation with what it might have been, and myself with those who have much greater reason to complain than I have; not envying those who are more fortunate and ought to be more happy.

"Possibly this letter may find you removed from Aire, and probably upon your march to England . . . When you are settled in quarters, the gulf between you and London may easily be passed, et peut-être j'aurai l'honneur en deux mois d'ici de vous voir briller chez Madame l'Ambassadrice de Venice; but let me advise you to prepare yourself for the affront of being taken for a foreigner by every body that is not acquainted with you.

"The stay I am to make in this country is yet uncertain; the 18th November the Parliament meets. If members are wanted I suppose we shall be sent for, the beginning of next month. If business is likely to go on quietly, they may possibly not care to give us the trouble of so long a journey—Quant à moi je suis content. My present motto is, *in utrumque paratus,* and all I pray for is that I may never have occasion any more to visit these Northern Hills, for I think nothing but a Rebellion can ever call me there again. An acquaintance of yours bears me company in this place, Cunninghame[1] is his name, if that is not sufficient to call him to your remembrance, il a une soeur au Chateau de Stirling qui n'est pas laide . . . You will forgive the length of this stupid letter, but it is a fault I am not often guilty of, therefore I may expect to have it the easier excused, for I could in much fewer words have assured you of my regard ann esteem for you, and my sincere wishes for your happiness wherever you go, and whatever you undertake. —Adieu."

[1] Another close friend of Sackville's, already referred to in Chapters III and IV. He was afterwards Adjutant-General of Ireland. His name is variously spelt.

By the end of the year the campaign was ended and Sackville was sent with his regiment to Dover Castle. After Christmas he was back at his house in Whitehall, and from there wrote to Younge at Kilmarnock another of those letters, too few of which have been preserved, debonair, engaging, young, with youthful vigour under easy control, and with the kind of light auspicious satirical touch that he never lost control of, even during the most inauspicious times of his later life. One French expression in this letter seems to show that he was a reader of Rabelais. Disclosures of Lord George's light-hearted interest in social life, in current gossip or scandal, in love-affairs, in the stage; of those propensities which gained him the reputation of the gayest man in Ireland, are not so frequent that apology should be needed for quoting the letter almost in full.

" I should have wrote to you sooner had I been in London, but you must know it is now become so fashionable for Colonels to do their own duty, that I have diverted myself, during the holidays, in living with my regiment in Dover Castle; and as I thought dating a letter from thence would not make so good an appearance as dating from Whitehall, I deferred it till I came hither, not that I think I am the least wiser than I was before . . . Your letter was the best performance of the kind I ever read, and, indeed, I am much obliged to you for it. I don't know whether Cunninghame will say as much, for he never will outlive the name of ' aimable bonbon ' . . . De quoi parlerai je? les opéras ne valent rien, les assemblées ne brillent point jusqu'à present, il ne reste donc que les comédies pour toute ressource, et il faut avouer qu'elles me plaisent, nonobstant que le grand Quin n'est point employé . . .

On débite que Milord Anson doit epouser Mademoiselle Yorke, fille de Grand Chancelier; il ne se porte pas bien à present, et la Demoiselle s'impatiente, qu'il ne se trouve pas encore en état de bander comme un Carme. Qu'avez vous fait, mon cher Major, que vos amis sont privés si long tems de votre compagnie? Vous avez trouvés peut-être des charmes invincibles en Ecosse que vous fassent oublier vos autres attachements. L'amour ne se borne point aux pays fertiles, il se retire souvent aux montagnes, et se pique même de soumettre des sauvages à son empire—si en chemin faisant il vous a rencontré, ne s'est il pas arreté un peu à rallumer le feu dans un coeur qui lui a fait tant d'honneur? mais badiner à part—vous avez été assez long tems auprès de votre regiment, pour demander un congé de quelques mois, venez au plutôt; autrement vous ne vous trouverez plus au fait des affaires, et bien des nouvelles modes seront passées avant que vous les ayes donnés votre approbation.

"Your old acquaintance, Colonel Howard, is going to be married to Lady Lucy Wentworth, Conway has pretty well recovered his looks. My Lady Ailesbury still looks fatigued. God knows what they have been doing together. It is expected the Duke will soon think of returning to the army. We ave had no letters from Holland for some days, so we do not know whether the French have attempted anything. My regiment is to have the happiness of serving abroad this year, we envy you that indulge in ease and plenty, you must pretend to envy us for the honour we attempt to gain. When I last heard from poor Jocelyn, he was rather better; he still flatters himself with the hopes of being able to serve this campaign, but I want faith. I think you ought to be ashamed to suffer a lieutenant of foot to be in possession of the best thing in Stirling Castle [Cunninghame's sister?]. You Field-Officers are so wise and cautious that you will not marry, without a woman brings a great sum of money along with her. Some people say I am wrong to attribute it to prudence, and insist upon it that your caution proceeds from want of vigour. Though you may want vigour it is no reason you should not want patience, and I am sure I have tried yours so sufficiently, that if my modesty does not, at least my paper forces me to release you, with only just room to assure you how sincerely I am

"Your faithful servant,

"Geo: Sackville."

As he anticipated, Sackville had again " the happiness of serving abroad " in 1747 and 1748; in Flanders with the Duke of Cumberland for the concluding campaigns of the War of the Austrian Succession. It was at the end of the war, during peace negotiations, that the Duke sent him to arrange a general armistice in conference with Marshal Saxe at French Headquarters. Cumberland's instructions, for Colonel Lord George Sackville, dated May 2nd, 1748, from Headquarters at Hellinroveck, are that " You will proceed with your pass and with a French trumpet and an English drum, and on your arrival at the first French post, you will, in case you should be stop'd, send the trumpet forward with the pass to inform the Marshal of Saxe of your arrival at their posts charged with a letter from me. As soon as you shall arrive at the Marshal of Saxe's quarters you will deliver him the letter you are charg'd with for him, desiring at the same time that he will consent to your going into Maestrecht, which, if he agrees to, you will immediately do, and deliver the letter you are charg'd with to the Commandant, Monsr d'Aylva, or to the commanding officer, whom you will desire to open it in case of any accident hapned [*sic*] to the other.

" You will represent to him that as the preliminarys for a peace are already sign'd, and that in consequence a cessation of arms has been agreed to with an exception to the siege of Maestrecht, I am thereby deprived of the means of being able to second the bravery of their defence, and that it is therefore my advice that he accepts an honorable capitulation in order to save the lives of so many brave men, and in case that cannot be obtained, I need prescribe no rule of conduct to an officer who has already shewn so much gallantry and conduct."

Four days later Sackville wrote an account of the event to his father, in a style, as might be expected, different from that of letters to friends of his own age on less serious topics, but bearing none the less some marks of himself.

> " Tho' I was there but one day (he writes), I saw so many new and diverting scenes that it will furnish me with material for consideration for some time. The ridiculous

figure I must have made in riding blindfolded for about half a league in the French camp, the remarks of the soldiers upon me, my being unblinded at the headquarters in a court fill'd with French officers, before I recover'd my eye sight carry'd into a great room where the Maréchal stood at his levée, my being obliged to introduce myself, and then retiring immediately with him and beginning upon business. These sort of things when they are over are entertaining to relate, tho' when they happen one does not feel quite so pleasant under. The Maréchal made excuses about my being blinded and the officer was not a little abused by the whole court."

Lord George found the Marshal "not at all pleased with what M. St. Severin had done" in the peace negotiations. They had long discussions. De Saxe said he had no orders to agree to an armistice, he must wait for the return of a courier, but, if he did have orders, he would not object to Cumberland's plan. Sackville's letter to his father, with its detailed report of all the difficulties and delays; both with De Saxe and at Maestrecht, is in the Appendix, pp. 278-280. The Duke of Cumberland, although he was by no means friendly to Lord George, was much pleased by his conduct of this mission. "You may imagine that I thought myself greatly honour'd in being thus distinguished by the Duke, but I own I was frightened when I found so many unexpected difficultys, and that instead of carrying a letter and receiving an answer, I was obliged to become a negotiator. However, I had the good fortune to do nothing that H.R.H. disapproved of, and indeed he was pleas'd to say much more to me than I deserved."

There is one expression here which is of some significance in view of the charge of cowardice so frequently made against Sackville after the battle of Minden. A coward is not likely to bring himself to say or write the words, "I own I was frightened."

After the peace in 1748 Lord George was again in England. In 1749 he was appointed Colonel of a regiment of Dragoons in succession to Major-General Cholmondeley. At that time he and Wolfe[1] " of Quebec " were serving together as Major Wolfe and Colonel Sackville. They were on intimate terms. Later, Wolfe wrote him long letters from Canada. His opinion of Sackville was a high one. " We are to lose him without hopes of finding his equal."

It was not until 1755 that Lord George was made Major-General, immediately after his four years in Ireland. It was a year or so later that Percival Stockdale[2] was under his command in camp at Chatham and " was honoured with a share of his social and convivial attention." Stockdale was himself a man of civilized intelligence: he and his commanding officer no doubt agreed on some things, on political chicanery, for instance. " Sensible and good minds," writes Stockdale, " might, at any time, easily frame a simple, but salutary and efficient political code; by obvious and prominent analogies to private life. But what room would there then be for the state pedantry of politicians; for the difficulties, and mysteries, which are by themselves created; for the unrestrained workings of their corrupt hearts; for the lawless gratification of their insatiable passion for wealth, and dominion; a passion which never hesitates to insult, and break down, the most sacred and invaluable rights of our species ? "

Stockdale describes Lord George as " rather tall, and well formed," and as having " an elegance, a dignity of deportment." " He was very conversant with books, and men . . . and eloquent, often poignant, in conversation." But Stockdale, who was writing his reminiscences after Minden and the court-martial, allows sometimes, perhaps, the image of the later tragic and persecuted Sackville to blur his memories of Sackville as he knew him in camp at Chatham. Or it may be that this kindly and sensible clergyman, as he was after he left the Army, was unduly sensitive to what he describes as " a reserve and haughtiness in Lord George's manner, which depressed and darkened all that was agreeable and engaging in

[1] Further account of their relations is given on pp. 124 and 125.

[2] Stockdale's defence of Sackville's conduct at Minden is quoted on pp. 120 and 121.

him." "It shaded," he says, "those talents which were worthy to be admired; it naturally, and very fairly, hurt the reasonable self-love of his acquaintances and friends. His integrity commanded esteem, his abilities praise; but to attract the heart was not one of those abilities . . . For want of this flexibility . . . for want of a social gaiety, and affection, which one ought to cultivate, the publick were not interested in his good fortune—his elevation gave them no pleasure; and they did not regret his fall."

Stockdale remembers one observation, characteristic of Sackville's critical clarity, on the qualities of Lord Tyrawley as a *bel esprit* compared with those of Lord Chesterfield. "The first time," said Sackville, "I heard Lord Tyrawley converse, I thought him very entertaining; the second time, very well; and the third time, very indifferent. That is not the way with my lord Chesterfield; *he* never flags."

In 1756—the last peace with France had, of course, not lasted long—Lord George went with the then Duke of Marlborough on an expedition against St. Malo and Cherbourg. The next year Pitt decided on another of these expeditions, this time against Rochfort, and Sackville was offered the leadership of the land forces. He refused the offer. Sir John Mordaunt then accepted it. This expedition was, as Sackville foresaw that it would be, a failure. After the event many shared the opinion that "the generals were undoubtedly wrong to accept a command so little promising as one against that strong town and fortress; a command indeed so evidently tending to miscarriage, and of so sure an ill consequence to themselves." Pitt was blamed for allowing his "too sanguine desire to raise the glory of his country" to lead him on to such an attempt "without having even a moral certainty of its success." An anonymous "Officer in the Army," in a "Letter to the People of Great-Britain," summed up what was Sackville's view of the whole business in a vigorous and lively style :

"The design against Rochfort was purely chimerical . . . If we had been able to force that place—nay, and to burn all shipping, docks, magasines and arsenals—all this would have been but scratching a finger of France instead of running her thro' the body . . . And what were the English to pay for this enterprise? Why, a million and a half of money, and ten thousand souls, for I will venture to affirm that if our brave soldiers had landed on the Gallick continent and proceeded to Rochfort not one of the whole body would have returned back."

Sackville, late in 1757, took part in the Enquiry ordered to be held into General Mordaunt's conduct of the expedition. But it was, so Sackville felt, not Mordaunt's conduct that deserved censure, but Pitt's plan.

After the 1751-1755 Irish period Sackville, in his late thirties and early forties, became important in political as well as in military affairs. He had since 1741 sat in the House of Commons for Dover, and had made his first recorded speech in 1750, on the Mutiny Bill, showing full knowledge and full ability to use it. But "he was now rising," as Walpole says, "to a principal figure"; and the letters he received at this time show very clearly the regard and deference that were paid to him by the political notabilities of the day. In September, 1755, Henry Fox wrote to tell Sackville that "the King has declared his intention to make me Secretary of State, and give me the conduct of his affairs in the H. of Commons. If I might flatter myself that your lordship approves of this and would support me in my new station, I should be happy and oblig'd to a very great degree. I know your lordship's abilitys, and should esteem your friendship and be proud of it." He proposes "to wait on yr lordship as soon as I see you are in town."

Lord George was never at all anxious to be either the patron or the client of politicians. To this letter he replied diplomatically and non-committally. He "heartily wishes" that Mr. Fox's measures may be such "as may enable me to convince you of the sincere desire I have of deserving your good opinion and friendship."

There are several letters of Henry Fox to Lord George,

letters in which he begs to see him, and writes, in some agitation, of the critical state of political affairs.

"Three months domestick quiet," he writes towards the end of 1756, "is as necessary to this country as ever a night's sleep was to a man dying in a fever." "Mr. Pitt is arrogant, and I think dishonest, if not mad, to take the whole upon him." "I will do anything to join with Pitt," he had written a week before. Now he will "endeavour to make his administration as little detrimental as may be." These letters must have amused Lord George.

Pitt himself is almost fulsome in his compliments. "Nothing," he writes to Lord George in the autumn of 1757, "can be indifferent to me about which you can form a wish. The favourable and kind sentiments with which your Lordship is so good to accompany your commands to your humble servant must ever be rank'd among my most valuable possessions, and I assure your lordship that however ill I know my title to be, this is the property I intend the longest to defend." In this letter Pitt refers to "the unhappy retreat from the coast of Rochefort, *re intentata,*" and says, oddly, that it has sunk him into little less than despair of the publick. He sees no end of "the train of mischiefs," considers the state of the nation "indeed a perilous one, and fitter for meditation than discourse; at least not subject matter of a letter by the post;" and hopes "it will not be long before I have the succour and consolation of full conversation with your lordship on a scene of distress and danger that demands all the ability the age can furnish and the best portion of which your lordship has to give."

This was a very different tone from that of Pitt to Lord George after Minden. As Lord George observed, he became very "ministerial" then.

At the end of 1757 Sackville became Lieutenant-General of the Ordnance. Lord Temple, writing to him on that occasion, abounds in eulogy. "I cannot possibly let the messenger return with your commission sealed by me and not avail myself of this pleasing opportunity of expressing to you with how much satisfaction I executed this part of my office. I rejoice for my own sake as one poor individual of the public at large of every step that your lordship takes towards the head of your profession because it affords me the flattering prospect that I may live to see the military glory of this country once again retrieved . . . Add to this every private consideration of friendship and esteem.''

A letter from Sackville to the Duke of Newcastle in 1755 shows unmistakably his attitude towards the political intrigue into which it was sought to draw him. He will have nothing to do with it; he will not seek advance in his own profession as a soldier by such means. It is a diplomatic letter, though hardly so diplomatic as the Duke might have wished. The candour and force of the expression completely achieve their aim of making misconception impossible. The writer's character is alive in every line. After thanking the Duke of Newcastle for '' the honour he does me in thinking me worthy of his attention,'' Lord George continues :

> '' I hope to deserve the king's favour by expressing the strongest zeal for his service, but I desire to remain free from a particular connection with any of his ministers. I cannot ask for distinction or emolument in my profession, since I am to obtain it by resolving to support future measures of which I cannot have the least knowledge, and defend those that are past, which I cannot yet comprehend.
>
> '' I trust that by saying this I shall not be represented to his Majesty in the light of a person discontented or desirous to dismiss those ministers he may please to employ. I heartily wish I may be able to join in the support of every measure they may propose, for I do declare that I have neither political connection or engagement with any party or person whatsoever, and I farther hope that I shall not be driven into it by being misrepresented to the King, and consequently debarred from those marks of his favour which my rank in the army or my services may give me reason to hope for.''

This is not the kind of letter than any politician would care to receive. There is no reason for surprise that leaders in the political world should not have been anxious to help Sackville to his feet after the court-martial had gone against him.

In 1758, the year after he had sat on the Rochefort Enquiry, Sackville was again engaged in one of Pitt's "buccaneering" expeditions, scoffed at by Horace Walpole as they were by Sackville himself. Pitt was still "determined to strike some mighty stroke," and "unfortunately his mind was not purged of its vision of Rochefort." Marlborough was the general of this new expedition, and Sackville, as before, was obliged to go with him. They sailed from Spithead to St. Malo, reconnoitred there, and landed in the Bay of Cancale. Sackville marched in command of the first columns. A large French army approached and chased the adventurous English back to their ships. "The French learned that they were not to be conquered by every Duke of Marlborough." Admiral Howe was discouraged from making an attack by the weather: the expedition landed ingloriously at the Isle of Wight, and the leaders returned to London. The Earl of Shelburne, one of Lord George's most determined and vindictive enemies, lays the blame for this failure upon Lord George's incompetence and lack of spirit. Detailed descriptive letters from General Irwin and from Alexander MacDowall which, though written from different standpoints, supplement and verify each other, show that this charge is without any foundation.

The expedition, abortive though it was, had at least the effect of diverting French operations from Germany. Some of Marlborough's troops were now sent to Germany to be commanded by Prince Ferdinand of Brunswick, and in September Marlborough arrived in Hanover with Sackville as his second-in-command. When he died the next month of an epidemic at Munster Sackville took command of all the British forces, horse and foot, serving on the Lower Rhine. He was, from this time, for about ten months, on highest ground, with full prospects now of a career of military greatness which Minden broke beyond any reparation.

Chapter VI

MINDEN

At the Battle of Minden in August, 1759, Lord George Sackville was thus Commander-in-Chief of the small British force allied with the Germans, in defence of Hanover, against the French. The German Prince, Ferdinand of Brunswick, was in supreme command. When the battle was begun, Ferdinand sent Sackville orders by Captain Ligonier to bring up all the cavalry. Immediately afterwards Colonel Fitzroy[1] brought from Ferdinand another order, that Sackville should bring up the British cavalry only, and to the left. Sackville always especially disliked any sort of ambiguity. Lest he should mistakenly obey either of these almost simultaneous orders, and gravely doubting the second one—" Would he have me break the line?"—he sent his aide-de-camp, Captain Smith, to lead on the British cavalry, and, at some risk, rode over to the Prince for an explanation. When, after this delay, Sackville advanced, he did not do so quickly enough for the British cavalry to engage in the battle, and he twice halted Lord Granby who was under his command. The battle was won by artillery, the first to be won so; but victory was not as crushing as it might have been if British honour and glory had been gained at the cost of British lives. These are the admitted facts. As soon as we go further, there is controversy.

It is perhaps best to begin by turning back. Sackville and Ferdinand were not good friends. That Sackville did not like Ferdinand, that he did not care to be deferential to or even tactful with him, is evident enough from a single incident. Two nights before the Minden battle, at supper at headquarters, Sackville was praising the Maréchal de Contades. " Mais

[1] Sackville's letter to Fitzroy, written immediately after the battle, and Fitzroy's reply, are in the Appendix, pp. 280–283.

Minden Cartoons.

pourtant," observed Ferdinand, "j'ai vu le dos du Maréchal de Contades; il n'a jamais vu le mien." Sackville enquired where it was that the Prince had seen the Marshal's back. "À Crévelt? But Crévelt, Monseigneur Prince Ferdinand, was only an affair, not a battle." The Prince's brag fell flat: he was not used to such strokes, he resented them. The Duke of Marlborough had treated him very differently; with him he had always had the upper hand. In the company of the Duke's successor he could not feel so important; he was bound before long to suspect this, and then, with rapidly increasing chagrin and annoyance, he was bound to be sure of it.

The correspondence between the two men during the first seven months of 1759 is as might be expected, their official relationship being as it was. They frequently exchanged military information; and, early in July, Ferdinand had written to Sackville, telling him of the French capture of Minden and asking his immediate advice, which was immediately given. But, although it is clear that Ferdinand valued Sackville's military judgment and that Sackville did not fail in his obligations towards the supreme commander, it is equally clear, though not from this correspondence, that the essential incompatibilities between these two were too strong to be suppressed.

Sackville had always mistrusted as well as disliked the Prince. Scrupulous in integrity himself, he resented Ferdinand's prodigal appropriations of British funds[1] which were never

[1] It was not long before Ferdinand's misappropriations became generally known. Dodington, in his *Diary*, reports a conversation of his, early in 1761, with Lord Bute: "I told him that I thought Prince Ferdinand was become as unpopular in the Army as he was once popular; that he was accused of three great heads of malversation. The first was that he had exacted complete pay for uncomplete corps; the second, that not one shilling of all those devastating contributions had been carried to the public account; the third, that he had received good money and had paid the troops in bad to a very great amount, and at a great discount." It does not appear that any satisfactory rebuttal of these charges was ever made.

"His Highness might have served us better," writes Walpole, "had he had no interests to serve but ours. The sums which were never refused to him, and for which, not being a Briton, he could not be called to account, will perhaps outweigh the glory he procured to our arms, the benefits that resulted from his success, or the share which he made us take in saving the King of Prussia from destruction. Should the last-named Prince," Walpole continues in prophetic inspiration coupled with irony, "prove oftener our enemy than our Ally, we must comfort ourselves with having guarded the Protetsant religion in Germany."

accounted for. He resented the preposterous exactions of German agents, and he did not disguise what he felt. "Too honestly, too indiscreetly, too insultingly" he let the Prince see that this unwarrantable German freedom with British gold "had not escaped his observation." In Sackville's mind, when he had that second order, to bring up the British cavalry alone, there may well have been the thought that Ferdinand now intended to waste British lives as lavishly and as unjustifiably as he had wasted British money, a thought followed at once by the determination that this should not happen if he could help it. He knew, as Walpole did, that Ferdinand put his own interests and German interests first, but he did not share Walpole's opinion that the Prince was "intituled most deservedly to the character of a consummate general." No doubt his opinion of the abilities of Ferdinand, who was, at the least, among the ablest lieutenants of Frederick the Great, was too low; and no doubt he should not have allowed his opinion to affect the routine of his military obedience. That it did so, that Sackville at Minden acted as he did not only because he was in doubt over the two contradictory orders, can hardly be disputed; nor can there be much question that, when he had ascertained that the British cavalry was to advance, it was not solely from a pedantic adherence to correct procedure that he forebore haste and halted Lord Granby. It was not, as some thought, because he wanted to spite the Prince by depriving him of victory—or, at least, of overwhelming victory—for that would have been entirely out of Sackville's character, but rather because of his mistrust of the Prince, because he was determined to go no further than he had to go in co-operation with the plan of a foreigner for taking what he believed to be unnecessary toll of British lives. Angered, made obstinate by anger, but certainly not in the least subjected to any fear, he found it impossible to play the part assigned to him by military discipline. One resolve, not a reasoned one but of high emotional colour, stood in the foreground of his temper: that this boastful, swindling German, who had just shown that he did not know his own mind for two minutes together, should not blunder English troops into needless slaughter if he, an English Sackville, could help it. That he should have felt as he did and behaved as he did was incorrect; but no one who can remember the kind of incompatibilities that could sometimes exist between allied commanders in the two world wars will find it difficult to understand either the feelings or the behaviour.

If, as a result of such disobedience to a foreign commander as Sackville's at Minden, an *advance* were to be made, and the disobedience were to find its issue in bloodshed and honour and glory, even in glory misadventured, the heroic event would be held to justify what would then appear as a mere breach of propriety and not as the felony of a traitor and a coward, covering his name, as Carlyle observed of Sackville, with eternal infamy. But "the world, which readily pardons the excesses of intemperate courage, never forgives the least appearance of backwardness in the field": and this was why Sackville, after Minden, was with such violence censured and disgraced. Such protests as that of George Dodington[1] in his favour were not then to be entertained for a moment by any man of spirit.

It was as easy to admire and praise Lord Granby, Sackville's second-in-command, as it was to despise and condemn Sackville himself. Granby, pliant, dashing, affable, hard-drinking—appropriate godfather, indeed, to so many of the taverns of England—was utterly unlike Sackville in almost every particular. While Sackville "never had the art of conciliating affection," Granby was generally beloved both by officers and men. He was by nature destined for extreme popularity.[2] Thirty-two young officers ardently desired to be his aide-de-camp. He and the reserved, ungregarious Sackville could never get on well together. Granby, however, was open and generous. At the court-martial he was not in the least vindictive. Walpole notes, indeed, that he "showed honourable

[1] "He . . . is made a sacrifice to a German general, whose displeasure he had incurred for not suffering without remonstrance the British Army to be squandered, and the British Troops to be destroyed by undue preference in the defence of Hanover."

[2] "Lord Granby has entirely defeated the French! The foreign Gazettes, I suppose, will give the victory to Prince Ferdinand, but the mob of London, who must know best, assure me that it is all their own Marquis's doing."—Horace Walpole.

and compassionate tenderness," that he "palliated or suppressed whatever might load the prisoner." But Ferdinand could and did use him with deadly effect against Sackville at Minden.

With Ferdinand Granby was a great favourite. The Prince could drink with him, brag with him, do what he liked with him. Granby did not care how much English money passed into German hands. He had no sense of the value of money. He was extravagant, unsuspicious, unexacting, amenable, himself spending or flinging away all the money he could, out of his "unbounded good nature and generosity." He was skilful and brave, but, like Ferdinand, lacking in integrity. The man who was later to be so savagely assailed by "Junius" for degrading the office of commander-in-chief to that of a broker in commissions was not one to complain of the rapacities of the Prince and the German agents, as Sackville so emphatically was.

Granby's position as Sackville's second-in-command is a circumstance only second in importance to that of Sackville's position under Ferdinand. Granby, with his ardent and unreflective obedience to the Prince, was the very man to throw Sackville's "hesitations and equivocations" into the blackest, or drabbest relief. Ferdinand took care that his favourite should shine in all possible lustre so as to push to extremity Sackville's discredit. During the battle he ignored Sackville's position as commander-in-chief by giving orders direct to Granby to advance the second line of cavalry, thus exalting Granby at the cost of Sackville's humiliation, a behaviour not of the kind to encourage the commander-in-chief's own nicety in observance of military proprieties or conventions. The real error of Minden, it has been contended, was the "unpardonable *bêtise*" of Ferdinand in sending his commands to a subordinate over Sackville's head.

After the battle Ferdinand in his Orders made it almost grossly plain that things would have gone very differently and very much better if only Granby had been in Sackville's place:

> "His Serene Highness further Orders it to be declared to Lieutenant General THE MARQUIS of GRANBY, that

He is persuaded, that if he had had the good Fortune to have had HIM at the Head of the Cavalry of the RIGHT Wing, his Presence would have greatly contributed to make the decision of that day more Complete, and more brilliant."

Imputation of guilt[1] is equally patent in the following Order; and again the imputation seems deadlier, or more ominous, because Sackville is unnamed:

"And his Serene Highness Desires and Orders the Generals of the Army, that upon all Occasions, WHEN ORDERS ARE BROUGHT TO THEM BY HIS AIDS DE CAMP, that they be OBEYED PUNCTUALLY, and WITHOUT DELAY."

That Ferdinand was very angry, that his praise of Granby was prompted chiefly by his wish to punish Sackville, would be evident, if from nothing else, from his use of capital letters for forcing emphasis.

At the court-martial emphasis in capital letters of the heaviest type was laid, by the witnesses who favoured Ferdinand, upon Sackville's alleged delinquencies, his vacillations, his cowardice, his pretended misunderstandings. It was remembered that, before Captain Ligonier came up with the first order, Sackville had deliberately lost time by affecting not to understand a message delivered to him by a German aide-de-camp and had thus shown in advance his obstinate and pusillanimous disposition to obstruct. Colonel Sloper, whose evidence was marked throughout by extreme hostility to Sackville, made much of the "confusion" remarked by him in Sackville's demeanour when Ligonier brought the order. "For God's sake," he declared that he had urged Ligonier, "repeat your orders to that man that he may not pretend not to understand them, but you see the condition he is in!" Ligonier himself was also a hostile witness, sharing the animosity of the veteran Lord Ligonier. When Lord Holdernesse had replied to Sackville's request for a court-martial by saying that he must wait, as his officers were away in Germany, "My

1 "*Ce n'est pas une règle que puisque je loue l'un que je blame l'autre,*" Ferdinand very disingenuously wrote to Sackville after these Orders were issued.

lord Ligonier was more squab." "If he wants a Court-Martial," he said, "he must go seek it in Germany."

Two witnesses, Lieutenant-Colonel Hotham and Captain Smith, threw doubt upon the accuracy of the reporting of the conversations held when the first and second orders were delivered. These two officers were indeed extremely doubtful whether there had been any conversations of the kind; and it is not inconceivable that the imaginations of the witnesses to them may have been fired to conscious or unconscious invention by punitive animus. Ligonier, Sloper, and Fitzroy were in full enjoyment of the opinion which had so easily and inevitably come into fashion, that Sackville was a coward: the opinion that Captain Cartwright, more rankly abusive than any, had expressed when he declared Sackville "a damned chicken-hearted soldier—in short, Sir, Lord George was a stinking coward!" Determined to give no quarter, Cartwright continues: "I knew when I took the order for the last time to him to advance with the Cavalry, he would not do it: and I took the liberty of telling His Highness so before I galloped off to him. His friends said, Sir, that he misapprehended the order. He could not misapprehend *my* order to him, Sir, for I said, 'Lord George, it is his Highness' orders that you advance immediately with the Cavalry,' and I galloped away again. I spoke loud enough for all the Cavalry to hear me."

It is convincing proof of the sincerity of Sackville's conviction that he was not a culprit at Minden that he should have insisted upon a court-martial when he must have known how violent and wide-spread was the desire to condemn him; and how powerful were the forces working for his condemnation. He had to wait for the court-martial: he had time to reflect. But when the officers came back from Germany, at the end of 1759, he again demanded a court-martial from Lord Holdernesse, who gave again a delaying answer. The matter must be referred to the judges because it was doubtful if Sackville could be legally tried since the order that he was accused of disobeying had been given by a foreigner. There was the further point: as he had already been dismissed from the

Army, was he subject to military law? Both points were waived, not by the judges but by the Attorney General and the Solicitor General who were consulted instead, and Sackville was told that he might have his court-martial. But how would he like to have it ? Lord Holdernesse enquired, for there was no specific charge against him.[1] It was clear enough that Sackville was once again being given the chance to drop this obstinate demand of his and save face at the same time. But he stayed in his resolve. He was ready, he declared, to accept even Lord Tyrawley, a man of known brutality and one who had for long been his enemy, as President of the court-martial: and, when he was told that General Conway, who might be supposed to have ill feeling against him because of the Rochefort affair, would be on the court-martial, he replied that there was no man he would sooner choose. Conway was not his friend, but he was a man of integrity: it was not friends that Sackville wanted for his judges, he wanted men unprejudiced by friendship and honest enough to see the truth. To General Balfour he did object, because Balfour had already shown palpable bias.

As to the specific charge, it was not for him to say what it might be. " I have no business to accuse myself," he wrote to Holdernesse, " nor have I been guilty of any fault; but I conclude that Prince Ferdinand must have exhibited some charge against me ; otherwise, undoubtedly His Majesty would not have stripped me of everything in so ignominious a manner." Again Sackville repeated his petition for a court-martial. He would, he said, abide the event.

After that, there was nothing to do but to give this stubborn, patient man his last chance. In strict secrecy he was told that, even now, if he would stop, the Court, though it was already in being, would stop too. But, if he did persist, he must

[1] On August 22nd Ferdinand had written to Sackville that he had made no mention of him in his dispatches to England, "ni immédiatement après la bataille ni les premiers quinze jours suivants . . . Je n'ai écrit à Sa Majesté sur votre sujet que de Hadtbergen, après que je me fusse aperçu que les propos que vous tenies a l'armée pouvoient y alterer cette harmonie qui doit regner." There is nothing is this letter to satisfy the request received from Sackville, that Ferdinand should declare "sur quel point j'ai pu manquer si essentiellement pour m'attirer une punition mille fois pire que la mort."

remember that, however severe his sentence might be, the King was determined that it should stand. He must, in fact, remember Admiral Byng.

Even without this warning that he was risking his life by his obstinacy, Sackville could hardly have supposed that, if he were condemned to death, George the Second would be likely to reprieve him. He knew that George hated him, and he knew that he had many other enemies in high places. Fox was one of them: so was Pitt,[1] for all practical purposes; and so were all those who, like Pitt, were on the side of Ferdinand, either from self-interest or from other motives. Granby's popularity, as well as Ferdinand's influence, swung the Army strongly against Sackville. Among the aristocrats there were few who could or would be his allies: his former friend, the Duke of Newcastle, had, characteristically, stepped aside, and the Bedford family was antagonistic because of a quarrel between Sackville and the Duchess of Bedford's sister, who was his brother John's wife. His father, the Duke of Dorset, was an old man, retired, worn out, no longer in favour; not many friends had survived for him and his Duchess. As to public opinion, it was emphatically hostile. To the average citizen, not deeply reflective, and easily misled, as always, by emotional appeal and surface argument, the disgraced commander was a poltroon who had tarnished Britain's name and must be punished for it. Mass-prejudice was as unreasonable and

[1] After wishing Sackville all success in jusifying his conduct by a court-martial, Pitt writes later on in the same letter dated September 9th, 1759 : " Give me leave to say that I find myself . . . under the painful necessity of declaring my infinite concern, at not having been able to find, either from Captain Smith's conversation or from your own State of Facts, any room (as I wish't) for me to offer to support, with regard to a conduct, which my incompetence to judge of military questions leaves me at a loss to account for." Sackville, enclosing a copy of this letter to Lord Bute, rightly interprets it as a " strong declaration against me." " It would have been more kind," he adds, " had he first permitted me to have explain'd my own story to him or even admitted Capt. Smith to have spoke more fully upon the subject." Earlier in this letter Sackville wrote that he had heard that " I might expect no assistance from any of the Ministers because whatever tended to my justification must in a degree reflect upon the character of P. Ferdinand, and that it was necessary to support him in the fullest glory . . . This appeared natural and so ministerial that I saw notwithstanding the justice of my cause the infinite difficultys truth wou'd have to struggle with." Having received Pitt's letter, Sackville observes that " I find my intelligence about ministerial support too well founded."

" Tell him, I will stand or fall with him," was a message sent through Fitzroy by Pitt to Ferdinand.

as merciless against Sackville as it had so lately been against Byng.[1] The same menacing street noises were heard now as, before Byng's execution, were heard by the author of *A Modest Apology* :

> " Hearing a hoarse noise behind me, I turn'd round, and observed a naked Head, bolted thro' a Cobbler's Stall, from which issued the following incoherent Expression : " Damn my Blood, if Byng don't deserve to be scragg'd for not beating the French Fleet to Mummy, and landing his Forces at Mahon." Upon which it immediately began to roar, " Instead of a Ribbon he shall have a String, etc."

Yet for all these ill omens Sackville believed that he would be acquitted. " I must live in hopes of better times," he wrote to his brother-in-law, Lord Bateman, in September, '59. " If under all the disadvantages of being prejudged by the King, in being dismissed from my employments before trial, and under the popular prejudice I now stand, I could obtain a court-martial, I flatter myself I must be acquitted." " Thank God," he had written to Lord Bute a week or so before, " I do not yet feel myself sink under my misfortunes, and I still trust that truth will prevail." At about the same time he writes, in his published *Apology* : " I can have no hopes of establishing my character but from the force of truth."

Sackville's pertinacity, under the circumstances, in " pushing on " his trial, amazes Walpole, who cannot help admiring him for it, although, as usual, he tempers his admiration. " If here ambition preponderated over fear, at least he was not always a coward." He sought danger that he must have seen and weighed, says Walpole, who discounts the report that Lord Mansfield had assured him he could not be convicted.[2] " For my own part," Walpole continues in a notable sentence,

[1] Sackville had strongly opposed the sentence on Byng.

[2] " But do General Officers weigh legal niceties in the scales of Westminster Hall ?—are not military men apt to pique themselves on showing antipathy to every suspicion of cowardice, unless they are very brave and sensible indeed ?" Walpole also notes the observation of Pitt, who had heard that Lord Mansfield was connected with Sackville, and that the law intended to support him. " The law," said Pitt, " has nothing to do with that question."

"I would sooner pronounce Lord George a hero for provoking his trial, than a coward for shrinking from the French. He would have been in less danger[1] by leading up the Cavalry at Minden than in every hour that he went down to the Horse-guards as a criminal." Sackville, to Walpole, is a brave man (sometimes, at least), but a fool: and he paid for his folly all the rest of his life.

That Walpole's opinion may be justified we are asked to believe that Sackville "never afterwards recovered spirit enough to act with dignity, nor to display the parts which had been so conspicuous in his early life." If only he could have waited (people so soon forget) and trusted to time to heal his wounds! If only, in fact, he had had less spirit then, he would have had more later on. Why could he not be content to make the best of it and settle down quietly to some civilian career? After all, a different George would soon be king, and then, discreetly and gradually, Sackville would come back to favour. If only Sackville could have seen, as Walpole did, that the declaration that there was no specific charge against him was *quite enough,* and indeed even better than an acquittal after the sad scandal of a public trial. But this perverse man lacked the circumspection which Walpole held so dear, he lacked the "judgment," he was an ambitious fool, restless under the ruin of his fortune. That was why he insisted upon a trial which was certain to end in his condemnation.

The true explanation is surely simpler. Sackville, it is very evident, did not believe that he had done wrong. When the facts came out, when his defence was clearly set against the charges, as the court-martial would ensure that it should be, then even his enemies must see that he was not guilty and they would declare accordingly. He would be reinstated in the offices of which he had been unjustly deprived: his name would be cleared. Such confidence was no doubt *naïf*, too *naïf* indeed, for a man of Sackville's worldly experience to

[1] The poet Gray, in a letter to the Rev. James Brown, says much the same: "To be sure, nothing in the field of Minden could be half so dreadful as this daily baiting he is now exposed to; so (supposing him a coward) he has chosen very ill."

have given it constant trust. In such a matter few men would be constantly of the same mind, and, for all the natural sequence of "They must see it!" upon "I am in the right!" Sackville must have very often realized that, though the truth of his cause was great, it might not on that account at once prevail, but he must risk that. Even should he be condemned, and condemned to death, he must be heard. The courage that Sackville showed in the unwavering course of his repeated claims for a court-martial was not the foolhardy courage of an almost insanely ambitious man who knows, but deceives himself into thinking that he does not know, that his conviction is inevitable: it was the courage of one well aware that what he is doing may, not must, have a disastrous or a fatal issue.

Towards the end of January, 1760, Sackville was at last informed that he should have his trial, with General Onslow as President, and a messenger was sent to Prince Ferdinand to ask that evidence should be dispatched. Rather more than a month later Lord Barrington announced to the House of Commons that Sackville had been put under arrest for disobedience to orders. The Speaker strongly opposed the court-martial of a member of the House who was no longer in the army; but Sackville's brother-in-law, Lord Milton, assured the House that the prisoner urgently desired to be put on his trial.

At the beginning of the proceedings an incident occurred which threw the vindictiveness of the reigning sovereign, and the indecency of its expression, into violent relief. Lord Albemarle asked if it were open to the court to pass anything less than a capital sentence. George the Second, incensed beyond measure by an enquiry which might put the idea of clemency into the judges' heads, struck out Lord Albemarle's mother's name from the list of those invited to his private evening parties and commanded that she should not be spoken to in the morning Drawing-Room. The next thing that annoyed the King was that the President of the court-martial suddenly died in an apoplectic fit. This meant delay, and George, almost apoplectic himself with impatience and rage, ordered the Secretary of War to make out a new Commission that same evening, and to add four more members so as to be on the safe side. Not a day must be lost: what would his kinsman Prince Ferdinand think of him, what would he think of his authority, if he could not get Sackville tried and sentenced with proper expedition? "Prince Ferdinand's narrative," says Walpole, "has proved to set out with a heap of lies. There is an old gentleman of the same family who has spared no indecency to give weight to them." George the Second, unlike George the Third, was a thorough German.

On March the seventh the court-martial began again. But it was to take longer than the King wished; longer, indeed, than was generally expected, for it lasted till the third of April. The judges were eleven Lieutenant-Generals and four Major-Generals, under the Presidency of Sir Charles Howard, with Charles Gould as Judge Advocate.

The report of the trial, full of repetitions, often makes tedious reading, and it is not intended to attempt synopsis here. The general trend of court-martial and other evidence, and of other indications, for and against Sackville, will, it is hoped, appear in this chapter. Against him the burden of the charge is, of course, that there was neither excuse for his doubt about the orders, nor for his slowness, subsequently, in marching: that his delays, deliberately obstructing Ferdinand's plan, amounted to disobedience, and that they resulted both in baulking the British forces of glory and in letting the French off lightly by saving their army from complete destruction.

The chief examiners, Lieutenant-General Cholmondeley and Lieutenant-General Lord Albemarle, although not on the whole unfair to Sackville, were evidently rather against him than for him; but Albemarle was as evidently unfavourable to Prince Ferdinand, his questions being often designed to show that the battle took Ferdinand by surprise, as indeed it did, which may have accounted for the confusion of his mind when he gave his first orders.[1]

[1] The Prince of Anhalt had heard from four deserters that the French forces were marching, but he sent no word to Ferdinand. The first information was given by the French cannonade. Sackville was one of the first on horseback at this warning.

Throughout the trial Sackville himself behaved like an innocent man, aggressive, indeed, in his confidence in his innocence. Walpole, recording his conduct and demeanour, is amazed. No diffidence, no humbleness, no sort of timidity. He was disdainful and authoritative, he called Sloper a liar, and he " used the Judge-Advocate, though a very clever man, with contempt." The poet Gray, in a letter written just after " the old pundles who sat on Lord George had at last hammered out their sentence," describes " the unembarrassed countenance, the looks of revenge, contempt and superiority which he bestowed upon his accusers," and says that they were " the admiration of all." Not of Walpole. " Lord George's own behaviour," he writes, " was extraordinary." It certainly was the exact reverse of what would have been Walpole's own behaviour in such a case. After speaking of the superiority of Sackville's abilities, he says that " most men would have adapted such parts to the conciliating the favour of his judges, to drawing the witnesses into contradictions, to misleading and bewildering the Court, and to throwing the most specious colours on his own conduct, without offending the parties declared against him. Very different was the conduct of Lord George. From the outset, and during the whole process, he assumed a dictatorial style to the Court . . . " That he had more spirit and more force than anyone there is Walpole's implied conviction. " He prescribed to the Court and they acquiesced. An instant of such resolution at Minden had established his character for ever."

Walpole seems not to have reflected that Sackville's lack of resolution to commit what he thought would be an error was fully compatible with his resolution in pursuing a verdict that he was sure was right. And it was resolution, not the lack of it, that accounted for his conduct at Minden: he was, there, too firmly set for his own good in his resolve to be as deliberate and as cool as Granby was hot and impetuous. That he was a criminal in this resolve was the opinion of such hostile witnesses as those already cited; and, outside the Court, this opinion was echoed and re-echoed, in general talk, in the news-sheets, and in open letters addressed to Sackville. " We looked for a commander, and we find a commentator. We depend upon an active warrior, and we meet with an idle disputant; one who, in the field of battle, debates upon orders with all the phlegm of an academic, when he ought to execute them with all the vigor and intrepidity of an hero."

This censure is passed in the first " Letter to a late Noble Commander of the British Forces in Germany." The " Second Letter," now striking occasionally a more satirical note, again marks Sackville's coolness and caution for especial blame. He is reproached for his lack of that " Warm Enthusiasm which Cold Caution disavows," and reminded that no one ever achieved eminence without it, and that " there are moments, my Lord, when what the World calls Prudence must give way to Passion." " Pyrrhus, you know, my Lord, used to say that if Valor were lost, it might be found in the Heart of a Roman. If the spirit of Caution and Procrastination is wanting, we know, my Lord, where to find these tranquil Qualifications."

" You was ordered to advance," the writer of the Letter addresses Sackville less obliquely, " to advance, but not to creep, my Lord." " Never till now, perhaps, did we meet with so much Caution about the Regularity of a March in the Heat of Battle." " It is vain to pretend that you was perplexed about the Meaning of your Orders. Such Hesitation," he adds, being evidently of the same mind as Colonel Sloper and Captain Cartwright, " might almost lead us to suspect, that you was pre-determined not to understand any." " If you received two orders contrary in their Directions, it was your Duty to have obeyed the last; or that, at least, by which, from your Survey of the Field, you thought it most probable for his Highness to have directed." " Instead of leading them [the British Cavalry] on to the Theatre of Honor you detained them in a place of inglorious Security, where we do not find that a single Man was either wounded or bruised."

This " Fellow-Citizen and Freeman of Great Britain " thought, as Walpole did, that Sackville was not suited by temperament to command in the field. Against this particular command, indeed, " your Nature seems to have revolted." Let him, then, confine himself to civilian service, he who could not understand that " it is more glorious for a Soldier to mistake than to defer his Duty." " I respect your talents and give Credit to your integrity. There are many Offices which you might fill with Reputation to yourself, and Service to your Country." " It is greatly to be lamented that your Lordship should have been so little acquainted with the true Bent and Propensity of your Genius, as to undertake a Command of such Hazard and Importance."

At the court-martial this same charge of unmilitary propensity to inglorious hesitations and dishonourable half-heartedness bore its full weight upon the prisoner. According to Ligonier's evidence as well as according to Sloper's, Sackville had hesitated before Fitzroy came up with the conflicting order. " That means the whole wing should come away," Ligonier reports Sackville as saying, an observation to much the same effect as that addressed by Sackville to Fitzroy : " This cannot be so, would he have me break the line?" Sackville was represented as impeding Ligonier and Fitzroy just as, later, he impeded Granby. According to the evidence, he told Fitzroy not to be in a hurry. " I am out of breath with galloping!" Fitzroy replied, " which makes me speak quick, but my orders are positive. The French are in disorder, here is a glorious opportunity for the English to distinguish themselves." But Sackville hesitated still, repeating that it was impossible the Prince could mean to break the line. Fitzroy insisted that there was no doubt about the Prince's orders. "Well, then," Sackville enquired, " which way is the Cavalry to march, and who is to be their guide?"—" I! " cried Fitzroy.

Even that display of ardour did not affect Sackville as it should have done. He went on pretending to be puzzled; there was nothing for it but that he should see the Prince: he would not even take the whispered hint from his favourite, his aide-de-camp Smith, to obey and say no more about it. After the totally unnecessary visit to Ferdinand, even worse followed: the holding back of Granby, Sackville's own slow and miserable pace of advance and the final calamity of a victory gained in defence of Hanover without the German George the Second's English cavalry having taken part in it at all.

Ferdinand had expressed his own sense of the matter in a letter written to Sackville from Minden on August the third, replying to a letter in which Sackville had defended himself. After saying that he is mortified by having to make any explanation on so disagreeable a matter, and referring to a conversation "*déjà très désagréable,*" with General Haddam, who had spoken to him on Sackville's behalf, Ferdinand continues, wording his letter so as to express extreme displeasure while avoiding making any charge in form:

> Je vous dirés dorè tout simplement que je n'ai pu voir avec indifference ce qui s'est fait avec la Cavallerie de la droite. Vous commandés tout le Corps Brittannique, ainsi votre poste fixé ne devoit pas être tout la Cavallerie, mais vous deviez egalement conduire les uns et les autres suivant que vous en trouvies l'occasion pour coöperer à la reussité d'une journée si glorieuse pour l'armée.
>
> Je vous ai fourni la plus belle occasion, pour profiter, et pour decider le sort de cette journée, si mes ordres avoient été rempli au pied de la lettre . . . Il ne me peut pas être indifférent si mes ordres ne s'executent point, et qu'on ne veut ajouter foi aux porteurs de cet ordre. Je vous prie, my lord, de me despenser d'entrer dans un plus long detaille. Ni de revocquer à l'ordre des choses de la verité de la quelle je suis persuadé, et du sens que j'y attache. Je crois, my lord, que je vous ai toujours donné des preuves distingués de ma façon de penser sur votre sujet, et avec le même droit j'ai lieu d'être très peu satisfait de l'inexecution de mes ordres. A quoi je dois l'attribuer je l'ignore, et j'en suspens mon jugement."

"You did nothing that I told you to do, and you have no excuse," is what Ferdinand means. It all sounds bad enough: but Sackville's self-defence and the evidence given in his favour make it appear at least improbable that it was nearly so bad as it sounds. It is clear, even from the evidence of Ligonier,

Sloper, and Fitzroy, that Ferdinand's orders, if not contradictory, must have been misunderstood or misrepresented by those who delivered them. Three witnesses, Lieutenant-Colonel Hotham, Captain Smith, and Captain Lloyd, who was another of Sackville's aides-de-camp, were positively and unreservedly of opinion that no guilt or blame attached to the prisoner. Captain Smith was all the while on the spot, up to the time when Sackville rode over to see Ferdinand, and he puts things in a very different light from that thrown by Sackville's accusers. He observed no trace of confusion in Sackville. "As to any alteration in his lordship's looks or behaviour that day, I am sure there was none, but that he would have gone to death if it had been needful."

Smith explains what seemed to him the justifiable reasons for Sackville's orders to halt, and for his slowness in marching. In this connection account should be taken of the danger from the known disposition of Granby, who, it is not difficult to believe, "was posting on with less attention to the rules of a march, but with more ardour for engaging." Smith's testimony is that:

> By orders of the Prince the Cavalry was first formed into Squadrons, and then into line. While they were forming I was on a rising ground from whence I observed that by the time four or five Squadrons were formed Lord George Sackville marched them, which occasioned disorder in the rear, they not being able to keep up, which I went and informed his Lordship of, who, upon that, made them halt, and I returned to my post. Soon after, they moved again, when a Hanoverian officer whom I knew came up to me, and said that they marched so fast in front that they could not keep up, and that their horses would be blown, which I went again and told Lord George of, who then said that he would halt no more, but that he would march slow, and that then the rear, when it was formed, might soon overtake him, but he desired them not to hurry. The place where they were forming the line I observed was not wide enough, but, riding forward, I observed there was room enough a little further, which I mentioned to

his Lordship, who then ordered them to move on, and the line was soon well formed.

Smith was no doubt predisposed in Sackville's favour, but he was not the kind of man to distort the truth. "Captain Smith I very intimately knew," writes Wraxall, describing him as "strictly conscientious, and incapable of asserting any fact that he disbelieved." The Rev. Percival Stockdale, who had been a soldier before he became a clergyman, and had been under Sackville's command at Chatham, also knew Smith well, and also testifies, in his Memoirs, to the honesty of this man "with whom no consideration upon earth could ever prevail to suppress the truth." Like his son, Sydney Smith the famous wit, he was "a man of sense and spirit," and "his testimony at the Court Martial . . . was unreserved, explicit, and ardent:—however impartial he was, he must have been ardent."

Stockdale goes on to report a conversation which showed that neither Smith's ardour nor his conviction of Sackville's innocence had cooled with the passing of time. He spoke on this occasion very much as he had spoken at the court-martial.

> Walking with him, one day, along Wych-Street, we renewed the memorable subject; I seriously asked him, if it was his real opinion, that the conduct of Lord George Sackville deserved no censure on the MINDEN-day?—He emphatically answered, that his conduct, on that day, was perfectly accurate, and what it ought to have been; and that he merited no more blame, as a soldier, than *that* child ;—pointing to a little flaxen-headed boy that passed as we conversed.
>
> I asked Mr. Smith, if he did not advance too slowly, when he *did* march?—He insisted that he could not, circumstanced as he was, march faster; and he gave me clear, and satisfactory reasons for that assertion . . . He added that the orders which were brought to Lord George by prince FERDINAND's *aides-de-camp*, were contradictory to each other, confused; and consequently necessarily embarrassing to any man. He further observed that

when he [Sackville] rode himself to prince FERDINAND, to get an explanation of his orders, he was exposed to more danger than he would have been in the pursuit[1] of the French.

Stockdale adds that Lord Grey also told him that he did not consider Sackville guilty of the least misconduct at Minden; and that Captain Sutherland, who had fought at Minden, expressed to him "his warm indignation against the malignant prejudices and false testimonies" of the court-martial.

A later writer, one qualified to pronounce upon military matters, Lieutenant-Colonel Whitton, in his *Service Trials and Tragedies,* has pointed out that the staff work at Minden was very bad, that the orders were confusing enough to put others than Sackville in doubt, and that Sackville's conduct was certainly not due to cowardice. It is a pity that another writer of recent times, the author of *Gentleman Johnny Burgoyne,* should, in contrast with Colonel Whitton, have given the Minden affair so little consideration as to commit himself to the statement that Sackville was "cashiered for cowardice." Cowardice was never the formal charge, and Sackville, therefore, did not seek to refute it.

What he did seek to prove, in his letters to Ferdinand, in his published *Apology*, and in his defence at the court-martial, was justification of his uncertainty about the orders, and the necessity of preserving the alignment by halting and by avoiding such haste in marching as would have destroyed it. On August the second,[2] writing to Ferdinand from Minden, after observing that the Orders just issued (those in which he had been censured by implication) had struck him like a "coup de foudre," Sackville continues:

J'ai reçu ordres de former et d'avancer toute la Cavalerie. Peu de tems après, un autre ordre me vint de faire avancer la Cavalerie Brittannique seulement. Ces deux ordres

[1] Would that danger, in comparison, for example, with the danger Sackville was in at Fontenoy, have been so considerable? Common soldiers and lesser officers would have been killed or maimed or mutilated as usual, horses would have been disembowelled; but Sackville, in his superior command, must have known that it was not so likely that anything of the sort would happen to him.

[2] Sackville's letter of the same day to Fitzroy (Appendix, pp. 280–282) may be compared.

suivèrent de si près qu'ils m'embarrassèrent un peu; j'envoiois cependant la faire faire le detour du Bois, et apprennant que Votre Altesse n'était pas eloigné je pris le parti d'aller moi même lui faire rapport de ce qui passait, et demander ses instructions ulterieures, ce qui ne tarda nullement l'execution des premiers.

L'ordre que je donnois à mylord Granby de faire Halte c'était toujours dans le dessein d'obeir aux votres en gardant l'alignement, qui ne dura surement que très peu de tems. Je lui donnai après pour la même raison le même ordre : il me fit dire qu'il avoit reçu ceux de Votre Altesse de s'avancer, et il le fit effectivement, et je me pressai avec la droite pour m'aligner avec lui, jusqu'à ce que nous arrivâmes où nous étions ordonné derrière l'Infanterie, et il me parût même dans ce moment qù'il ne me devança point.

Sackville goes on to say that Granby will do him justice on these points, and that " il m'autorise de dire qu'il est prêt à rendre son temoignage là dessus à Votre Altesse en ma presence." Granby, as has been already noted, was generously fair at the court-martial: his evidence did not charge guilt.

The letter concludes by requesting that Ferdinand, in his Orders of the following day, should re-establish Sackville's reputation in the eyes of the army and of the world. This favour was demanded because, as Sackville expresses it with great restraint, " the Orders of to-day seem to condemn me without naming me."—" If your Highness had *yourself* seen my situation and all that I did in it, you would not have thought me culpable, and, if I have been, it was surely my misfortune and not my intention." It is no doubt of himself that appears in those last words, but a characteristic detachment, an objectivity of view that he could sustain even here.

Quotation has been made from Ferdinand's evasive reply to this letter.

In his *Apology* Sackville emphasizes the fact that he had already, before riding over to the Prince to ask what he was to do, ordered Smith to bring up the British cavalry through the wood, so that time should not be lost. " I should not have gone to him at all had it not been in order to avoid the possibility of a Mistake, which might have arisen from my taking upon myself to decide which of them [the aides-de-camp] brought His Serene Highness's intentions."

At the court-martial Sackville pursued the same defence as he did in his letters and in the *Apology*. Instant obedience to the second of those two conflicting commands did not seem to him to be justified. "Had I then acted a cautious part with regard to myself it had been easy for me to have made either of these two gentlemen [those who brought the commands] answerable for the step I should have taken, but, entrusted with such command as I bore, it became me not to consider my own security, but the public service." At the most he had lost eight minutes[1] by the visit to Ferdinand: his slowness in marching was further accounted for by obstruction from the wood: his readiness for action was shown by his having been one of the first on horseback on hearing the French cannonade.

It was a cogent, spirited, and most evidently honest defence: but that it failed in face of the powerful forces of prejudice opposed to it is not surprising. Seven of the fifteen judges voted for the capital sentence. This was three less than the necessary two-thirds majority. Among the other eight judges, opinion was not, of course, in Sackville's favour; but most of them had come, probably, to the "Tertium quid" conclusion formed by a certain number outside the Court, and indicated by Horace Walpole. To them Sackville's coolness under such circumstances was censurable, they

[1] As to the time lost, Walpole admits that "it is doubtful whether, if employed, it would have been of much consequence." Fitzroy deposed that the distance over which he and Sackville had to ride to reach the Prince was about four hundred yards. "What pace did he go towards the Prince?" Sackville asked him, and he replied: "Half a galop." Lord Albemarle asked Fitzroy: "How long was it from the time you delivered the Prince's orders to Lord George to the time of Lord George's sending Captain Smith back to the Cavalry?" The answer was "I believe about a quarter of an hour." To a further question from Lord Albemarle: "How far had Captain Smith to go back to the nearest point of Cavalry?" Fitzroy replied, "About a hundred or a hundred and fifty yards." The Duke of Richmond's statement in the House of Lords twenty-two years later, that the time lost in obeying the orders was an hour and a half, is an extreme example of the many exaggerations which malevolence prompted on this particular point. The Duke, to make himself credible, declared that he "held his watch within his hand" all the time.

felt that " enough was evident to prove that Lord George at least was too critically and minutely cool in a moment of importance," but that he did not really mean to play the traitor for the sake of spiting Ferdinand; that " the swiftness of the victory forestalled his ultimate acquiescence," that, in fact, he meant to behave badly only up to a certain comparatively harmless point.

Sackville, found guilty of having disobeyed Prince Ferdinand's orders, was pronounced unfit to serve His Majesty in any military capacity whatever.

Chapter VII

HATRED, PERSECUTION, AND ABUSE

BEFORE Minden, Lord George had been extolled. As a soldier, he had indeed met with little else but praise and enthusiastic recognition. " Such cannon-proof courage as you showed at Fontenoy " is a phrase that fits well to the fact. The Duke of Cumberland testifies that Sackville was not only a brave commander, but an exceptionally able one: " I am exceedingly sorry to lose Lord George as he has not only shown his courage, but a disposition to his trade which I do not always find in those of higher rank." " Wolfe of Quebec," who, before he became famous, was Major and Lieutenant-Colonel under Sackville's colonelcy, admired greatly and was in " agreeable companionship " with the man to whose judgement of character and talent he owed his own promotion.[1] In 1749 Wolfe wrote from Glasgow, deploring that Lord George was soon to be transferred: " We are to lose him

[1] " I think myself much obliged to Lord George Sackville, and have writ him the strongest assurances of it. What he said some time ago to H.R.H. left, no doubt, a favourable impression, and forwarded this succession." (1750)

without hopes of finding his equal . . . and unless Colonel Conway falls to our share . . . none will be found that can, in any measure, make amends for the loss of him. For my particular I may expect his assistance, whether he is in this regiment or not; he has given such strong marks of his esteem that there can be little doubt."

When Sackville, the year before Minden, succeeded Charles Spencer, Duke of Marlborough, as Commander-in-Chief of the British forces in Germany, Lord Bute " rejoiced extremely at your having the command, it was your due every way," and expressed his "indignation that it was given by halves," owing to George the Second's determination always in future to withhold the power of " posting officers upon vacancies." " Ligonier assures me every method was taken by your friends to make it [your appointment] compleat." Even so soon after the court-martial as 1763 Sackville's high distinction as a soldier was sometimes allowed to be remembered. In the *Annual Register* for that year his " such admirable talents " are recalled, and it is added that, but for " the error or misfortune of a moment," he might have ranked with the Marlboroughs and the Brunswicks.[1]

His fall was, as Walpole said, " prodigious." " Nobody stood higher, nobody had more ambition and more sense . . . I suspend my opinion until Lord George speaks for himself." Opinion was not, however, generally suspended. " The mob . . . are now grinding their teeth and nails to tear Lord George to pieces the instant he lands . . . Admiral Byng was not more unpopular."

Both Byng and Sackville were hated, abused, and persecuted for the same reason; because both had fallen suddenly, and far. The public, in the one case as in the other, was able to enjoy one of its rarest satisfactions of envy by accusing, attacking, and reviling a disgraced hero. The distinguishing quality of this satisfaction is especially evident in the *Second Letter to a late Noble Commander,* published shortly before the court-martial. The public in a free kingdom, so runs the argument of this Letter, are entitled to demand explanations

[1] See p. 9.

and justifications from *anyone* who has injured them. Lord George's addressing them in self-defence "was no more than they had a Right to expect." "If they think themselves injured by the highest personage in the State, his Eminence does not place him above the obligations of explaining or justifying his Conduct." Sackville might think himself innocent, but, the writer ominously adds, so did Byng. "No man could express a stonger Conviction of his own Innocence, a greater Consciousness of having done his Duty to the utmost of his Abilities, than a late unhappy admiral."

No! Inward conviction of rectitude is not enough. But the writer of the Letter implies that Sackville is not even self-deceived. "How many have counterfeited all the Symptoms of Innocence, and braved Conviction, who at length have been found Criminal by their own Confession." In any case, Lord George must expect, now, to suffer as though he were guilty: and why should he not? Others of lower rank, many of them, are treated as guilty though they may be innocent, then let *him,* the nobleman, the high one, have a taste of this plebeian medicine for a change, let *him* "go through with it," too! The writer, well content, bids his Lordship to consider that "it is an unavoidable Imperfection in Government that Persons accused, or even suspected of Delinquency, must, till they have an Opportunity of manifesting their Innocence, undergo many of the Inconveniences of Guilt . . . Reflect on the number of your Fellow-citizens confined in loathsome Prisons and laden with heavy Irons on suspicion of Crimes, of which several of them will probably appear innocent at their Trials." How familiar is the ring of those words that follow, how common to political persecutors at all times the contention that "their crimes are trifling in comparison, for yours endangered the Peace and Safety of Society."

Shortly after the court-martial Lord Ferrers was hanged with a silken cord for murder. Walpole, at variance with the view just quoted, calls him a more atrocious criminal than Sackville. The scenes at the hanging of Ferrers suggest to Walpole that mob-vengeance would have been satisfied if Sackville had been shot. "The mob was decent, and admired him, and almost pitied him: so they would Lord George, whose execution they are so angry at missing."

Walpole notes that punitive hatred of Sackville was equalled in intensity only by adulation of Granby. "The world, which pardons the excesses of intemperate courage, never forgives the slightest appearance of backwardness in the field," for both the pardon and the unforgivingness make most men feel brave. Smollett, with a conviction as sure as Walpole's, writes that "an abhorrence and detestation of Lord George Sackville as a coward and a traitor, became the universal passion, which acted by contagion, infecting all degrees of people from the cottage to the throne; and no individual who had the least regard for his own character and quiet would venture to preach upon moderation or even advise a suspense of belief until more certain information could be received." The words describe a state of mind usually to be found only when some sexual offender is on prominent trial, or in time of war.

Illustrating the general animosity, but tingeing it with a certain minor skill and minor humour, Lord George Townshend, who had been friendly with Sackville, caricatured him in flight at Minden, and circulated these caricatures among his friends. "I shall be kill'd, Oh, I shall be kill'd!" he represents Sackville as exclaiming in panic terror, while in the act of making his "mistake" near Minden he "shews his Rear." Junius accuses Townshend of cowardice at the Battle of Dettingen, where he served with Sackville. The caricatures face page 102.

The army treated Sackville no better than the mob did. Even Lord Shelburne, one of Sackville's most malignant enemies, described the conduct of the army as scandalous. "He was universally deserted. Those who had favoured neglected and insulted him. No one would speak to him in the Commons or anywhere else."

George the Second himself, with uncontrolled spite, had done all that he could to set example for copy. Gray, the poet, writing to Wharton in April, 1760, when the court-martial was over, says that "everybody blames *somebody* [meaning the

King] who has been out of temper and intractable the whole time.'' The King's stubborn and unreasoning malice stretched beyond the victim, to his friends. Witnesses for Sackville were punished at once. Captain Smith, his aide-de-camp and principal witness, '' had no sooner finished his evidence but he was forbid to mount guard and ordered to sell out.'' '' Smith's honesty did him no good,'' says the Reverend Percival Stockdale, and with the same mildness he refers to Captain Sutherland, who '' was very strong in favour of Lord George; and I believe he afterwards found that it was not serviceable to his promotion.'' Walpole, less mildly and more truly, writes of the '' cruelty '' with which Sackville's friends and witnesses were treated. '' Hugo, a Hanoverian, was dismissed on his return to the army. John Smith was obliged to quit it here; and Cunningham was sent to America, though he had been there three times already.'' In every instance '' thwarting the inclinations of the Court '' led at once to what was little short of persecution.

It was as bitter a disappointment to George the Second as it was to '' the mob '' that sentence of death was not passed on Sackville. The King, in his ungenerous chagrin, did what he could to make amends, he insulted Sackville to the best of his ability. He decreed that the court-martial verdict should be given out in public orders to the army and a homily added to it, and that it should be recorded in every regimental order book. He blotted Sackville's name from the roll of the Privy Council, commanding that this dishonour should be published in the *Gazette*. He forbade Sackville's appearance at Court, and saw to it that the Prince of Wales and the Princess Dowager and (to make all safe) Lord Bute as well were apprised of this. Walpole writes of this royal conduct as '' impotent,'' because it was '' circumscribed in narrower limits than his wishes; and unjust, as exceeding the bounds of a just trial; since no man ought to be punished beyond his sentence.''

Walpole writes often forcibly and fairly about Sackville; but it is sometimes difficult not to conclude that he is cunning in his fairness, that he hides a hostile motive, that the impression which he means to convey is that he is *as fair as he can be*, and that, because he is so anxious to " make allowances," and to " do all he can," whatever he has to say against Sackville must be well heeded. That Walpole was, at the least, more an enemy than a friend to Sackville can hardly be doubted. He was not at first an open enemy, he did his damage in his own way, he was like himself in giving an impression at which he did not seem to aim. Towards Sackville Horace Walpole's attitude shows three main phases. It is a mutable moon. For the young Sackville, aristocratically insolent and rash, but abounding in high promise for himself and likely well to reward his followers, Walpole has an almost servile admiration. But, even before Minden, he had misgivings about him. He did not at all like his offending Pitt and George the Second. When Pitt offered Sackville the St. Cas command, Sackville made his characteristic reply that he was tired of buccaneering. Pitt, Walpole feels, will not forget that sarcasm on his expeditions. Nor was it less imprudent of Lord George to treat the King as he did. He went to war in Germany without the royal approbation, and even without waiting on His Majesty. Such lack of decorum was, to Walpole, alarming. Really, even for a Sackville, this was going too far. None the less, to Lord George in disgrace, Walpole is cautiously just. He was not sure that he might not again be one of the great, he " suspended opinion," he was careful not to be too much for him or too much against. His cue then was to wait and see what the verdict was: not only the verdict of the court-martial, but the verdict of the years that followed. But when Lord George Germain, Secretary for America, ignored Mr. Walpole's ceremonial call upon him, affronted vanity vindicated its rights. It was true, Walpole admits, that etiquette did not oblige ministers to acknowledge such a courtesy as he had paid: but Lord George might well have acknowledged it. How ungrateful, after all that Walpole had done for him. "I stood by him in his disgrace, I even sat next to him in the theatre without wincing, and now he takes no notice of me!" Some such thought may well have been harboured by Walpole's mind, as he determined not to write anything " nice " about Lord George, ever again. In petulant bitterness, realizing that he had backed, however warily, a loser, or one, at least, by whom *he* could not gain, he turned to his early memoirs to alter and annotate what he had written about Sackville. He describes him in his middle age as a man " of desperate ambition and character," as a scheming politician ousting his enemies and promoting his friends, urgent in private pursuit of unworthy aims, but ineffective and intimidated when he appeared publicly as a minister. In January, 1776, Walpole writes : " However dictatorial Lord George was in the Cabinet, he had recovered so little spirit, was so afraid of inviting personal reflections and was so cowed by his conscious unpopularity that he nowhere appeared the Minister so little as in the House of Commons, and never shone there with so little lustre." In his later journals Walpole prophesies that George the Third's displeasure will fall on this man for his insolence, which " bore him above all his disgrace." He is horrified by the heights to which Lord George Germain carried this " overbearing humour," as when he told his Sovereign that the two heaviest and worst Sailers were *The King* and *The Lord North*. " And," writes Walpole, " he bragged of having said this. If ever he falls into disgrace the King will remember it." (" Yes, indeed, and how I hope he will! ")

Walpole, in this third phase, exposes his hatred of Lord George, he does not ambush his attacks. There are other passages in which there is still less concealment or control. " Though his restless ambition incited him again to aspire to high employments and honours, both which he attained, he will never figure in history as an admired character, since he acquired no successes, no glory for his country by his councils. He strengthened rather than effaced the suspicion of his courage, almost forfeited the general opinion of his parts, and obtained no honours that were not balanced by redoubled disgraces and mortifications . . . Not long after the commencement of the fatal American War he was suddenly hoisted to the management of it; in the course of which he was frequently exposed to most bitter apostrophes on his former imputed timidity, and did but give new handle to that imputation by the tameness or feebleness with which he bore or repelled those attacks; while the want of vigour in his defences, void of any emanations of parts, made his abilities as much questioned as his spirit by those who were too young to remember his former exertions." Walpole goes on to suggest that Lord George's "councils and plans" may have been "ill-grounded, impolitic, or unwise," and emphasizes the "ill success" which "attended almost every one of the measures he recommended or promoted." It is impossible to mistake the nature of Walpole's gratification when he writes, a little later, of Lord George being "*tumbled* in a moment from a height which he decorated so ill," or to overlook his animus as he declares that "the partiality or obstinacy of a Sovereign, whose passions he implicitly obeyed, compensated his fall by the extravagant reward of a Viscount's coronet." Walpole, after his manner, with his constant motive, inserts in this passage craftily tempering clauses.

It is interesting to compare Horace Walpole's famous letters with the ignored letters of Lord George. They are often in revealing contrast. After George the Second's death Sackville strove for rehabilitation. This is a letter that he wrote to Sir Henry Erskine in 1763:

> . . . I certainly was very impatient to know what his Majesty's intentions were in regard to me. I could not doubt of his gracious disposition in general from the moment I was assured that he was sensible of the hard usage I had met with, and I rely'd with confidence that I should *now* have received marks of the King's favour because that period was come which my Lord Bute himself had fix'd for my being released from that situation to which I was reduced by the violence and iniquity exercised against me in the late reign.
>
> I now perceive that many untoward circumstances are said still to prevent his Majesty from doing me that justice which the goodness of his heart and the benevolence of his mind would naturally incline him to, for I am persuaded

that the injured and the oppressed are particularly entitled to the King's compassion and protection, but if I am to continue unrelieved till every part of administration should wish to see me restored to favour and employment, I may pass the remainder of my life in vain expectations, for I am sensible that till his Majesty declares me not unworthy of his countenance, those who from the fashion of the times or the malevolence of their own hearts are conscious of having injured me will never wish to see my persecution cease, and when I was formerly promised support, I could not understand it as depending upon the circumstances now mentioned.

His lordship [Lord Bute] is pleased to say that if I went to Court I should soon be convinc'd that the King declined to do what I desired, not from want of esteem but from reasons of state alone. You know very well[1] why I have not pay'd my personal duty to his Majesty. It was not from choice but from want of knowing whether my appearance there would be proper after the hint I had from you about it. If I now am to depend upon being look'd upon with that graciousness which his Majesty usually shews to those who are honour'd with his approbation, I should be most happy in receiving that as the first mark of his favour, for you may be sure after what happened at his first coming to the throne I should be most cautious of even risking my returning to the King's presence without an assurance of such a reception as might be a credit and honour to me.

Sackville then refers, with undiminished calm, to this startling passage at the end of the letter which he is answering; a letter from Lord Bute to Sir Henry Erskine:

And now let Lord George, Sir Harry, seriously reflect on this, and on the part you tell me he meditates if not humoured at present. What, join the greatest enemy ever man had, who aimed at no less than his blood, because the most benign of princes cannot do for him now even what

[1] See pp. 135–136.

that prince himself wishes, without shaking an administration that is his last resource. If these be Lord George's sentiments, if he be so [MS. defective here] he is the man his enemy took him for, and unworthy of the opinion I have instilled into the King about him, and one whose very name he will never suffer to be mentioned to him again.

In reply to this, Lord George continues :

As to the latter part of the letter it must have been in answer to something you wrote from your own ideas of what I might be reduced to do, as I do not recollect I desired you to mention anything relative to my further conduct. I hope my behaviour for many years past may have convinced my Lord Bute of my ever having acted in support of the Crown upon just principles. I will go farther, I have lately acted not only from duty, but, if I may be allowed the expression, from affection. I have admired the King's character, I have respected his virtues, and I trust nothing will ever induce me to enter into faction for the distressing the Crown. My particular circumstances prevent my correspondence with those who were the authors of my misfortunes. Nothing but the utmost necessity shall oblige me to give any degree of opposition to such ministers as the King may employ. But if I am sensible that those about his Majesty shall persist in preventing me from receiving those marks of the King's justice which his own benign and amiable disposition would incline him to shew to the meanest of his subjects, surely I may be allowed to declare in Parliament my disapprobation of the measures of such men as the only constitutional resentment which can be shewn by individuals to the servants of the Crown without being thought deserving of such terms of reproach as are express'd and insinuated in his lordship's letter.

The effects upon Horace Walpole of doubt and perturbation and of the need for self-defence were very different. This is how, six years earlier, whining in a fuss, he wrote to Lord George about his little worry:

I am perhaps doing a very impertinent thing, and very malapropos, giving myself an air of consequence; but it is of consequence to me not to forfeit your good opinion very innocently. I came to town last night, where I have not been two days together these three weeks or more. The bookseller, who printed my simple Chinese letter, told me with a very significant look that he heard I had writ something else since, with which it seems I had not trusted him.

This was a letter from the Elysian fields. It struck me that the Speaker had a few days ago with more earnestness than I then minded, pressed me to tell him who did write it. I told him very honestly that I neither knew nor had ever enquired.

I read it when it came out, and did not admire it enough ever to enquire. Since I came home I have sent for it and read it, and that makes me now trouble your Lordship. I would flatter myself even as an author that it is not like me. In the impertinences to some for whom I have the greatest regard I am sure it is most unlike me. I can guess no reason for its being imputed to me but its being a letter like the Chinese one.

My dear Lord (I hope I may say so), I am not apt to be serious: I am on this head, and very much hurt. I never thought any kind of my writing worth preserving. I should beg this letter may be, that if the most distant day could bring out the least trace of that Elysian letter being mine, my honour, which I most seriously give you that I know not the least tittle relating to it, and my own hand and name may rise in judgment against me. When I have said this, I hope you will not tell how much I am punished for my writing follies, and that I, who care not a great deal for what is said of me that is true, am so liable to be wounded by lies.

The falsetto note strikes shrill: egotism and vanity in their usual disguise of false humility inform the letter. Reading it makes it clearer still why Walpole, who had so much to say about Lord George, should have been so little able to understand him.

The "extravagant reward of a Viscount's coronet" was bestowed upon Lord George Germain more than twenty-one years after George the Third's accession. Lord George, as his letter to Sir Henry Erskine shows, gained no favour or employment during the earlier years of the reign of that sovereign, who, though "admitting and condemning his harsh usage," was "prevented by state reasons from affording him the redress intended." It was too dangerous for a new king to favour a man whose disgrace was so notorious and so recent, a man who was still the object of a general malice sharpened by disappointment at his not having been shot. In the first days of George the Third's reign a paper was posted on the Royal Exchange: "No petticoat Government, no Scotch Ministers, and no Lord George Sackville."

Sackville's behaviour, as soon as the court-martial was over, made it clear that he was still strong in his certainty that "nothing could be justly alleged against him." "You may think perhaps that he intends to go abroad and hide his head: *au contraire,* all the world visits him in his condemnation." Though Thomas Gray obviously exaggerates, there was no doubt some reaction in Sackville's favour after George the Second, with Teutonic thoroughness, had delivered every possible kick to the man who was down. In his own "world" Sackville had sympathisers, although some people must have visited him out of mere curiosity. "He says himself, his situation is better than ever it was." Lawrence Sterne is more ambiguous. Writing a month after Gray, he says that "Lord George was last Saturday at the Opera, some say with great effrontery, others with great dejection." That he was often in great dejection it is impossible not to believe. It could hardly have been with sure confidence that, immediately on hearing of George the Second's death, he wrote to Lord Bute asking "whether it were proper to pay his duty at Court as early as possible." When, soon after the accession, he did appear at the Court of the new King, "this was considered so great an indignity to the memory of the late King, and those ministers who had the management of the German war, that an enquiry was set on foot to ascertain who invited him. It was traced to Lord Bute, who was officially informed that such an invitation was a great breach of decorum. The same was signified to Lord George, who . . . never went afterwards during that administration."[1]

But, from the time of George the Second's death, Sackville continued to hope and to work for deferred rehabilitation, in spite of repeated rebuffs and disappointments. At last, in 1765, he was made a member of the Privy Council and appointed Vice-Treasurer of Ireland, but he was dismissed a year later through the efforts of his enemies. Real rehabilitation did not come till 1775, when Lord George (now Germain) was made Secretary of State for the Colonies.

For the five years after Minden, although Sackville remained a Member of Parliament, he had to stand in the background of public life, and only on one occasion, in 1762, did he speak in the House. It was not, indeed, until 1770, early in the session, that, as Lord George Germain, he became conspicuous in Parliament, making frequent speeches, always against the Ministry, speeches remarkable for their force of reasoned argument and for their formidable satire. It was then, and later, that he exposed himself to attack, not during the 1760-1770 decade. But his enemies, during what has been called his " ten years' interregnum," were not inactive: if they could have turned him out of the Commons, they would have done so. They could not, because, as Lord Shelburne said, Sackville " represented a family borough," and, if expelled the House, he might have been " chosen and re-chosen again and again, in spite of repeated expulsions." Lord Shelburne also observed that he himself, and others, had taken great exception to Sackville's first rehabilitation in 1765. It is clear that Lord George would have been neither Member of Parliament, Vice-Treasurer for Ireland, nor Member of the Privy Council if his enemies could have possibly prevented it.

At Hythe, the family borough, Lord George's nominee for mayor was opposed, in 1767, and Lord George's own representation was threatened.

I am just returned from Hythe (he writes to General

[1] From George Coventry's *Memoirs*.

Irwin) where I have withstood a most violent attack. Lord Holdernesse assured the ministers that my family had no other interest in that place than what arose from the influence of the Ld. Warden, and he claim'd the support of Government, that he might have the nomination of two members there, which he could obtain without difficulty as he should have the assistance of many gentlemen in that neighbourhood. Mr. Evelyn was one of his candidates, and he was set forward to declare himself for the general election . . . The Ld. Warden and Mr. Evelyn set up a nomination in opposition to the person they knew I was engaged to, [as candidate for the mayoralty] and carry'd it on with the same eagerness as if there had been the election of a member . . . Threats, promises, and money were us'd in their full extent. The contest was not fair as I could pretend to have neither the means of rewarding or punishing and had nothing to set against present interest and future expectations but personal attachments or gratitude for past favours. However, to the honour of my constituents, my friends would not forsake me, and upon the poll I carry'd my mayor by 51 against 34, and I had the pleasure of seeing most of those in Custom House employment vote with me, and all of those who were under the Ld. Warden, tho' they were assured in the most positive manner that they would be immediately dismissed from their offices. This sort of violence gave offence to all moderate people . . . What Ld. Holdernesse [who had put forward Mr. Evelyn as candidate] will do I know not. If he begins with that sort of work the previous threatenings shall be publickly proved and he may take the credit of avowing them. Had I lost the first question I should soon have been over-run, but they will now see that I am more firmly established there than they imagined, and that the place is not to be carry'd by a *coup-de-main*."

Lord George Germain's occasional submission, on which Horace Walpole comments, to repeated insults, innuendoes, and jibes in the House of Commons after 1770, may seem surprising. It is perhaps disappointing that he did not always fiercely retaliate. But to these continual attacks upon his honour, courage, and ability he had grown accustomed. The campaign was of long standing, it was not something new to inflame him and of a sudden to try his temper. He was able, therefore, to meet these attacks not with violent reprisals, but with a dignity, contempt, and reserve which few men could have sustained after his fashion. He did not meet them with the "tameness and feebleness" that Walpole imputes to him. There are instances, certainly, of lack of composure on his part, but they are few, considering how well calculated were the repetitions and the trivialities of his assailants to put him out of patience. Indeed, he could go a step beyond normal composure on occasion: his humour could prompt him to relish of a jibe with any wit in it. When Wilkes said in the House that "the noble Lord might conquer America: but he believed it would not be in Germany," Lord George "repeated this sarcasm on himself in Council and commended it."

The first serious attack made upon him in the Commons was by Governor Johnstone in December 1770, and his resentment of it could not have been more drastically expressed. This particular "apostrophe on his former timidity" had consequences more dramatic than any of those that were to follow. Lord George Germain had referred in a Commons speech to his interest in the honour of the nation, to which Governor Johnstone, replying in Lord George's absence, said that he "wondered that that noble Lord should interest himself so deeply in the honour of his country, when he had hitherto been so regardless of his own." Coventry's account of what came of this throws into strong relief the composure and the fixity of purpose of both the men concerned. Governor Johnstone must have been the sort of man Lord George liked.

> Lord George Germain . . . declared he was sorry that he had missed the opportunity of making an instant replication; but that, however, he would take proper notice of it. On Monday, 17th theDecember 1770, Governor

Johnstone was attending a Committee . . . when Mr. Thomas Townshend[1] came to him, and desired to speak with him: he took him into another room, when he told him . . . that the reflection he had cast on the character of Lord George Germain, though not heard by himself at the time, had been communicated to him by his friends; and that in consequence, Lord George had begged him to wait on Governor Johnstone to desire that he would retract what he had said: that for his own part he should be exceedingly sorry to have a quarrel happen between two gentlemen whom he knew, and for whom he had a great respect, and he therefore hoped that to prevent the consequences, Governor Johnstone would retract what he had said respecting Lord George.

The Governor said, it was very true, he had made use of such and such expressions in the House; that they conveyed his opinion, and that he would maintain and support it. Upon which Mr. Townshend said, in that case, Lord George demanded the satisfaction of a gentleman from him, which the other declared he was ready to give his Lordship at any time. Mr. Townshend then said, Lord George was in an adjoining room, and, if the Governor pleased, they would go to him. The Governor assented; and Mr. Townshend conveyed him to the room in which Lord George repeated the cause of quarrel, and the demand of satisfaction, which the other acquiesced in, desiring his Lordship would appoint his own time and place. Lord George then mentioned the ring in Hyde Park; and as, in affairs of that kind, all times were alike, the present was, in his opinion, as good a one as any. Governor Johnstone entirely agreed with Lord George as to place; but said, that as he was now attending his duty in a committee, on a subject he had very much at heart, he hoped the meeting with Lord George an hour hence would make no difference. Lord George said, no; and then spoke as to seconds, informing the Governor at the same time, that he had desired Mr. Townshend to attend him in that light.

[1] Afterwards Lord Sydney.

Governor Johnstone said there was little occasion for seconds, and that therefore Mr. Townshend should stand in that light as to both of them. Governor Johnstone further said, that as he had at that time an open wound in his arm, and his legs very much swelled, he could wish they would use pistols; to which Lord George saying it was equal to him what the weapons were, they separated, and Governor Johnstone returned to the committee.

In this conference, as well as through the whole affair, both the gentlemen behaved with the greatest politeness to each other, as well as with the greatest courage.

At the appointed hour, Lord George and Mr. Townshend were in the ring; and soon after, Governor Johnstone, accompanied by Sir James Lowther, whom he happened to meet on his way, and had requested to go with him. Lord George accosted Governor Johnstone, and desired he would mention the distance, declaring that he was then upon his ground, and the Governor might take what distance he pleased. The Governor was taken back by the seconds about twenty small paces. The antagonists having prepared their pistols, Lord George called on the Governor to fire, which the Governor refused, saying, that as his Lordship brought him there, he must fire first. Upon which Lord George fired, and then the Governor. Neither of the shots took effect. Lord George then fired his second pistol, and as he was taking down his arm, the Governor's second ball hit his lordship's pistol, broke some part of it, and one of the splinters grazed his Lordship's hand. The seconds immediately interfered, and the affair was ended. Governor Johnstone afterwards declared to his friends, that in all the affairs of the kind which he ever knew, or was ever concerned in, he never found a man behave with more courage and coolness than Lord George did on this occasion.

No harm was done. It was all almost as innocuous and polite as some of the later French duels. But it might easily not have been: both Johnstone and Germain were risking their lives with those bullets that might by equal chance have hit or have missed. The public was impressed by this adventure. "He challenged and fought Governor Johnstone," says Walpole, "with a coolness that with almost all men justly palliated or removed the imputation on his spirit." Walpole, in face of this change of general opinion, and, by the balance of his expressions, playing, as usual, for safety, is inclined to feel that "Lord George Germain is a hero, whatever Lord George Sackville may have done."

Though Lord George Germain's duel served his reputation well at the time, it by no means prevented others from following the example set by Governor Johnstone and by so many others before him. The insults publicly thrown out in the House were repeated with evident relish or with apparent regret, while the news-sheets gave eager and lively thrusts:

The Americans are cowards and will yield
Sooner than face our forces in the field:[1]
And then in brave commanders how much richer,
We who have Mansfield, Sackville, Jemmy Twitcher.[2]

This rhyme appeared during 1775 in the *London Evening Post*. Lady Sarah Lennox, writing in 1779, might well feel that Lord George was still fair game. In the new weekly paper, *The Englishman,* she finds "no spite but at Lord North, Sandwich, and Germain, and one may without scruple give them up, I think, and call the paper a fair one." Lord George continued to provoke the same kind of attacks, the same kind of malicious or curious gossip. Since Minden he had been a target exposed to the same shafts, to more or to less of them, according to the position he was in. Eleven years before *The Englishman* appeared, Lady Mary Coke had written, in the pained tone so commonly chosen for the recounting of others' misadventures, of "an answer that was made Lord George Sackville while he was speaking with great violence against Sir James Lowther. Very inadvisedly he said something about avoiding the combat, and as if these words threw him into

[1] The first two lines are meant to represent Lord George's opinion as expressed in the House.

[2] Lord Sandwich.

confusion he stopped and could not go on, asking those about him whereabouts he was; upon which one that sat before him said, '*About avoiding the combat,* my lord.' Why will people so unnecessarily lay themselves open to have disagreeable things said to them? Not that I hear that he seemed to mind it."

It would have been unlike Lord George not to have smiled ironically, at least in retrospect, at such a lapse of his own.

One of the most important of Lord George Germain's assailants was Charles Fox, who, in 1777, attacked him "in his highest manner." "An ill omened and inauspicious character," he called him, truly enough, and (Walpole continues),

> . . . besides blaming the choice of a man pronounced unfit to serve the Crown, dwelt on his ignorance and incapacity for conducting a war. The attack was by moderate men thought too personal and too severe. It was felt in the deepest manner by Lord George, who rose in the utmost consternation and made the poorest figure. Lord George said the man in the world who he chose should abuse him had done so.
>
> Lord North handsomely defended Lord George, and said he was glad Fox had abandoned him, an old hulk, to attack a man-of-war.

Lord North said the same thing differently to Fox, when the debate was over. "Charles," he said, "I am glad you did not fall on me to-day, for you was in full feather."

Later in 1777 Fox again attacked Germain, comparing him to Dr. Sangrado who would persist in drawing blood because he had written a book on bleeding; and, after the capture of Burgoyne and his army, he told Lord George that he hoped to see him brought to a second trial. He put the whole blame for Burgoyne's capture upon Lord George, although Lord North, with his usual "decency," claimed his share of it. That was in the spring of '78. Fox made his charge publicly in the House, alleging that Lord George had not "given orders sufficiently explicit to General Howe to endeavour to meet and assist Burgoyne." Orders, in fact, of the same character as Lord George had himself received from Prince Ferdinand nearly twenty years since. Fox, in his speech, was measured and calm, in contrast with his former bitterness and violence. Walpole comments on his "extraordinary temper and judgment, without any acrimony." He had come now to the view that "too many of the King's Servants were involved in criminality to make personal bitterness to any single man excusable." But, after Lord George had "defended himself in a good speech, though many thought he did not clear himself,"[1] Fox's self-command deserted him. In a passion he tore up his motion of censure upon Germain, left the House, and declared to many that he would not return to it.

The debate on General Burgoyne's services in America had begun the month before, in February. Many professed to believe that Germain had recalled Burgoyne and Howe so that blame might fall on them instead of on himself. Mr. Temple Luttrell[2] spoke in justification of Burgoyne, calling him brave but unfortunate. "But," he added, "that [his bravery] is sufficient ground for accusation in the eyes of *some*: had he turned his back instead of going forward he would have met with a different reception from the noble Lord whose military conduct was certainly the reverse of the gallant officer's whose conduct they were about to enquire into." Speaking of Lord North, "then did he seize," said Luttrell, "the glorious opportunity to recommend to his sovereign a war minister whose public incapacities for every vigorous exertion of mind, whose disgrace at the Court of George the Second, was founded on the most decisive censure of a court-martial; whose loss of the nation's confidence and his own character, is on public record. What had that nation then to expect from his councils ? What plan of his, since in his office, dare he expose to the public eye,

[1] The familiar equivocal balance of the words proclaims their author.

[2] He had attacked Lord George some two years earlier, "abusing him in the grossest terms and for a long time in the House of Commons. He said flight was the only safety that remained for the Royal army, and he saw one who had set the example in Germany and was fit to lead them on such an occasion. Lord George said not a word in reply." —Walpole.

and say it has succeeded ? Why then should we give him a partial acquittal to the prejudice of a gallant officer, whose only crime has been avowedly that he was too zealous, too brave, too enterprising, too anxious for the good of his country; had strictly obeyed his orders; and done all that British valour was capable of, to carry the minister's plan into execution. Had he, instead of that, receded from his colours, disobeyed the commands of his superiors, and hid himself from danger, he might have had pretensions to one noble Lord's patronage, and to the other's dignities and emoluments."

Lord George's reply to this was certainly not tame or timid. He declared that "he never was personal in the House to anyone, that he never, by any conduct of his, had merited such an attack. He could not silently endure it. He despised the honourable member, but would level himself with his wretched character and malice." "Old as I am, and young as is the honourable member, I will meet that fighting gentleman and be revenged."

At this spirited rejoinder the House was thrown into general confusion. There was a tumult of cries: "Order! Order!" and "Chair! Chair!" The Speaker undertook to keep order if the House would support him, and Lord North admitted the delinquency of Lord George. He had made a personal attack, he was therefore out of order. Fox made an attempt to speak to order, and Lord North called him one of the most disorderly of members. The Speaker could do nothing, fifty members were standing up and trying to talk at the same time. Luttrell, under cover of the riot, tried to get away, so as to avoid having to apologize, but members were told to stop the doors against him, and the Speaker ordered the sergeant-at-arms to bring him down from the gallery, where he had sought refuge, to his seat.

The Speaker then said that "he was desired by the House to call upon the two honourable gentlemen who had spoken such high and harsh words to each other to stand up in their places and pledge their honour that the matter should go no further." There was to be no second duel, if the more prudent members could prevent it.

Lord George rose to acknowledge that he had been out of order. If he had used any improper expressions, he was sorry, and he hoped the House would excuse it. Mr. Luttrell, however, in various speeches which recurred at intervals over a period of some two hours, went back to Minden, arguing that his attack was not personal. He would not, he said, be bullied out of his privilege as a member; he had a right to say publicly what he thought about a public character. He, like so many others, felt that Lord George's disgrace after Minden was something that could be dragged up on any occasion to give point to any attack. "The sentence of the court-martial," he declared, "is a public record, relative to a man in a public post of trust. . . . I have not alluded to the noble lord's private vices or virtues." "If, after being insulted for doing my duty, I am to be committed for delivering the sentence of George the Second, I should prefer being committed to giving up the privilege of parliament and promising to take no notice of a personal attack. . . . I shall give no other answer, and abide by the decision of the House." Fox supported Luttrell, saying that he wished not to irritate but to settle the present dispute, but there was certainly a difference in the two attacks, the first being a general one on a public character, the last a personal one on a private character; and therefore he recommended the noble Lord to say a word by way of extenuation to that gentleman as he had done to the House. Others expressed the same opinion as Fox did, but Lord George had a good many to speak on his side. Those who were for him held that he could not be expected to make any further apology, and that Temple Luttrell should be committed. A motion was made for his commitment, and he himself surprisingly seconded it, in order that the House might go on with its important public business as it could not do till "this altercation was settled." "I shall make no apology for public severity of language, but an apology I must seek for personal insult to myself."

At this point, as Temple Luttrell was about to be taken into the custody of the sergeant-at-arms, Lord George chose the best counter-move that could have been made in face of the manœuvres of this skilful and determined adversary. His practical sense defeated his stubbornness, his chagrin, and his pride; he addressed Luttrell directly, in regret for "certain improper words addressed to him in the warmth of debate." Luttrell then replied that "Now that the House is satisfied that sufficient apology is made for the personality they have heard spoken against me, I shall out of respect to the House comply with their injunctions that it shall go no further: and I beg leave once more to observe that what was said by me of the noble lord was meant as public matter, not as private abuse or enmity."

So the matter ended. The distinction between public and private abuse may seem, to some, a fine one. Luttrell had deliberately, in cold blood, pointed to a long past disgrace, and pointed to it with a gesture and emphasis by which, as he surely knew, Germain would be intolerably goaded. Germain, taken unawares, in hot anger, retorted. Who was formally in the right, and who formally in the wrong, is not very important. These continued references, year after year, to the distant Minden disgrace, may have been "in order," but they were not made with the purpose of enforcing legitimate criticism. They were made meanly, vindictively, cruelly. Their purpose was to exacerbate, to wound; venom was their life-blood.

The Germain-Luttrell affair made a great stir outside the House as well. The *London Chronicle* and other papers wrote it up, and it made good copy. Rhymesters were incited by an event so entertaining, and so distasteful and discomfiting to Lord George:

Tho' records speak Germain's disgrace,
To quote them to him face to face,
(The Commons now are *si honnête*,)
They voted, was not etiquette.

Less spectacular and less protracted was the unquestionably personal attack made early in 1778 upon Germain by Sir Alexander Leith. Walpole records that he "abused Lord George in the grossest terms in the Commons, and told him he was not fit to serve the King.'' The *London Chronicle* of February 9th of that year states that Sir Alexander Leith '' was called to order by the Chair, whence it was observed that such liberties were extremely improper.'' Walpole's account that '' Lord George answered with great spirit and said that any man had a right to accuse him in form, but that no man should say such things to his face without a formal charge and proofs '' is supplemented by the *London Chronicle,* where it appears that Germain showed self-control as well as spirit.

> Lord George said he could never sit silent and hear such unbecoming personalities made to his face. He begged leave to assure the honourable member that, if they were sincere, they must be founded upon prejudices and were ill founded. He was a very old member of that House; and he defied any gentleman to say that he had ever used personalities himself. He always carefully abstained from them, and, whatever his provocation to retort might be on the present occasion, he should give one more proof of the same mode of conducting himself.

The proceedings in the House relative to Burgoyne's services in America began in February, 1778, (the month after Lady George's death) and they dragged on until May. The Government's enlistment of savages to fight against the Americans was also a subject of debate, and the blame for the barbarous and bestial conduct alleged against these Red Indians was charged solely to Germain. Lurid and horrific details were given by Colonel Barré. '' Not only did they dig up the buried bodies of the slain to get their scalps, but even after they had obtained their beloved trophies of glory, the skulls of their enemies, they sucked the congealed blood out of the mangled carcasses.'' Colonel Barré, in his thick theatrical voice with its emphatic Irish brogue, enunciated accusingly these revolting atrocities.

It was four years later that Lord George's enemies had their last chance to make a really intensive and protracted attack upon him, and to rake up Minden yet once again. When, early in 1782, George the Third created Germain Viscount

Sackville, the experienced hounds were at once in full cry. Walpole writes of the Duke of Grafton's " great indignation and bitterness on the report that Lord George was to be called up to that House; he that had been employed though degraded, and who had done nothing to deserve reward, but the contrary." It was, however, the Marquess of Carmarthen who acted as spokesman against the new Viscount in the House of Lords. He " proposed . . . to protest against the admission into their order of a man stamped by an indelible brand, and by a sentence that had never been cancelled." " The positive Monarch precipitated the patent in defiance. The Marquess, as unshaken, pursued his hostility, solicited the peers to condemn the indignity offered to them." " The exaltation was as abruptly and cruelly the occasion of recalling the former stigma," " and the new Viscount was reduced . . . after taking his seat, to hear his former sentence read to his face, and to combat in person for the Sovereign's prerogative right of giving, and his own competence of receiving, the conferred honour."

Lord Carmarthen made the familiar disclaimer of personal animosity, but

> [1]he considered it derogatory to the honour of that House to admit a person still labouring under the heavy censure of a court-martial. The language of the Earl of Shelburne, the Earl of Abingdon, and the Duke of Richmond on this occasion, was beneath their dignity as Peers of the realm. They heaped upon Lord George unmerited insults, which at any time would be unfit for the debates of such an assembly. Even provided they had any cause of enmity against him, as Junius,[2] of which character they strongly suspected him, that was not a suitable place, nor a suitable occasion for such resentment. The whole proceeding was pronounced by Lord Thurlow, extra-judicial and irregular. Lord Sackville's reply was so powerful, so animated, and so much to the point, that they had cause to blush at their

[1] From Coventry's Memoirs.

[2] Coventry was convinced that Lord George was Junius, and so were many others, both at that time and later.

unmanly behaviour, and it was universally admitted, even by his enemies, that a more dignified speech was never made within those walls. The Marquess's motion was lost a second time.

Lord Carmarthen, on the first occasion, before Lord George, as an admitted peer, could answer him, argued that " the creating such a person a peer, a person who had in his military character been publicly degraded, was a disgrace to the House." He went on to speak of his " sincere pity " for " the individual who laboured under such a heavy load of stigma as was contained in the sentence in question: a copy of which," he added, whether in a mournful, compassionate, or whether in a triumphant tone, is not known, " I hold in my hand." He appealed to their lordships " to feel, as men jealous of their honour must necessarily feel upon such an occasion."

No one responded to this, there may have been some slight tension of uneasiness, so Lord Carmarthen got on his feet again, and put his motion of protest, reading the court-martial verdict aloud, also George the Second's highly sympathetic and embroidering confirmation of it.

Lord Thurlow, the Lord Chancellor, then spoke, and after describing the motion as altogether irregular and disorderly, reminded the House that they were at that moment, in point of Parliamentary form, utter strangers to the facts. He appealed to their lordships not to act inconsistently with their usual liberality and candour.

The Earl of Abingdon responded to this appeal by declaring that Lord George had been the greatest criminal this country ever knew: and he continued his speech in the same totalitarian vein. Were they to admit to the contamination of their House a man who " had been the author of all the calamities of the war, and all the distresses which Britain now groaned under? It was to his blood-thirstiness, his weakness, his wickedness, and his mismanagement, that the war had been prosecuted at so large a waste of blood and treasure, and with such a miserable repetition of ill-successes." It is not surprising that Lord Abingdon should have been afterwards imprisoned in the King's Bench for a libel. In a second speech he was threatening as well as abusive. He assured their lordships that he would " do his business," if this man were sent up to the House. " He had in his own house, ample materials to make the groundwork of an impeachment; and which he would certainly produce, if the person in question attempted to come among them." Of the effect of this threat upon Lord George he professed to have no doubt. " I hope there are those in the House, who are ready to run to their Master . . . If they give him a true account, the effect will be a rescue of the House from the taint that menaces it."

Of the other speeches in support of Lord Carmarthen's motion Lord Shelburne's is the most interesting. He began by a noble explanation of the " extreme pain " caused him by his taking part in the present debate; the intensification of this pain, which in any case he would have felt, was due to his having suffered many professional injuries from Lord George. Those injuries had made him smart, and there had been, as a result, " a sort of enmity " between himself and " the person in question "; but from the very moment that Lord Shelburne saw the sentence of the court-martial, his heart, it seemed, had melted, and with emphatic vigour he now called upon God Almighty to witness his chivalry. From the moment of that condemnation he had " neither privately nor publicly, directly nor indirectly, in thought, word, or deed, done that person the smallest injury, or bore hard on him on any occasion whatever." The slate was wiped so clean, indeed, that Lord Shelburne's friends had noticed it, and he had had the opportunity of giving also to them this creditable explanation. He hoped, now, that no one would think that he spoke from hatred: every spark of animosity was long since extinguished. He went on to talk about the King, drawing the attention of the House to his own constant endeavour to " treat his Majesty with that profound respect due to his person, and with that reverence so infinitely due to his estimation." He enlarged on his loyalty. Nothing could be more repugnant to him than any undue infringement of the royal prerogative, but, for all the intensity of his loyal devotion, he could not but see that there was such a thing as an *extraordinary stretch of prerogative*, and the House of Peers was entitled " to right itself " against that. When the King proposed to make Lord George Germain a peer, there was too extraordinary a stretch of prerogative even for so humbly respectful a subject as Lord Shelburne, even for one who had so freely, so charitably, and so long since, forgiven Germain for all the harm he had done him. Yes, it was all " very extraordinary," the present motion had been called " very extraordinary," but, " Good God! were not these very extraordinary times?" Lord Shelburne proceeded to speak of the recent catastrophes to British arms in America, and of Lord George's restoration, seven years since, to the Privy Council, and of the design to expel him from the Commons. That design could not be carried out; but, he argued, there was all the difference in the world between " allowing a person to sit in the other House and suffering him to come up here ": though, of course, no one thought more highly of the House of Commons than he did. " With regard to the person now designed to be created a peer, I call upon the learned adviser of the Crown, and I ask why? " He ought never to have been made a Secretary of State, and, indeed, in appointing him, and in " entrusting him with the management of the war, they in a manner began the war with the greatest insult to America that could possibly have been devised."

Such was the effect, upon Lord Shelburne, of the " extinction of every spark of his animosity " towards Lord George. After his speech the House divided, twenty-eight voting for Lord Carmarthen's motion, and seventy-five against it.

Notwithstanding the small minority in favour of his motion, Lord Carmarthen brought forward one of the same kind when Lord Sackville, now having taken his seat in the House of Peers, could be there in person to hear what the Marquess and his supporters had to say about him. The Marquess said more or less the same things as before, emphasizing again the court-martial sentence, and adding an expression of his astonishment at the noble Lord's own conduct in accepting the honour of a Peerage.

Lord Abingdon, feeling perhaps less sure of himself now that his threat of impeachment had failed to strike terror, or sickening of the infection of Lord Sackville's actual presence in the House, was not, to begin with, violent. " Surely we *must* have a right of exclusion " was his early, almost plaintive tenor, though later he did approach, if not attain, the level of his former rhetoric. " Against everything that has been said, against common sense, against common decency; in the face of all public virtue, and in encouragement of every private vice, we find a man foisted in upon us, and with the reward of nobility made one of ourselves . . . I fear my Lords . . . are ready to sell their birthright for a mess of porridge." This admission of Lord George Germain to the peerage was " no less an insufferable indignity to this House, than an outrageous insult to the people at large. It is an indignity to this House, because it is connecting us with one, whom every soldier as a man of honour is forbid to associate with. It is an insult to the people at large, for, what has he done to merit honours superior to his fellow-citizens? I will tell your Lordships what he has done; he has undone his country. . . . "

This association, quite a natural one, of Lord George with the ill success of the American War was certainly not enough to account for the rancour of his enemies. Others equally responsible on such a count were not attacked in the same fashion, nor near it. His " mismanagement " of the war was a serviceable weapon against him, but it was not because of this that he was hated with such bitterness, with such fury. Lord Abingdon slips in a reference to " private vice," as Luttrell had done four years earlier, showing his personal, his undiscriminating animosity. There is hardly a single attack upon Lord George, either as Sackville or as Germain, which is not, in its essence, flagrantly personal. Not personal as a retaliation for personal injuries inflicted by Lord George, for none of his enemies, including Lord Shelburne, could have been so strongly urged by any injurious words or actions of his, real or imagined. The punitive hostility against Lord George was personal in another sense. It was his individual qualities, his idiosyncratic combination of them, his pride, his remoteness, his intransigeance, his indifference, his irony, his disdain, his self-command and self-assurance, that inflamed mean minds with irresistible incitement to destructive attack. Sackville's personal appearance, his tallness, his massive solidity of frame, his handsomeness, his aspect of inbred authority, his demeanour of dignity and reserve, were added and notable provocations to petty resentment.

This man, naturally an object of uneasy envy and malevolence to little people, was by the tremendous mishap of his life marked out as one to be safely aimed at, and more than safely, with moral credit to him who aimed, credit of honour. Made vulnerable from chance of circumstance, he lacked those faculties by which he would have evaded, stepped aside, intrigued; manœuvring and diplomatizing himself out of a position in which he was so dangerously, so conspicuously exposed. He was now no less incapable than he ever had been of that kind of slim political agility that would have, long ago, tricked his enemies and made him after awhile into an accepted man, even a popular one. In his speech of self-defence before the peers Sackville spoke like himself, with calm and reason, with honesty and patience, with directness and logical force. He spoke immediately after Lord Abingdon.

Early in his speech he referred to the court-martial sentence; he contended that "the sentence amounted to no disqualification whatever." Speaking of "the peculiarly hard and unfair circumstances that had attended his being tried at all," "What had been the temper of those times?" he asked. "Faction and clamour predominated; they both ran against me, and I was made a victim of the most unexampled persecution that ever a British officer has been pursued with. I was condemned unheard, punished before trial. Stripped of all my military honours and emoluments upon mere rumour, upon the malicious suggestions of my enemies, without their having been called upon to exhibit the smallest proof of their loose assertion and acrimonious invective, I stood pointed to the world as a man easy to be run down by clamour, and to fall a sacrifice to faction. Thus cruelly circumstanced, thus made to suffer in a manner equally unparalleled and unjust,

I did not choose to flee like a guilty man and hide myself from the world. I challenged my accusers to come forward, I provoked enquiry, I insisted upon a trial . . . Determined to clear my character at any hazard, I . . . resolved to abide the consequences, and what could your Lordships imagine induced me to persevere [in provoking the court-martial] but a consciousness of my innocence? . . . I well knew that, had the sentence been more severe, had it been capital, it would have been executed . . . It does not become me to say a word of the court-martial, or of its proceedings; I have submitted to my sentence . . . At present, neither the charge, nor the defence, nor the evidence, nor any part of the proceedings, is before your Lordships; and yet you are called upon to put the sentence a second time in force against me. Not that I mean to express any, the least objection, to the whole of the proceedings being examined. I should have been happy, indeed, if the whole of the case had been submitted to your Lordships' investigation."

Sackville had been ready to challenge Lord Carmarthen to a duel on account of the speech by which he brought forward his first motion: he was, indeed, "with difficulty restrained" from challenging the Marquess; but he spoke of him in the House with marked temperance, with a free generosity. "I have no doubt that the noble Marquess meant nothing but what was consistent with his own honour, and his sense of what was due to the honour of the House. He has certainly acted in a way that is manly and fair, to take it up while I am present, and not behind my back."

Continuing, Sackville pointed out that his election in 1765 to the Privy Council constituted a virtual repeal of the sentence of the court-martial. He reminded the House of his later appointment as Secretary of State, and asked them to "consider the hardship of the court-martial sentence being urged against me as a disqualification for a seat in this House, which had been deemed no disqualification whatever of my being a Privy Counsellor and a Secretary of State; two situations surely of more dignity and of more importance . . . than even a peerage." As to making the sentence a ground of censure, "Would your Lordships sanction, confirm, and aggravate a sentence, pronounced by a court-military, without having the whole of the case before them? That would be to make the military law, sufficiently severe as it confessedly is at present, ten times more severe, by annexing to its judgment the censure of a civil court of judicature."

Sackville further objected to the addition to the court-martial sentence, in Carmarthen's motion, of George the Second's comment. "To the sentence of the court-martial I was bound by the laws military to submit . . . but would any man of honour say that I am answerable for the comment of the executive government? . . . The court-martial alone was competent to pronounce upon what they thought my conduct had been. I was tried by them, and not by the executive government."

He spoke of his past endeavours to serve his King and country to the best of his judgment, though "I cannot pretend to cope with any man in respect to abilities : there are many, I am persuaded, more able than myself." Then again he spoke of the court-martial, pointing out that he could not possibly get its sentence revised. "It happened two-and-twenty years ago, and every member who sat upon it, except two . . . were dead and buried long ago. Any attempt to investigate the motives which actuated the several members of the Court is now impracticable." "It is neither expedient, necessary, nor becoming," he concluded, "for this House to fly in the face of the indisputable prerogative of the crown, merely because the crown thinks proper to bestow a reward on an old servant."

This was Sackville's last act of self-defence. He had now only three more years to live. Lord Carmarthen's second motion was lost, as the first had been, by a large majority.

Chapter VIII

AMERICA: 1765-1775

BRITAIN's war to suppress the American Rebellion was for long generally regarded not only as a disastrous failure but as the least justifiable, the most foolish, and the most incompetently conducted of all our wars ; as, in the main, a tragic farce of errors. In later years the inevitable reaction against this view took place, and the case for England has been more and more favourably presented, by American historians as well as by others. The whole question has been so fully debated that it does not seem necessary to attempt to lead the reader now over that well trodden ground. It may however be suggested that a review of Lord George Germain's[1] political, military, and personal correspondence at the time, and of the debates in which he took part as American Secretary, might well qualify earlier judgments, though it would hardly remove all the basis for all of them.

It is important to remember, when considering the part now played by Lord George Germain, that, at the time, sane and understanding Englishmen,—men of genius, even,—necessarily lacking the perspective that we cannot help having now, and befogged by misinformation and consequent misunderstanding in place of the clear incontrovertible evidences which came later, were convinced that force must be used against the American colonists. Even at the end of the war Edward Gibbon continued to vote for Lord North. Doctor Johnson was well weighted always by conviction of the justice of the British cause and wanted to sit in Parliament to support it. "If the King would make Lord Chatham dictator for six months," he declared, "nothing more would be heard of these rebels." Lord Chatham himself, who has been so

[1] Germain, in place of Sackville, was his name from 1770 to 1782.

often cited as a friend to American liberties, was at no time in favour of American independence, and he supported England's right to make financial or commercial regulations for the colonies, also to impose port duties or customs on anything sent to America. During a critical period of over two years, from August, 1766 to October, 1768, he was the head of one Ministry and Lord Privy Seal in another. He did not do much good.

Lord Chatham's views about America were not so clear and simple as some have thought them. He contended that England could not, in order to raise revenue, tax the colonies, but he firmly upheld her right to govern them, and this involved everything short of actual "taxation for revenue." This, in the view of others, was a merely metaphysical distinction, "very ministerial," to use Lord George's phrase. In a letter of January, 1766 Lord George writes that "It seems we have all been in a mistake in regard to the Constitution, for Mr. Pitt[1] asserts that the Legislature of this country has no right whatever to levy internal taxes upon the colonys; that they are neither actually nor vertually represented, and therefore not subject to our jurisdiction in that particular; but still as the Mother Country we may tax and regulate their commerce, prohibit or restrain manufactures, and do everything but what we have done by the Stamp Act; that in our representative capacity we raise taxes internally and in our legislative capacity we do all the other acts of power. If you understand the difference between representative and legislative capacity it is more than I do, but I assure you it was very fine when I heard it."

George Grenville, who was responsible for the famous Stamp Act, acted on his belief that England had the right to levy any sort of tax upon the colonies, which, as Junius put it, having "benefited most by the expenses of the war [against France] should contribute to the expenses of the peace." While most of the American provinces were chartered by the crown and exempted from taxation, others were not; and the case for Grenville was that this chartering and exemption issued from an undue stretch of the prerogative of the crown, and that

[1] He was not made Earl of Chatham till about six months later.

" the entire colonization " should now be " equalized." Confusion and vacillation prevailed in the minds of many on the whole matter, as well they might. Some, like Lord Rockingham, held that we had a right to tax, but that it was not expedient to exercise it; others veered continually, like the Duke of Grafton, who sometimes sided with Pitt, sometimes with Rockingham, and ended up by supporting taxation, no matter what the risk. The real division, among politicians and the politically-minded, was on the question of expediency. Was it wise, as a matter of practical politics, to tax the colonies, or was it not? Very few would have been against taxing them if the thing could have been safely done.

In the view of Grenville and his supporters it was not the Stamp Act but the agitation of British politicians against it, and the ensuing repeal, neutralized, in attempt at compromise, by a provocative preamble, that brought about the calamities which followed. In March, 1774, Lord George Germain spoke in the Commons of Burke's having " taken great pains to . . . extol those who advised the repeal of the Stamp Act . . . I was of opinion that it should not be repealed, and voted accordingly. It is now contended, that that measure [the repeal] produced the desired effect, and that on its passing, everything was peace and tranquility. I know the contrary was the case, and we have evidence at your bar, which proved that the Americans were totally displeased, because in the preamble to the repeal we asserted our right to enact laws of sufficient force and authority to bind them. I am on the whole fully convinced that the present situation of affairs in that country would never have been; and that the people there must and would have returned to their obedience, if the Stamp Act had not been unfortunately repealed."

Junius thought exactly the same. He wrote, about four years later, that " if the pretensions of the colonies had not been abetted by something worse than a faction here the Stamp Act would have executed itself. Every clause of it was so full and explicit that it wanted no further instruction; nor was it of that nature that required a military hand to carry it into execution. For the truth of this answer I am ready to appeal even to the Americans themselves." "It is truly astonishing," Junius wrote in an earlier Letter, "that a great number of people should have so little foreseen the inevitable consequence of repealing the Stamp Act, and particularly that the trading part of the city should have conceived that a compliance which acknowledged the rod to be in the hand of the Americans, could ever induce them to surrender it . . . We have not even a tolerable excuse for our folly. The punishment has followed close upon it."

Junius, like Lord George, believed in Grenville, not in Chatham, and was convinced that Chatham and those others who, in Lord George's phrase, "took an avowed part with America," were the real authors of the war. "Unfortunately for this country, Mr. Grenville was at any rate to be distressed, because he was minister, and Mr. Pitt[1] and Lord Camden were to be the patrons of America because they were in opposition. Their declarations gave spirit and argument to the colonies, and . . . they in effect divided one half of the empire from the other." Junius emphasizes, as Lord George does, the weakness and inconsistency of withdrawing a tax and proclaiming at the same time a right to impose it: "They have relinquished the revenue, but judiciously taken care to preserve the contention." It was not taxation, but "a series of inconsistent measures" that "had alienated the colonies from their duties as subjects, and from their natural affection to their common country."

When, after the repeal of the Stamp Act, such custom-house duties as those upon glass, red-lead, and tea were put on as an experiment, to see how the Americans would take them, Junius was for the repeal of those duties because, following as they did the surrender of the Government, they were "impolitic," not because they were "oppressive": although he regarded them as "more offensive to the colonies, more

[1] Junius's own note here is, "Yet Junius has been called the partisan of Lord Chatham!" Those who believe that Sir Philip Francis, who had Pitt for his patron, was Junius, emphasize all that Junius writes in favour of Pitt and declare that the Letters in which he most violently attacks him are not genuine. The authenticity of the Letter now quoted has never been in question. It is unlikely that Lord George was Junius; but that Sir Philip Francis was is more unlikely still.

directly exerting the right of taxation." "The tea-duty," Junius wrote to Wilkes, "preserves the contention between the mother country and the colonies, when everything worth contending for is in reality given up." Lord George, too, was, as a matter of policy, for the repeal of these taxes, but only if there was no talk of their being oppressive. "If the Americans would petition for their repeal, I would stretch forth the first hand to present it ; but, on the contrary, if they claim such a repeal as a right, thereby disputing the authority of the mother country, which no reasonable man ever called in question, I wish it may be enforced with a Roman severity."

These were prevalent opinions. Even Charles James Fox voted for the Boston Port Bill, which shut up Boston Harbour to punish the Bostonians for emptying the taxed tea into it. In February, 1767, Lord George wrote that "the Chancellor of the Exchequer [Charles Townshend] declared yesterday that if we once lose the superintendency of the colonys this nation is undone." "It is believed," he writes about a fortnight later, "that Ld. Chatham has changed his ideas about America and means to act with vigour." In another letter of some seven months earlier, Lord George states that "Mr. Pitt inclin'd to have George Grenville," the author of the Stamp Act, "consider'd for office." The shadow of that dreadful alternative to which Junius,[1] in the summer of 1768, saw England reduced, was already cast, and deepening. Either there must be war with the colonies or they must be independent. That not one or the other but both of these events would happen if "timidity, weakness, and distraction" continued to prevail, was clear to Junius writing then "on the brink of a dreadful precipice," though "far from despairing of the republic," and knowing that "we have great resources left, if they are not lost or betrayed." He, like Lord George and many others, was divided between hope and the gravest misgiving.

It was in the brief Rockingham Ministry succeeding the

[1] An abridgement of this Junius Letter is in the Appendix, pp. 284–287. The greater part of the Letter might have been written, *mutatis mutandis*, at the end of August, 1939, by an opponent of the Chamberlain Government.

1763-1765 Ministry of George Grenville, that Lord George took a minor office as one of the Vice-Treasurers. The Rockingham Ministry dated from July, Lord George's appointment from December of the same year. In July he had written to Charles Townshend that "the opinion of permanency cannot be established in favour of this ministry till you have the avowed and real management of the House. Whenever that happens it will be a mortification to me if I am not permitted to assist." But as things were, he added, he could not say that his anxiety to assist was great. He makes it clear, as is to be expected from one whose view of the American crisis matched so closely with that of Junius, that office would not tempt him to any change of front. He had not given "the slightest hint that I should act in support of Administration upon the expectation of any subsequent arrangement, but directly the contrary." He held his office only till the end of July, 1766, which was immediately before Chatham's Ministry succeeded Rockingham's. Charles Townshend wrote to express his regrets, and implies that Lord Chatham was responsible for Lord George's dismissal. "Everything proceeds entirely from Lord Chatham to the King, from thence without any intermediate consultation to the public, and I am confident that no other man has the least previous knowledge or influence." Lord George in reply expresses his mistrust of the Ministry, doubting if Townshend, who was now Chancellor of the Exchequer, would be able to execute the parliamentary part of his office to his own satisfaction unless he had a greater share in advising the measures that he might be expected to support.

Lord George did not take office again until November, 1775, under Lord North, when he succeeded Lord Dartmouth in the newly created Secretaryship for the Colonies; or "for America," as it was often called. By that time the American War was begun, and was going very badly for England. Lord George, says Horace Walpole, was adopted to repair Lord North's indolence and inactivity, and he adds that, till Lord George took office, there had been no spirit or sense in the conduct of the war. Certainly the new American Secretary, knowing very well how things were, took office unwillingly. Writing to his old friend General Irwin on November 4th, he says that he fears he will soon be in Lord Dartmouth's place. "I have try'd and cannot avoid it. Pity me, encourage me, and I will do my best."

For the last ten years he had felt the greatest uneasiness over the policies adopted towards America; he knew well how hard it was to put any "spirit or sense" into them. In December, 1765, he had written to this same friend: "Everybody is distress'd about America. The spirit that rages there is beyond conception. God only knows how it will end, for as yet I have heard no human reasoning that promises a happy issue to it." For Pitt's "strange doctrine" he had, as has already been noted, a contemptuous antipathy; and he thought such doctrine highly dangerous. "Mr. Pitt," he wrote early in 1766, "said one thing which I was sorry to hear, that if he was an American he would not thank the Parlt. for the repeal of the Act if it was not done upon the principle of our having no right to lay an internal tax upon that country. In the temper the colonists are now in, such a declaration will be seized with eagerness, and his authority will be quoted as a sanction for their wildest pretensions of an exclusive legislative right of taxing by their assemblys." Lord George wanted a policy that would avoid war by reconciling the colonies without surrender of what he believed to be British rights. "Nothing is so easy as to declare war," he wrote, "nothing so difficult as to make peace," And, again: "Every fool can pick a quarrel, but I do not remember any minister wise enough to end a war without forfeiting his own credit with the bulk of the people." In February, 1766, he was anxious that the resolution "desiring His Majesty to carry all the laws now in force in America into execution" should not be passed in the House of Commons, and he voted accordingly, because that would have amounted to an immediate declaration of war. Four years later he was afraid that the Ministers might make an example of Boston and act with too much severity.

Unlike many others, Lord George was consistent in his view of the troubles in America. To him it seemed that

British political pusillanimity and vacillation, and pro-American treachery, were playing into the hands of the seditious American few who were striving for an independence which would be ruinous both to Britain and to America, and who were thus enabled to succeed in misguiding more and more of their fellow-colonists. "The Colonys are growing worse and worse," he wrote early in 1767. But in America there were those who were not seditious; and the part of Great Britain was to support them to the utmost of her ability, and to prevent the outbreak of what would be not only a revolutionary, but a civil war. How ill we were requited for our extraordinary lenity and indulgence, to those who were undutiful children! The consequences of yielding to riot and ill grounded clamour had been foretold, and were now apparent. Perhaps Administration would now be obliged to exert a degree of vigour. The loss of the American colonies would ruin England. But, as the year 1767 wore on, no necessary rigours were exerted; the political situation grew more and more perplexing. When the Act for quartering the troops was disobeyed in New York and Boston, the Ministers would not exert executive authority, but proposed to bring the matter up in Parliament, The Chancellor (Lord Camden) held stout language in the Lords, and general abuse of him followed. He was told that he and his friends had encouraged the Americans; Lord Temple said that such encouragement was criminal and treasonable, and Lord Talbot tartly remarked upon the change of the Chancellor's tone. "New converts," he said, "were always the most zealous." "Something must be done in support of the authority of the Mother Country," says Lord George in the letter in which he gives an account of these proceedings. He could not have thought it likely that anything effective would be done. That "this sort of Government cannot continue" is his only consolation. It continued only till December of that year. Meantime, during the summer, since the country gentlemen could not, as Lord George ironically observes, be kept in town then, the business of the Commons remained at the mercy of the Court. "I left the ministry as unsettled as usual, Ld. Chatham not in a condition to attend to business, and by all accounts no system form'd for future operations."

So it went on. In December the Duke of Grafton's Ministry succeeded Lord Chatham's, with Lord Chatham retaining his office of Lord Privy Seal for nearly a year longer. No one did anything. Chatham was ill, but at the end of December was said to be better. "If Ld. Chatham is as well as your friends upon the road think him to be he will not long remain in this state of inactivity." But a few days later Lord George writes again to General Irwin, telling him that the Ministers all continue out of town, and there is not the least news stirring. "The great man at Hayes [Chatham] remains shut up."

From Boston, however, a livelier state of things was reported. The Commissioners of Revenue had arrived there, and on an unfortunate date, the Fifth of November. Lord George describes what happened. "When they landed, the populace were carrying in procession the Pope, the Devil, and the Pretender, in order to commit them to the flames in honour of Protestantism. Mr. Paxton's name being Charles it was fixed in large letters upon the breast of the Devil, and these figures met the Commissioners at the water side and were carry'd before them without any insult thro' the streets, and whenever they stopp'd to salute an acquaintance the figures halted and faced about till the salutation was over, and so accompany'd them to the Govr. Hutchinson's door where the Devil, &c., took their leave with loud huzzas from the mob, and were immediately conducted to the destined place of execution."

Lord Chatham continued to "hide himself," and the general opinion was that, owing to his ill health, he could "never appear in business." Spring and summer passed, with nothing better to report from America. In August Lord George writes sceptically that the Ministers "profess" acting with firmness and vigour. "If the first declaration of the Ministry do not check the turbulent spirit of the Americans I shall dread the consequences, for nothing is so likely to produce confusion as vigour unably exerted." By September the accounts from America were more and more unfavourable; and Lord George could not learn what measures the Administration were taking. "They talk of vigour." Two regiments were embarked for Boston: but everything depended on what the Governors were told to do with them. Lord George doubts whether anything will be done properly.

Lord Chatham, "a miserable, decrepid, worn out old man,"[1] from under whose "gouty legs" the Duke of Grafton had "crept into the elbow chair," gave up the post of Lord Privy Seal about a month after Lord George wrote this unhopeful letter. He had not for some time been able to fulfil the duties of this post. The miscellaneous Letters ascribed to Junius and written during 1768 give the same picture of ministerial incompetence as is given by these letters of Lord George's written at the same time, when "the state of the colonies evidently demanded some extraordinary measures of wisdom and of vigour."[2] "Governed as we are, our constant prayer should be, *Give peace in the time of these ministers, O Lord!* There is certainly some dreadful infatuation which hangs over and directs the councils of this country. Our ministers drive us headlong to destruction."[3]

The Duke of Grafton's Ministry lasted two years, and was succeeded in January, 1770 by the long-lived Ministry of Lord North. During 1769 Lord Chatham, though out of office, was still a figure of power. Lord George was of opinion that "the late great commoner" would have the credit for whatever change of ministry might take place. His influence with the King continued; he was better in health. Lord George's mistrust of and contempt for the men in office is unabated. Towards the end of 1769 he is sure that Wedderburn must have spoken admirably well as the ministerial writers treat him so roughly. He pictures the Ministry as dependent and instable; no one could tell who might be the leaders a few months hence. "Where could His Majesty find a set of men more observant of his orders or of less

[1] From a doubtful Junius letter, April 23, 1768.

[2] From a letter signed "C" and considered an authentic Junius. July 23, 1768.

[3] From a doubtful Junius letter, October 15, 1768.

consequence as individuals if he should think proper to change hands ?"[1]

Under Lord North, in 1770, many of the same Ministers held office: Lord George did not feel that things were any better. The Government, he thought, was likely either to be unwisely yielding or tactlessly severe. If only George Grenville were in office! There was no one else with his knowledge and firmness. But Grenville was dying. After his death, which "will be the greatest misfortune and loss," what will the opposition try to do? "I hope not to make Ld. Chatham minister? You cannot suppose I should be very sanguine in such a cause." After Grenville's death Lord George seems to have given up hope that anything effective could be done against the folly of the Government. "The more I think of the bad consequences of his death, the more alarming they appear to me. His presence in Parlt. was such a check upon Ministers that I shall expect when he is no longer among us that all decency will be lost." It is, then, not surprising that Lord George, a year or so after Grenville's death, should impatiently write, "As to politics, I think little about them." He saw no good in opposition, things being as they were, but when the time came he would try to do the best he could, "and show that I am not apt to change my sentiments about men or measures."

Horace Walpole's statement that American affairs were loosely managed before it came to actual war in 1775 is certainly not exaggerated. It is not a baseless contention that if George Grenville's policy had been carried out firmly, and with discretion, the colonies must, as Lord George said, "have ultimately returned to their allegiance:" and that it was Lord Chatham who, while his "wretched ministers served at the altar . . . offered up his bleeding country as a victim to America."[2] If our Governments, during those tedious unprofitable years from 1765 to 1775, had shown statecraft instead of doing practically nothing except feebly

[1] This is one of many indications that Lord George was not, as he has been described, "a Courtier of George the Third."

[2] Miscellaneous Junius letter of December 19, 1767, thought to be genuine.

and indeterminately to irritate the Americans as they became, year after year, more unsettled by their discontents, the colonies might not have been lost.

It was probably the speech made by Lord George in the Commons on March 28th, 1774 which first gave Lord North the idea that he might be useful in helping the Government out of their increasing difficulties in dealing with America. Lord North publicly recognized the value of this speech, declaring that it was " worthy so great a mind." Lord George, through his friend Lord Amherst, and through his nephew Lord Thanet, was well informed on America, or certainly better informed than most were. The speech had a tone of authority and decision. He is especially concerned with the " internal government of Massachuset's Bay." " I wish," he said, " to see the council of that country on the same footing as other colonies . . . I would wish to bring the Constitution of America as similar to our own as possible . . . At present the Assembly of that province is a downright clog upon all the proceedings of the governor, and the council are continually thwarting and opposing any proposition he may make for the security and welfare of that government. You have, sir, no government—no governor; the whole are the proceedings of a tumultuous and riotous rabble, who ought, if they had the least prudence, to follow their mercantile employments, and not trouble themselves with politics and government, which they do not understand.

" We are told by some gentlemen, Oh! do not break the charter! do not take away their rights that are granted to them by the predecessors of the Crown! Whoever, sir, wishes to preserve such charters, without a due correction and regulation—whoever wishes for such subjects, I wish them no worse than to govern them. Put this people, sir, on a free footing of government; do not let us every day be asserting our rights by words, and then denying our authority, and preventing the execution of our laws. Let us persevere in refining that government which cannot support itself, and proceed in the manner we have begun, and I make no doubt, but by a manly and steady perseverance, things may be restored from a state of anarchy and confusion to peace, quietude, and a due obedience to the laws of this country."

A little later in that year Lord George's private letters about America are less unhopeful. "I like the American news which I now see in the papers," he writes in early July. "Virginia's refusing to join with the Bostonians in the agreement for not importing goods from Fngland is decisive, and there is nothing left for the mob of Boston but to decide between ruin and submission." On the eve of the war, in spite of the news from Massachusetts, Lord George, though apprehensive, is not pessimistic. What he fears is ministerial delay. At the end of the momentous month of May, 1775 he writes of the great stir caused by the news from America. "By the first report I was afraid the troops had misbehaved, but upon reading the account from Salem I was satisfy'd that the party having done what they were order'd at Concord, marched back towards Boston, and possibly may have lost some few men. However," he adds with his usual detachment, "the Bostonians are in the right to make the King's troops the aggressors and to claim a victory." He says it is strange to see how many joyful faces there are upon this event, and explains it by the hopes which people have that Rebellion will change the Ministry. Decision and firmness will succeed, thinks Lord George. "This blow, if follow'd up, will soon bring that province into order."

A fortnight later he is afraid that the Secretary for America will take fright and refuse to order decisive and vigorous measures. But that would not mean a change of Ministry. He sees not the slightest chance of that. Now, as so often, he sets his hopes on the American loyalists. "How much more mischief must be done before we avail ourselves of local force?" The marching of the loyal part of the province, and sending a body of Canadians to the frontiers of New England is what he wants. This could, he thinks, be done quickly, and would be much better than slow and repeated reinforcements from England. This letter ends on a note of grave doubt. "Tho' the losing of time may be fatal I still think we shall not dare to take bold and decisive measures till we are drawn into them by degrees, and when perhaps it may be too late."

At the end of June Lord George's misgivings are on the same ground. The ministry will not act, or will act feebly. "They love delay." "The news from America is as bad as possible, that is, it is come to that crisis which makes it necessary for administration to adopt real offensive measures or to resign their offices and leave the conciliatory plan of meanness and submission to those who wish to be their Successors upon such terms." Lord Suffolk, one of the Secretaries of State, had written to him, saying that the impressions made at New York by what had happened in Massachusetts were "disagreeable." But he told Lord George that he took comfort from the fact that the stocks were unaffected, and the respectable part of the city in very proper sentiments. Everything, Lord George would be glad to hear, was all right "*at this end of the town*." The italics are Lord Suffolk's : he means St. James's. Lord George in reply emphasized the importance of New York. He did not share Lord Suffolk's complacency. The advice of Congress to the Committee at New York to admit British troops and not to send away British stores was, he said, the only visible symptom of moderation. It might mean that the "principal people were not yet ready to go into open and avowed rebellion; though they may give all possible encouragement to those who are actually in arms and block up Boston and seize Ticonderoga, &c. I am happy, however, that our generals are arrived, and I shall wait with impatience till I hear what effect their presence will have among the troops, and whether they will be able to take the field after driving away those fellows who presume to confine such an army within the town of Boston."

As the weeks went on, Lord George seems to have deliberately repressed his misgivings, feeling, no doubt, that there was nothing else to be done. At the end of July he writes that, if it is true, the report of an action at Boston under General Gage means that a most decisive blow has been struck against the Bostonians. There was news, too, that the Southern Colonies began to feel already the bad effects of their trade being stopped, "and Lord Suffolk writes me word that they cannot long hold out. The Congress, too, I hear, are not unanimous, and the Deputies from the Massachusets Bay are disappointed and disgusted. They say that even Dr. Franklin has lost his authority among the most violent from his excess of moderation. One decisive blow at land is absolutely necessary. After that the whole will depend upon the diligence and activity of the officers of the Navy."

September finds him writing in the same tone. "As there is not common sense in protracting a war of this sort, I should be for exerting the utmost force of this kingdom to finish this rebellion in one campaign." He mentions that the Ministry are busy looking for foreign troops, "but I should be sorry to see the British forces less than were promis'd." One good sign was the way in which the French and Spanish Ministers were expressing themselves. "They seem to think Europe is interested in preventing the independancy of the Colonies in America."

Immediately before his appointment as Secretary for America Lord George gives a vivid sketch of a sitting in the Commons which lasted "till past four this morning in the most crowded and hot assembly I ever remember to have been in . . . Barré drew a ridiculous picture of Lord North as having no will of his own, and adopting everything I had propos'd, so much that he expected he would have resigned his post into mine as into abler hands. Wedderburne spoke then and very ably; then Burke, passionate, long, and not so entertaining as usual; then Chas. Fox, very abusive and able, and full of those quick turns which he inherited from his father. Lord North then spoke well, but not one of his best days, as it was all serious."

The picture that Barré drew was not altogether ridiculous. Lord North had turned towards Lord George: in him he was seeking American salvation. The American policy of the Ministers had changed to Lord George's, not his to theirs. What he thought should be done in America and his opinion of them for not doing it are clear enough from what he said and wrote. But, when he came to office, it was, as he had thought it might be, too late.

Chapter IX

THE AMERICAN SECRETARYSHIP

THE new American Secretary summoned every hope that he could, but he knew with what good reason he had asked his old friend Irwin to " pity and encourage " him. American affairs were bad enough.

The incapacities of our admirals and generals were so disastrous that even at the time it was hardly possible to speak of them without seeking solace for anger, apprehension, and despair in the astringency of ironical humour. A letter of August, 1775, from General Burgoyne in Boston, could have left no doubt in Lord George Germain's mind, before his appointment as Secretary, as to the way the war was going.

After briefly observing that General Gage is an officer totally unsuited for the command, General Burgoyne continues:

> It may perhaps be asked in England, what is the Admiral [Graves] doing? I wish I was able to answer that question satisfactorily. But I can only say what he is *not* doing.
>
> That he is *not* supplying the troops with sheep and oxen, the dinners of the best of us bear meagre testimony, the want of broth in the hospitals bears a more melancholy one.
>
> He is not defending his own flocks and herds, for the enemy has repeatedly and in the most insulting manner plundered his own appropriated islands.
>
> He is *not* defending the other islands in the harbour, for the enemy landed in force, burned the lighthouse at noon day, and killed and took a party of marines almost under the guns of two or three men-of-war.
>
> He is *not* employing his ships to keep up communication and intelligence with the servants and friends of Government at different parts of the continent, for I do not

believe Genl. Gage has received a letter from any correspondents out of Boston these six weeks.

He is surely intent upon greater objects, you will think; supporting in material points the dignity and terror of the British flag, and where a number of boats have been built for the rebels, privateers fitted out, prizes carried in, the King's armed vessels sunk, the crew made prisoners, the officers killed, he is doubtless enforcing instant restitution and reparation by the voice of his cannon, and laying the towns in ashes which refuse his terms. Alas! He is *not!* The British thunder is diverted or controlled by pitiful attentions and quaker-like scruples, and under such influence insult and impunity, like righteousness and peace, have kissed each other.

I should have hesitated in giving an account that may appear invidious, had not the facts been too notorious to expose me to that censure, and my feelings in this great cause too sensible to observe them without some impatience. Upon the whole when the supineness of this department is added to the diffidence of the other, and the defects of Qr.-master Generals, Adjt.-Generals, secretaries, and commissaries are superadded to both, they will make altogether a mass of insufficiency that I am afraid would counteract and disappoint the ablest counsels in the world.

Throughout this very long and very illuminating letter General Burgoyne speaks his mind:

After a fatal procrastination, not only of vigorous measures but of preparation for such, we took a step as decisive as the passage of the Rubicon, and now find ourselves plunged at once in a most serious war, without a single requisite, gunpowder excepted, for carrying it on.

Howe's victory at Charlestown was the only good news that Burgoyne had to report. He quotes from two intercepted letters written by John Adams, whom he seems to mistake for Samuel Adams, leader of the Congress and Constitutional

Treasurer, to support his opinion that "the rebels are led by some very able men," and that Adams himself is "as great a conspirator as ever subverted a state." Adams in this letter shows how clearly, in what detail, and how far ahead, he foresaw the work that patriotic Americans would have to do for the creation and confirmation of their new State. Burgoyne may well observe that "the bare effort of investigating such subjects argues an aspiring and vigorous mind," "that such a man soars too high to be allured by any offer Great Britain can make to himself or his country," and that "America, if his counsels continue in force, must be subdued or relinquished; she will not be reconciled." Adams wrote, to his wife: "The busyness I have had upon my mind has been as great and important as can be entrusted to man, and the difficulty and intricacy of it is prodigous. A constitution to form for a great empire; a country of fifteen hundred miles extent to fortify; millions to arm and train; a naval power to begin; an extensive commerce to regulate; a standing army of twenty-seven thousand men to raise, pay, victual, and officer."

The other letter, to a friend, is no less "vigorous" and "aspiring."

> We ought to have had in our hands a month ago the whole legislative, executive, and judicial of the whole continent, and have completely modelled a constitution: to have raised a naval power and opened all our ports wide; to have arrested every friend of Government on the continent, and held them as hostages for the poor victims in Boston.

The only comfort that Lord George Germain could draw from these two letters was in the dissatisfaction expressed by Adams with "one of his tools"—Burgoyne thinks it is Hancock—whom he calls "a pidling genius." It could hardly have been much consolation to the future American Secretary to remember Lord Suffolk's reassuring letter of two or three months earlier about the stable conduct of the stock market. Everything, as Lord Suffolk had said, might be well in St. James's, but it was evidently not well in America.

Nor could Lord George, before his acceptance of office, have been greatly cheered by the communications of Mr. Eden (afterwards Lord Auckland), who wrote a good many letters to him on behalf of Lord North. In September, 1775 Eden announced that Admiral Graves was to be recalled, leaving the command with Shuldham. Shuldham, however, in spite of his important conviction that " he is to act in every respect as against an enemy," seemed likely, so Eden wrote next month, to be "by no means better than the wretched creature whom he supersedes." Eden writes as hopefully as he can. He evidently set store by the patriotic addresses, the " handsome " addresses, received from various provincial towns. (" More addresses! The nation is good enough.") He wonders, naturally, that " so spirited a people should be so civil after so dispiriting a campaign." The Government were " begining to exert themselves," that was something; even though he has to add that " much is wanting to make that exertion systematic and effective." Knowing something of the character and policy of the man to whom he is writing, Eden is careful to assure him that ministers do seem at last to realize " the danger of half measures."

Two or three days later Eden is solaced by the style of some letters from General Gage, even though " nothing had happened." The rebels had been dislodged from two or three advanced posts, that was all: they continued round Boston in great multitudes. Still, Gage's letters were written " with much spirit."

Both Lord George and Mr. Eden, dismayed though they were by Gage's incapacity, spoke of him as kindly as they could. " A worthy general with parts inferior to his situation," says Eden; and Lord George, with a more courteously elaborated gesture, " must then lament that Genl. Gage, with all his good qualitys, finds himself in a situation of too great importance for his talents." Writing some four months before he became American Secretary, Lord George shows full realization of the special dangers of incompetent command in this particular war. He must have faced the possibility of a fatal issue from the incompetence hitherto prevailing.

"The conduct of such a war requires more than common abilities, the distance from the seat of Government necessarily leaves much to the discretion and resources of the General, and I doubt whether Mr. Gage will venture to take a single step beyond the letter of his instructions, or whether the troops have that opinion of him as to march with confidence of success under his command."

The miscarriages of General Gage caused sorrow and dismay qualified by forbearing sympathy: Admiral Graves' negligent misconduct roused not only fear and misgiving, but resentful anger. "I shudder to think how ill the removal of troops, artillery, &c. from Boston will be supported by Admiral Graves." "A corrupt admiral without any shadow of capacity," Eden calls him in another of his letters to Lord George.

At home, though the Government might seem to be "beginning" to do something, Ministers were still inordinately slack. Contemporary observers, one after another, speak of the confusion and apathy and ineptitude pervading the important departments. Lord George, calling at the Admiralty soon after his appointment to office, found that the First Lord, Lord Sandwich, and everyone else except Palliser, were in the country for Christmas. "Lord North would have gone to his villa at Bushey," writes Walpole, "but Lord George Germain would not let him." In comparison, at least, with these others, Lord George, active continually with his plans for raising and hiring troops, for sending supplies and recruits and more naval forces, ambitious for the conquest of the rebels in one campaign, seems of indefatigable energy. It was an energy that made him unpopular amongst his colleagues. "The friends of Lord North chafed at his authority." The other ministers of the Crown were glad to remember Minden as justification for keeping Lord George at a distance; he could count on no friendly co-operation from them. He could not overlook the negligence and the favouritism of Lord Sandwich, with whom it was only to be expected that he should have been at "great variance from the moment he received the seals." Sandwich had not sent Howe the necessary supplies, and Lord George charged him with that neglect of his duty. Lord North, though he stood by the American Secretary, was not his friend; it was not unnatural that he should, however lazily and good-humouredly, have felt some antipathy to the man who was to repair his deficiencies. Lord George knew how he felt. He was under no kind of illusion about either Lord North or the King, those two "worst and heaviest sailers." Indebted to the King though he was, he knew his character well enough; he realized to the full the dangers of George the Third's obstinacy, narrowness, and insincerity. Walpole remembers that Lord George, in 1773, had told him of his fear that the King's reign, for his insincerity, would end unhappily. But the American Secretary, at the beginning of his term of office, may well have regarded the defects and disabilities of some of Lord North's ministers, notably of Sandwich, with his "jobbing partiality in the choice of admirals," as more actively detrimental to the conduct of the war than were the disabilities of Lord North or those of the King.

Lord George, however, was not a great statesman himself, and he never thought he was. He was far too critical to be any more illusioned about the scope of his own abilities than he was about that of other men's; from his youth his ambitions were military, not political. Under the sentence which forbade him to serve the King in any military capacity whatsoever, he had to do his best to serve him as a minister, in a post where he was circumscribed by his natural limitations, and by his ingrained conservative sympathy; where he was continually misled by gross misinformations, and where the whole political machinery at every turn handicapped or obstructed him. Lord George, aware of the obstacles against him, did not cling to his office: he made attempts to resign it, but it was not till the end of 1781 that he was allowed to do so. He had a task in which success was impossible, except perhaps for the greatest. It has been said that the elder Pitt, in his prime, would have been sunk by it.

But though it is impossible to represent Lord George as a statesman of superlative wisdom and vision in his conduct of the American War, he was at least superior to his colleagues not only in energy but in good sense. By the side of George the Third and many others of his contemporaries, he seems full of enlightenment. He realized that the *Americans* could never be conquered by force, and he said so, to the amazement of the House of Commons. It has already been indicated that it was a factious American minority which Lord George thought British force was attempting to subdue, by the will and for the benefit not only of Britain but of the colonies themselves. He thought that our governmental ineffectiveness, our military and naval ineffectiveness, not their broad-based resolve to resist on the grounds of justice and liberty, were responsible for the disasters that occurred; if only we could recover vigour and skill, then we could give the American loyalists the help we owed them, and both they and we would be saved. The rebellious few pretended concern for liberty, but what they really sought, from the first, was independence for its own sake. If, indeed, it should ever happen that these few, by their malevolent energy and cunning, and with the aid of British incompetence and sloth, were able to spread infection far, then the war was lost. But Lord George, when he became American Secretary, did not believe that this need happen. He hoped most deeply that it never would happen, and he was loth to relinquish the hope.

He was of course mistaken in his idea that independence was desired from the first; but his trust in loyalism was not, in the earlier or even in the later stages of the war, without foundation. There were very many loyalists in the American colonies: there was at one time a state that could justly be described as "civil war" in the south; and, when Howe landed at New York, many joined him. It was, however, impossible for Lord George to see American loyalism in true perspective; the persistence of his view of the war as a civil war, a persistence induced and encouraged by constant misinformation, led him again and again into error. When Prevost and Cornwallis found that they could pass freely through the Carolinas, Lord George saw, in that, proof of Carolinian loyalty, not evidence of the rebels' policy of leading on the enemy dangerously in a country that he did not know, the "Fabian" policy of retreat and delay. He wrote to Clinton that the feeble resistance Major-General Prevost met with in his march was "an indubitable proof of the indisposition of the inhabitants to support the rebel government." But he was not unaware of the American reliance upon Fabian tactics. In the summer of 1775, four years earlier, he had written to Lord Suffolk that "the manner of opposing an enemy that avoids facing you in the open field is totally different from what young officers learn from the common discipline of the army." He explains how such an enemy should be dealt with, recalls the unfortunate experience of Braddock in the last war in America, emphasizes General Howe's understanding of the instructions that should be given to the troops. "Genl. Howe . . . will, I am persuaded, teach the present army to be as formidable as that he formerly acted with." But when he heard about Prevost and Cornwallis, he forgot American strategy and thought only of the loyalty of the South. As so often, this prevailing preoccupation darkened his counsels.

Not only did Lord George fail to realize the extent of "rebellious infection" in America: he failed to realize the dangers ahead from French help to the colonists. He was convinced that they would get none of any value. "Dr. Franklin would not be able to procure any open assistance." So late as 1779, when Spain came into the war, he thought that Washington and his whole army could be bribed to join the British by promise of plunder of Spanish colonies.

It is easy, now, to ridicule the fantasy of such errors; but it may be doubted if some of the taunts against Lord George have not been too easily indulged. Some passages from the Germain Papers have led to the conclusion that the American Secretary forgot the duties of his chief office in his extravagant devotion to those of the other office which he held as Commissioner of Trade and Plantations. He thought of nothing but sugar and tobacco. Sugar was really important. So he sent repeated requests to the West Indies to guard well the sugar plantations, in the conviction that "the security of the Sugar Colonys would give great pleasure to all ranks in this Country." The picture is drawn of the American Secretary with absentee owners of West Indian plantations crying in panic at his doors and driving him to the conclusion that it would be a pity to send to Clinton troops that would be so much more usefully employed in protecting sugar. Clinton, Lord George reflects, is careless about his bills, so it would be a very proper answer to his demand for troops and supplies to remind him that the stores sent out for sale in the canteens had not been paid for, and to tell him what promotions he ought to make. Lord George is represented as putting aside his dispatch ordering Howe's co-operation with Burgoyne, so as to be free to turn to what he thought much more pressing, a letter commending to the Commander-in-Chief a man who was coming out to speculate in captured tobacco.

Irony may be expected to play upon such provocation: but the West Indies were, after all, important: it was Lord George's business, as Commissioner, to regard them, and it may be unwise lightly to blame him for his solicitude about British possessions which it proved practicable to retain. If Lord George had always centred his energies upon the North American colonies at the expense of the West Indies, we might have lost both. He rightly anticipated attacks upon the West Indies by European powers, and he knew that failure or defeat in the West Indies might well involve failure and defeat in North America; that these were not separate, but related theatres of warfare. " A superiority at sea, " he wrote, " can not be maintained without considering the fleets at Jamaica, the Leeward Islands, and in N. America, as co-operating for the safety of the whole."

During his American Secretaryship Lord George's natural sagacity did not desert him. Circumstances, to a large extent, imposed his errors. All government officers, from the King downwards, lived in a fog of misinformation that rarely lifted. They could not check and verify as may be done now; though indeed even in our time, with our communications, it is easy to be deluded about what goes on in other countries, and to believe what we wish to believe. America, then, really was three thousand miles away. It took five or six weeks before news from New York could reach London. That Lord George did not see America steadily and see it whole is not surprising. He was inevitably in the dark, or dusk, but he was not an obstinate fool, blundering inexcusably, even when he described the American victory at Trenton as " the effects of dispair."

A weight of especial blame, during his lifetime and since, has been attached to him on account of the disaster at Saratoga. After Washington's successes at Trenton and Princeton at the end of 1776, Howe's plan of campaign was overruled by Lord George who had conceived the more ambitious plan of an invasion from Canada to result in the cutting off of New England from the other colonies. Howe was to co-operate by advancing up the Hudson and meeting at Albany the northern forces under Burgoyne. But Howe received no adequate instructions, thus there was no co-operation; and Lord George's plan, or the failure to execute it, may be blamed for what happened at Saratoga in October, 1777. In chapter V of this book reference is made to the charges brought by Fox against Lord George. Fox said that the orders given by the American Secretary to General Howe were not explicit enough. Undoubtedly responsibility for Saratoga must be borne by Lord George as well as by others.

Not only soon after Saratoga, but up to almost the end of the hopeless struggle, Lord George's faith in ultimate victory continued to receive apparently valid support. Proofs or assertions that rebel counsels were divided, that disaffection[1] might easily be promoted, that " we have many friends in the country," were offered, together with other good omens, to him at frequent intervals: by Clinton, reporting from New York early in 1779 that signs of disunion were apparent, and giving credit to " a report of Col. Campbell's command being landed at Savannah and the country having shown themselves friendly ": by Lord Carlisle, writing at about the

[1] Here again, there were grounds; there was André, there was Lee, there was Benedict Arnold. Treachery to Washington's cause did exist; there were disagreements in Congress; there was disaffection also in the American rank and file.

same time of arrangements for supplies for the loyal inhabitants of New York and Rhode Island: again by Clinton, in April, expressing confidence in the loyalists as " a party on whom we may depend": by Eden, later in the same month, declaring that the credit of the rebel Congress is beyond a doubt at the utmost stretch and actually breaking, and that his letters from New York are filled with hopes of a termination of the war: by the Bishop of Derry, in an undated letter from Passy, telling Lord George that Franklin is thoroughly dissatisfied with the Congress and more so with Versailles, that he would gladly contribute to a reunion of the Empire, that Turgot assures the Bishop that Congress has used Franklin shamefully and does not deserve him: by the same correspondent, emphasizing the reiterated assurances that he had had of de Maurepas' determination not to insist upon American independence: by Admiral Arbuthnot, from Charlestown in May, 1780, expressing his wish " to have one colony filled with the suffering loyalists as a deposit to depend on in future": by Arbuthnot in the same month, assuring Lord George that " if a loyal militia could have been encouraged under the gentlemen of this country I have no doubt but a force of this kind might have been opposed to Mr. Washington equal to his force, independent of the regulars ": by Governor Martin, in June, 1780, from South Carolina, asserting that " all accounts from North Carolina speak of the disposition of the majority to return to their allegiance," and confirming these accounts two months later by the " great proof " of loyalty afforded by fourteen hundred of the North Carolinians having joined the Army: by Eden, at about the same time, enclosing a letter written from New York by " one of the best observers that I ever met with, and representing the cause of the rebellion as hopeless ": by Admiral Rodney, from Santa Lucia at the end of that year, giving Lord George " a true insight " by informing him that if the rebel soldiers were paid up and given a little land, Washington would soon have no army, and stating his beliefs that " the man Arnold "— " Give him but a command and thousands will join him "— will do more good than " all our generals put together," and that "Washington is certainly to be bought—honours will do it": by Admiral Arbuthnot, in January, 1781, from the *Clinton*, off New York, giving news of a bloody revolt in Washington's camp, of "universal disaffection" breaking out into "open and violent sedition," and, in the following month, announcing that the rebels are "in the utmost distress and desponding": by Lieutenant-Governor Bull, from Charlestown, at the same time, assuring the Secretary for the Colonies that "nothing is more ardently wished for than being once more happy under the protection of His Majesty's royal favor, and former government, by known laws," and that "many gentlemen formerly under the usurpation have, and daily do come in to sue for and receive the King's protection": by Lieutenant-Colonel Benjamin Thompson, writing from an advanced post of a cavalry camp near Charlestown in January, 1782, about some prisoners he had taken from Washington's Regiment, and saying that they were "absolutely no better than children, their horses so fat that a long march would knock half of them up and that he would venture an attack upon the whole cavalry with only a hundred and fifty dragoons."

The confident tone of these reports is much the same as that of earlier ones, in which northern loyalty is the grateful topic and encouragement is found in various other delusions. Eden, in the autumn of 1775, tells Lord George that the British troops, leaving Boston, will be welcomed in New York and will act with advantage there: from New York every day came new reasons for this belief. The Congress, Eden was privately informed, "had disagreed much and did not separate in good humour with each other." In the summer of 1776 Burgoyne was writing to Lord George that the spirit and enthusiasm of his troops are extraordinary, and that "the Canadians appear overjoyed at the British successes." Another communication from Montreal reached the American Secretary at the same time, "a Paper of intelligence by a person whose veracity may be depended upon." From this he learnt that "Les troupes du Congrès sont frappés d'une terreur panique et dans la plus grande confusion."

By September, 1776 Lord Percy was writing to Lord George, from Long Island, hailing him as the deliverer of his country and " venturing to foretell that this business is pretty near over." Admiral Collier, from his ship at Halifax, in the summer of the next year, gave Lord George an exulting account of his capture of " the finest ship in the rebels' possession," and of Mr. Manly, the naval officer " in whom the Congress place all their reliance." The general joy at these events " exceeded everything before known at Halifax."

Misinformation and partial truth, striking the same apparently authentic note, from abroad and from home, were poured, early and late, into Lord George's ears. Eden, who as Lord North's secretary was an important source of news, had felt able to reassure him before his Secretaryship about English public opinion, now that Englishmen knew what the American War really was about. The cause of the war was now at last, by the autumn of 1775, generally understood to be· " the determined purpose in the New England colonies to seek independence at all hazards," with the happy result that the heart of the British Nation had become warmly engaged in it. The rebellion had been undervalued, it was true, but, so Eden's argument ran, since all the world had undervalued it, the nation, possessing the virtue of candour, felt no impatience with its rulers. None at all; they knew how natural, how inevitable, their rulers' mistakes had been, and all their resentment was reserved for those whose designs now appeared so much worse than they were supposed to be. The British public, Eden implies, and the American public too, when better nature is allowed free play, though they may sympathize with what they think is a struggle for rights and for freedom, can never sanction the criminal desire to cut adrift from the Mother Country. Now we knew just where we were, and " the business . . . bears, therefore, a more promising aspect." Eden is gratified by the reflection that not only duty, but the less elevated though sometimes no less serviceable human impulses of fear, interest, and fickleness, may well profit the British cause. If the four together bring any colony to submission, Lord North's idea is that a commission should be given to some proper person, with ample powers, to settle with that colony. Eden turns hopefully to the familiar contemplation of the loyalty of the South: the great probability of the southern colonies hastening to enjoy the benefits of such a commission was obvious.

Transported by his enthusiasm and by his determination to impart it to Lord George, Eden declares that there never perhaps was a commission of such importance for any individual in the annals of mankind. Why should that individual not be Lord George[1] himself? "I shall proceed to tell your lordship without form or flattery that Lord North (and I believe every person well informed and equally honest in wishes and declarations) thinks you the fittest man in the kingdom. He also *knows* that nothing would make your friend Howe so happy as to see you in such a situation . . . It is superfluous to add from Lord North that your lordship's sentiments on any part of his plan will be received with the utmost deference."

With what ironical contempt Lord George, so well experienced in adversity, so well acquainted with the manners and methods of politicians and with the nature of ministerial favour, must have received this fine tribute. The wording of it was calculated to give him a peculiar satisfaction, though not of the kind intended by Eden. Realism and clear judgment did not cease to be among his distinguishing characteristics during the American War. That he suffered from misinformation does not mean that he believed everything he was told. But he did believe that England would not survive the loss of the American colonies; and this conviction prepared him to accept indications that the American colonies would not be lost. It compelled him, though with increasing doubt and misgiving, to serve a purpose which he thought so momentous, so long as there remained the scantiest hope of his doing so with effect. It was the strongest necessity that he should hope as much as he could, and for as long as he could, that he should nourish the will to accept evidence against the prospect of the downfall of his country, against that final disaster. This was not, of course, the only evidence that he had before him.

[1] Lord George was made American Secretary rather more than a month later.

But in whatever degree he might be forced to credit the reports, the opinions, the warnings, and the unquestionably true information that disappointed or thwarted or endangered him, he could not, in a complete sense, accept them. They were received, not accepted. He knew they were true, or he knew that there was truth in them, but his knowledge remained ineffective in respect of the bearing of this truth upon the ultimate issue. It is not difficult to imagine his reception of such a communication as that of the Philadelphia merchant, sent on to him by Sir Robert Herries; his scrutiny of it, the degrees of distance at which he would have held and kept it, the assembling of it in his mind in relation and in subjugation to what was there already. The date of the merchant's letter is February, 1776; it reached Lord George in the following June:

> . . . we can assure you thus much: If any terms of reconciliation are offer'd, that the Congress ought to accept, they will be embraced. None but terms fit for freemen will be thought admissible either by the Congress, committees, or people at large, and should Great Britain prefer the destructive war she has plunged herself and this country into, for the sake of the shaddow when she possessed the substance, to the idea of doing justice to her colonial subjects, we really dread the consequences to both countries. In the event she will most undoubtedly lose this territory, and probably fall a prey hereafter to some of her powerful neighbours and rivals.

The writer then declares that the charge that America "aims at independency" is unjust: but that the way in which the war has been conducted, by burning of towns, by seizing of ships, by barbarity and cruelty,

> has prepar'd men's minds for an independency, that were shock'd at the idea a few weeks ago. This you may depend on, and should this campaign open with furious Acts of Parliament, you may bid adieu to the American Colonies. They will then assuredly declare for independency, and if

> they once make such pretensions they have no doubt of being able to support them, even without the assistance of foreigners; but it can hardly be imagined that the Court of France will refuse assistance . . . Surely the people of England are infatuated, that they permit such arbitrary and tyranical measures to be pursued by their rulers as must in their consequences destroy their immediate interests, and in the end ruin the nation; for our part we do most sincerely pray that such terms of reconciliation may be held out as can be accepted on this side. We are happy to know there is a disposition to receive such, and we believe this to be the only line that can possibly save the two countries from the most ruinous consequences . . .
>
> We have made such preparations for the preservation of the city, that we are pretty confident that neither your fleet nor army can ever get before it ; however, if this and every other city and town on the coast of America were destroyed, it would do more injury to Great Britain than America, and would totally put submission, reconciliation, terms, and treaties out of the question. In short, nothing can save or serve the true interest of Great Britain but holding out just and equitable terms before it is too late.

Identification of American and British interests was firmly set in Lord George's mind. He would never have disputed it; but in the good will of the rebels he had no trust. That any reconciliation with them might advantage either Britain or America he could not believe. And almost exactly at the same time as he read this Philadelphia letter he was reading also what he was assured was an unimpeachably truthful account of the panic terror and utmost confusion of Congress troops.

Everything that Lord George did and said about the American War is perfectly understandable in view of his convictions and the support that he had for them. It is not surprising that, while he realized the tremendous difficulties of his task in coping with inefficiency in the conduct of the war and with what he saw as the dangerous treachery of the "English rebels," he could not realize that what really made his cause hopeless was its dependence upon a policy conceived and executed in profound, incurable misunderstanding.

Of freedom for the people under the Constitution Lord George had always been a defender, and he wanted the colonies to have as much of it as the British had. He did not misunderstand because he was a selfish, unfeeling aristocrat, disdainful of the rights and careless of the well-being of the commonalty under British rule. In his Parliamentary speeches he shows concern for both. At the end of 1772 he spoke against a motion to send ten thousand troops against the Caribs on the ground that the climate was so bad that the soldiers would die there. He took this occasion to urge increase in soldiers' pay. "What encouragement have men to enter into the service? To live, pardon me, to starve upon sixpence a day! The soldier's pay since the first institution of an army has never been raised; the officer's has repeatedly, but the soldier's never . . . Indeed, sir, I am astonished how they live."

It was about three years earlier that Lord George was warning the House of Commons that "the minds of the people are alarmed . . . lest the influence of ministers should have so far operated as to surprise their representatives into a vote dangerous to their liberties . . . The freedom of election is the sacred palladium of English liberty; and when that is violated, it cannot be long before our constitution is in ruins . . . The people must be satisfied. Their all is at stake; they apprehend that is in danger, and therefore they have a right to demand security." Throughout this speech "the people" are continually invoked. "What will the people say of such a House?" Lord George emphasized his warning to the Commons by recalling the example of Denmark. "The subjects of Denmark once boasted of the protection of Parliament. The parliament betrayed their liberties, and they, in return, abolished the parliament . . . If once the representatives of the people . . . are capable of entering into league against the people, all confidence will be at an end; the authority of the House will gradually decline, and at length the people, growing indifferent, will patiently acquiesce in the arbitrary decrees of one tyrant, rather than submit to pay the hire of corruption for three or four hundred."[1]

As to the American colonists, let their liberties, under our constitution, be guarded as zealously as those of Englishmen. What invasion of their liberties was desired? Taxation, in Lord George's eyes, was no invasion. If the American colonists were to be allowed a freedom at variance with the rights of the mother-country, a freedom not appointed for them by King, Lords, and Commons, not subject to the British Constitution, then they would no longer be colonies, they would be lost to us. That was why the struggles that the colonists saw as struggles against "usurpation and oppression" were to Lord George only explicable as struggles to break the just and beneficent bonds of union with the mother-country. Franklin had categorically stated that defence of liberties, not desire for independence, was the cause of the war, and that there was not, at first, any expression of such a desire, nor any hint that it would be advantageous to America; but, so little faith had Lord George in the sincerity of anyone who could make such statements that, at the end of 1777, he discouraged William Pulteney from seeking conversations with Franklin in Paris, on the ground that Franklin might "decline any explanations and claim on that account a merit with the court of France." The American Secretary saw little hope in conversations with any rebel while he remained a rebel; for, whatever the matter he might pretend to negotiate, it could be only a cloak for his real aim of separation. Defeat of the rebels, that is, of those who "really" desire separation, is, therefore, always foremost in Lord George's mind.

"If that be true," he significantly writes to Clinton in early March, 1778, "if that be true which has been so repeatedly declared by the Colony Assemblies, and is still asserted by many persons who pretend to be well informed of the dispositions of the inhabitants, that the generality of the people desire nothing more than a full security for the enjoy-

[1]Readers interested in the authorship of the Letters of Junius will find on p. 287 of the Appendix expressions curiously resembling some of those quoted from this speech. The quotations in the Appendix are from a Junius letter of 9th April, 1771, fifteen months after Lord George's speech was made, and from the *Dedication*.

ment of all their rights and liberties under the British Constitution, there can be no room to doubt that the generous terms now held out to them will be gladly embraced, and that a negociation will immediately take place upon the arrival of the New Commission, and be so far advanced before the season will admit of military operations as to supersede the necessity of another campaign."

Lord George, with evident sincerity, writes in the same letter of the King's most ardent wish for the peace, prosperity, and happiness of all his subjects; but, although a speedy and happy ending of the war by negotiation would give the King the greatest pleasure, no preparation for carrying on the war can be slackened. Negotiations may seem likely to succeed, but the war must be prosecuted none the less with the utmost vigour, "in case the Colonies shall obstinately persist in their refusal to return to their allegiance, and pay obedience to the constitutional authority of Government."

This was rather more than four months after Burgoyne had surrendered his whole army to these obstinate colonists at Saratoga.

The measures to be now undertaken for the prosecution of the war are detailed at length; and faith in American loyalism, once again, is exercised: "The various accounts we receive from Georgia and South Carolina concur in representing the distress of the inhabitants and their general disposition to return to their allegiance."

It was important that the well affected in all the provinces should be armed and that every means should be employed to raise and embody them. Lord George's plan is for an "embodied militia, officer'd by their own countrymen." When communication is opened with Georgia "great numbers of the back inhabitants" would join the King's troops. Success in the south is seen by Lord George not only as a counterblast to Saratoga but as the prelude to complete victory, and then "the Northern Provinces might be left to their own feelings and distress to bring them back to their duty, and the operations against them confined to the cutting off all their supplies and blocking up their ports."

Lord George had always leaned towards optimism in his view of the strength and the nature of the opposition to British forces in America: it had always been the sloth and weakness of political half-measures, and the ineffective command of British forces that had brought him doubt. Of course he wrote hopefully to Clinton; but from his letters to General Irwin who was his intimate friend, it is clear that his doubts persisted. In February, 1779 he wrote to Irwin: "What you hear of confusion in America among the leaders of the rebellion is true. What consequence it will have God knows, for we seem to take no advantage of things which ought to operate in our favour." He was certainly less sanguine than Lord North, who, just at this time, was writing to him of the "great comfort" he had from the war news.

Whatever Lord George may have really felt, he continued to encourage Clinton. By June, 1779 Spain, as well as France, was England's enemy: but "I can with equal pleasure and truth assure you that the spirit of the nation appears to rise in proportion to the greatness of the exigence; that every effort will be made to oppose the united attempts of our numerous enemies." The American War appears, in this long letter, as a war involved by the determination to give "all possible protection to every part of His Majesty's dominions." By recovering the revolted provinces protection would be given to America: that was why the "speedy reduction of the rebellion by destroying the rebel force" and the consequent "recovery of the revolted provinces" was so "great an object."

Rather more than a month later Lord George was writing to Clinton a letter which throws into the strongest relief his conviction that England was, in America, fighting for the Americans. It is from Clinton's directions to arm and embody the loyalists that he draws hope for "a speedy issue to this unhappy contest." Without the loyalists nothing can be done, for "I am convinced," he writes, "that our utmost efforts will fail of their effect, if we cannot find means to engage the people of America in support of a cause which is equally their own and ours, and when their enemies are driven away or subdued, induce them to employ their own force to protect themselves in the enjoyment of the blessings of that constitution to which they shall have been restored."

There is characteristic clearness and precision in this expression of an opinion which was always deeply fixed in Lord George's mind, and in which he had been continually confirmed by intelligence from America. "Upon these ideas it was that the war was first undertaken," ideas which were as valid to him in the summer of 1779, and later, as they ever had been.

By the autumn of that year grave reverses had come: the islands of St. Vincent and Grenada had been lost. At the end of September Lord George writes in another of these "secret" letters to Clinton that our affairs in the West Indies were so changed that it was unsafe to send back any part of the troops to North America or to spare any naval force to convoy them. But, in the midst of these "heavy misfortunes," he can count on the loyalty of South Carolina as a pledge that "the possession of Charles Town would be attended with the recovery of the whole of that province, and probably North Carolina would soon follow." As a further justification for keeping troops in the West Indies there was the good news of Sir George Collier's severe blow against the rebel force at Penobscot; and news of the divisions in Congress was evidently as reassuring as ever. "I have heard with great pleasure, from Capt. Dixon, that the dissentions and jealousies among the members of the Congress continue to increase, and that the people's repugnance to serve in their army becomes every day greater." The dangers from France and Spain, though serious, were not unduly alarming. All was not well, but much was well. The French and Spanish fleets "are returned to Brest, to recruit their seamen, which were very sickly . . . Our fleet is now greatly reinforced and in most excellent condition; and so great a military spirit has lately diffused itself throughout the people, that the internal defence of this country was, I believe, at no time so well provided for."

In the summer of the next year, 1780, the surrender of Charlestown to the British, and the details given in Clinton's letter about it, were stimulating. From every quarter, Clinton told Lord George, men were coming to declare their allegiance to the King and to offer their arms in support of his Government. Often they brought with them prisoners, their former oppressors or leaders, "and I may venture to assert that there are few men in South Carolina who are not either our prisoners or in arms with us." Three or four weeks later confirmation came from Admiral Arbuthnot, who wrote about Charlestown's "most pleasing aspect," and of there being little doubt that the whole province would soon be loyal again without any further trouble. Cornwallis, on the same day, writes to Lord George in the same strain. Arbuthnot hopes for a proclamation to inform the whole continent that, when they do return to their allegiance, His Majesty will restore their civil liberty. Allegiance first, then civil liberty: that was always Lord George's own conception of the proper sequence. Arbuthnot is sanguine, too, about the French. This summer the French will attempt their "*dernier coup*" and, if that is defeated, then they and the colonies will be at odds. The colonies will "upbraid them with not affording them proper succours, and will return to their wonted duty, as there is great reason to believe the bulk of the people are really tired."

As Lord George had hoped, the privileges of allegiance were now to be restored to *North* Carolina. Cornwallis could assure him that this was what most of the North Carolinians wanted. In September there would be the greatest probability of, as he ingenuously expresses it, "reducing that province to its duty."

Less than two months later, in August, 1780, Cornwallis wrote to tell Lord George of his brilliant and complete victory over Gates' southern Army. "Everything is wearing the face of tranquility and submission." "Internal commotions and insurrections will now subside. But I shall give directions to inflict exemplary punishment on some of the most guilty in hopes to deter others in future from sporting with allegiance, with oaths, and with the lenity and generosity of the British Government." Cornwallis paints the successes of British arms in festival colours, and describes his despatch into North Carolina of " proper people " with directions to " our friends " to take arms, to seize all violent malcontents, and all military stores belonging to the rebels: and " I have promised to march without loss of time to their support."

That after Cornwallis's victory things did not go so well as expected was put down to France. France had, in Eden's phrase, " given new fuel to the rebellious fire." Eden gave Lord George this explanation in a letter of October, 1780. Owing to France, yet another " great change " must be made in the whole conduct of the war, or large and immediate reinforcements must be sent out, both ships of war and troops. Eden's letter is discouraging, but not long afterwards Lord George was informed from New York by his nephew George Damer that the rebels lack soldiers, and " that it is not possible for Congress to increase, either with us *or with the rebels,* the general detestation they are held in." And a fortnight later Arbuthnot was writing to Lord George from the *Royal Oak,* off Block Island, representing the French alliance as the greatest of the disadvantages under which the rebels were labouring. " The return of all the revolted provinces to their allegiance . . . will be accelerated by their repeated defeats, by their irreparable losses, and, above all things, by their detestation of the French alliance. Destitute of unanimity in the Cabinet, and in the field, their situation is hopeless." " The rebellion has in truth derived no one advantage from the arrival of Terney's armament. On the contrary they have met with defeat and disgrace: their councils have been blasted by division." Arbuthnot was always the most optimistic of them all. No doubt Lord George heavily discounted his confidence that universal loyalty in America was then only a question of time. It was not " absolutely attained," but it was " not far distant."

Even so late as the following summer, when the surrender of Yorktown impended, Lord George continued to get much favourable news, and none that could prepare him for disaster. Writing from Long Island in July, George Damer was able to give a gratifying account of his services in Virginia, where he had been "employed infinitely more to my satisfaction than at any time since I left England." He writes of an engagement in which the enemy lost three hundred and the British only seventy. The chance of cutting up Lafayette's army had, it is true, been missed, but the rebel forces were inadequate and good signs abounded.

But at the end of September Damer writes, from Staten Island, in a very different strain, foreshadowing the surrender of Yorktown. Cornwallis, he says, has about six thousand men there: the French and the rebels have at least fourteen thousand, apart from militia. "That they will be able to begin their operations against my Lord Cornwallis's posts the very beginning of next month I look upon as certain, and I do not believe the most sanguine admirer of my Lord Cornwallis or of his army could expect him to hold out any longer than from two months to ten weeks."

This proved an underestimate. Cornwallis surrendered on the nineteenth of October. American victory was now certain. Here at last was a catastrophe that could not be belittled, even by Admiral Arbuthnot. The only question, after this, was how long it would take before George the Third was forced to give in. Rebellion was now indeed Revolution.

Chapter X

PATRIAE INFELICI FIDELIS

THE failure of English commanders and statesmen to foresee the disaster of Yorktown was no indication of unwarrantable optimism. Cornwallis had well chosen his position there: he could reasonably expect to hold it against the Americans and the French. He had bad luck. If Admiral Graves's delay, and Clinton's, had been only a very little less, Yorktown might well have been saved. "Surely," wrote Damer to Lord George in grief mixed with indignation, "surely there never was an instance of such an army so commanded falling a sacrifice to the negligence, irresolution, or absolute infatuation of others." There was justification for Lord George's conviction that misfortune, not necessity, had played the chief part in bringing about this final calamity.

It was not till the 25th of November, a Sunday morning, that the Secretary for America received, at his house in Pall Mall, the news of Yorktown. In a hackney coach, hired to save time, he drove at once from Pall Mall to Lord Stormont's house in Portland Place; from Portland Place, with Lord Stormont, to the Chancellor's house in Great Russell Street, and then, the Chancellor accompanying them, to Downing Street to break the news to Lord North. Lord Walsingham, who happened to be at Lord George's when the news came, was of the party. Lord George and his companions saw Lord North at about one o'clock. He was not only deeply moved, but unnerved by their communication. Lord George said that he took it "like a ball in his breast." He knew, as Lord George did, that it was the end. "He opened his arms, exclaiming wildly, as he paced up and down the room, 'O God! it is all over!' Words which he repeated many times with the deepest consternation and distress." Lord George then sent a dispatch to the King at Kew, and went on to his Whitehall office, where he found confirmation of the Yorktown surrender.

Sir Nathaniel Wraxall describes how, ignorant of the disaster, he went that day at half-past five to dine at Lord George's. It was a dinner-party of nine; Lord Walsingham was the only guest who knew what had happened. Wraxall remarks elsewhere in his *Memoirs* that "no man who saw Lord George Germain at table or in his drawingroom would have suspected from his deportment or conversation that the responsibility for the American War reposed principally upon his shoulders." On the occasion of this dinner-party the host kept his accustomed calm. He looked grave, but not discomfited. Towards the end of dinner a servant handed him a letter which he opened and read. "The King writes as he always does," he said to Walsingham, "but he has not marked the hour and the minute of his writing with his usual precision." The guests were curious; they waited for the time when Lord George's three young daughters should withdraw.

The news that their host then gave them was that he had just heard from Paris that de Maurepas lay dying. On that Wraxall observed that if he were First Minister of France he would be sorry to die before he had witnessed the end of the contest between England and America.[1] "He has survived to witness that event," said Lord George, with some agitation. Wraxall, thinking that Lord George was referring to the recent indecisive naval action between Graves and de Grasse, said the same thing over again in other words. "He has survived to witness it completely," Lord George repeated. "The army has surrendered, and you may read the particulars of the capitulation in that paper." He was visibly affected as he took the paper from his pocket and put it into Sir Nathaniel's hand. He told him he might read it aloud. The company listened in a profound silence of gloom: but with some gratitude, perhaps, that their host, with characteristic consideration and restraint, had not permitted the news to spoil their dinner.

Lord George, after making some complimentary remarks about the letter he had just had from the King, read it to the company:

> I have received with sentiments of the deepest concern the communication which Lord George Germain has made me of the unfortunate result of the operations in Virginia. I particularly lament it on account of the consequences connected with it and the difficulties which it may produce in carrying on the public business or in repairing such a misfortune. But I trust that neither Lord George Germain nor any member of the Cabinet will suppose that it makes the smallest alteration in those principles of my conduct which have directed me in past time and which will always continue to animate me under every event in the prosecution of the present contest.

[1] De Maurepas might have written frivolous verse about it, as he did about Madame de Pompadour.

Wraxall examined this letter. The very handwriting, he says, indicated composure of mind. Yorktown, it was clear, had not weakened His Majesty's obstinacy; indeed, it seemed to have toughened it. "Not a sentiment of despondency or despair," says Sir Nathaniel. The American colonies were none the less to be reduced to the blessings of submission to the British throne.

Lord George and Lord North knew better; but they had to go on. Lord George, in a memorandum written soon after Yorktown, writes of the need for maintaining possessions still held and of taking every opportunity to annoy the rebels and to support and encourage loyal subjects. After "our late misfortunes in Virginia" we must consider what can be done. In what is no doubt a deliberate understatement Lord George recognized "the difficulty of supporting an extensive continental war in America." The memorandum, "submitted to the consideration of His Majesty's confidential Servants," is a long one. It outlines plans for operations in and near New York and about Charlestown. Lord George still has hopes of the loyalists in New York, in Maryland, and in Pennsylvania. But not so much hope; hope now "greatly damped." For the tenth article of the Yorktown capitulation had handed over to the enemy all the "friends of Government" in Cornwallis's army. So it is not surprising that Lord George, after emphasizing the need for giving loyalists all possible help, should with significant bitterness add, "if any should again be bold enough to trust to the protests of this country." "How far this spirit of loyalty exists," he writes now, disheartened, "it is impossible to know."

He defines and specifies plans and objects, but most evidently he doubts if they can be carried out. What if "we should have no encouragement to expect that the people will take arms in support of their antient constitution, or to avoid the oppression of their present Government?"

Once again, from these expressions, Lord George's continuing view of the American War as a civil war is evident; but now it is a civil war in which the rebels are winning or have won. The only thing, now, was to use our forces to save what we could. Let us, therefore, he repeats, maintain the posts we have. If we lay aside all offensive operations, we can spare our troops for the West Indies, forming expeditions against the settlements there of France and Spain much more conveniently from New York and Charlestown than we could from Great Britain. By such means, as well as by holding to our positions in America, we should be serving the important purpose of preventing the French from taking possession of the American colonies. Well! It was believed by some, perhaps not altogether unreasonably, that the Italians and Germans, after helping the rebels in the Spanish civil war of 1936-39, would take possession of Spain.

The colonies, Lord George concludes, must at all costs not be totally abandoned. That would mean not only " the dismembring the Empire . . . but you must reflect upon the additional weight and strength which France will derive from it; if the ill consequences stopp'd there, they would be sufficiently alarming; but we must not flatter ourselves that Canada would not immediately fall, and your fisheries at Newfoundland, and all your possessions in the W. Indies would also be at the mercy of your enemies." That we cannot now bring back the rebels to their allegiance by force is the implication of the argument which follows. Lord George's present hope is that they will return to us of their own free will, in their own interests, when they have realized their condition, and when they have broken with France. Their General is drifting from them, for he " becomes every day more independant of the Congress as he more closely connects himself with France. How long such a Government can exist it is impossible to say, but the restless spirit of the people, and the regret they must feel for the loss of their liberty, which they thought they were fighting for, their dislike of a military government, their natural aversion to the French nation, may incline them to return to their connection with this country, if we remain in a situation to receive and protect them."

American independence was formally recognized by Great Britain in August, 1782. Some months before then, in January,

Lord George Germain had resigned his office as Secretary for America. Lord North resigned as First Minister in March of the same year.

If it had not been for the King, whose constant appeal was that they should not desert him as the Duke of Grafton had, both of them would, of course, have resigned before. Shortly before his resignation Lord North in the Commons referred significantly to " certain circumstances which I cannot now explain " which had compelled him to stay in office. Lord George, having reluctantly accepted the Secretaryship, tried more than once to resign it before he was allowed to do so. In January, 1778, Lord Suffolk wrote to dissuade him, most strongly, from retiring: " Allow me to express my hopes that calmer and maturer reflection will have convinced your lordship that it can neither be for the King's advantage or your own credit that you should retire at such a moment as the present. On the contrary, I wait with anxious expectation to hear that you mean shortly to come amongst us again, and avail yourself of the best relief from private affliction,[1] public busyness. These are not only my sentiments and wishes . . . " Lord Suffolk, in a letter of five days before, had assured Lord George that he was indispensable. " Zeal for the public welfare urges me to endeavour to arouse your attention even in the first agonies of grief. I shall confine myself at present to saying that we won't be idle during your absence; but we can't go far without your assistance. We may make some little progress, but the execution must depend upon you. Every motive, public and private, calls upon you to bear up! It would imply diffidence in your resolution to say more." Wedderburn echoes Lord Suffolk, writing to Lord George of the " mischief that must attend " his resignation, and assuring him that it would be " fatal."

In the early autumn of 1778 Lord George was again anxious to resign and he wrote to tell Lord North so. The King ignored the request when it was laid before him, and Lord North made no reply till a year later. His letter begins by referring to " a seeming inattention to your commands,"

[1] His wife's death.

and assures Lord George that he did, "about a twelvemonth ago," submit his letter to the King, "and have several times since mentioned the same subject to his Majesty. I have never yet been able to bring your lordship any answer, his Majesty having always appeared desirous of your lordship's continuance in your office."

In his reply to this letter Lord George accounts for his request on the ground of his age, which was then sixty-three. "I cannot expect long to enjoy that state of health which might enable me to be as active and diligent in the execution of His Majesty's commands as the critical situation of this country requires from every servant of the crown." He gives this reason, it would seem, as a matter of form. He does not say that he was ill or tired, but that he thought he might become so. "When I had the honour of writing to your lordship last year I was really apprehensive that I should not have been able to have undergone the fatigue of the attendance in the House of Commons added to the business of my office." But Lord George's physique was exceptionally robust, and his faculties, as Wraxall noted, remained all his life singularly undiminished. It is unlikely that the man who, shortly after his appointment as American Secretary, travelled from East Grinstead, was presented to the Queen at the Drawing Room, and then "sat near fourteen hours in the House and did not suffer by the fatigue," the man who so remarkably kept his vigour till shortly before his death, should have felt such apprehensions as he expresses in his letter to Lord North. The real reason why Lord George had wished to resign may not be considered a creditable one: it was that he felt he had been slighted. "It was natural for me," he writes immediately after his reference to his advancing years, "to hope that I might have deserved some mark of His Majesty's favour. As that is not the case, I can only lament it as a misfortune, but I shall never presume to complain of it as the least injustice."

Nothing could express more clearly Lord George's convinced opinion that it was an injustice. To injustice he had been peculiarly sensitive, and with reason, ever since his court-martial. It is this special vulnerability that is now apparent.

He significantly continues:

> I entered into the King's service when affairs in America appeared desperate, and few I believe *then* envied the honour I received. I acted upon the principle of endeavouring to be of some use to His Majesty, always desiring when I could be no longer so, to return to that private situation from whence I was invited.

Lord George had accepted reluctantly what he knew would probably be an unrewarding and unprosperous office: he had done his best in it, he had been valued in it, and he felt that, if he was valuable, if he was to stay on as the indispensable officer that so many told him he was and that the King seemed to think he was, then he should have some recognition. If he was not worth recognition, it would surely be better for some one to take his place who was.

No doubt he was piqued, and some would say unworthily piqued. But his touchiness is not surprising, considering all that he had had to put up with since Minden. Now that his reinstatement had come at last, he not unnaturally felt that it should be made " compleat," and that it was not becoming in him to indicate that it should be.

In September, 1779, after that year's interval, he had cause again to feel affronted. Lord North had suggested that the offices of Commissioner of Trade and Secretary for America should be separated. Lord Carlisle was to be Commissioner, because Lord Gower wanted to give him a suitable political début. In his reply Lord George, with bitterness, makes his resentment clear. He was quite ready to resign both offices: but not to hold the one without the other. His resentment on another issue is also clear: Lord North, he felt, did not take him into his confidence. The astringency and irony of this passage in his letter to Lord North are tragically characteristic:

> The plan your lordship proposes is no surprise to me. I have known it had been thought upon many months ago by those who have the honour of being consulted by you. All I can say to it is that when the King tells me it is his pleasure

that such an arrangement should take place I have no reply to make but humbly to submit to what he may think most for his service, though I must feel it as degrading to me. But if my inclinations were consulted I had much rather that Lord Gower and Lord Carlisle should be fully gratified by Lord Carlisle's receiving the Seals with the Board of Trade.

This is another offer to resign: but Lord George thinks himself bound to point out the " public objection " to Lord Carlisle becoming Secretary for the Colonies: which is that " the expectations and demands of the rebellious colonies will be raised when they perceive that one of the late Commissioners will have the settling of any future treaty with them. The proposals made by their Excellencys will be considered as approved and adopted by His Majesty, and if that was the case I should think it a most alarming and fatal blow to this kingdom." "I beg pardon," Lord George adds, "for writing my mind so freely to your lordship, but there are times when men should speak out."

Such a time indeed it then was. France and Spain were at war with Britain: in America, by sea and by land, reverses had been continually suffered. Lord George had to make the best he possibly could of it in his letters to Clinton of the same date, but to Lord North he wrote, as well he might, of " the depression of Great Britain "—" the present embarrassed situation " is what Lord North calls it—and added warningly that " the situation of this kingdom cannot be too soon the object of most serious consideration." In this important letter to Lord North he states his belief that " the resources of this country will still enable us to withstand all our enemies and even to act offensively against them. But we must proceed upon plan and system and we must remember that whatever is undertaken will be attended with great risk, but I am certain exertions must be made, for no measure can be so fatal as a tame defensive war which must end in the destruction of this country. As long as I remain in office your lordship may command my best endeavours for promoting what you may think for the honour and safety of this empire, and when I cease to be in his Majesty's Council my most earnest prayers will ever be offered for His Majesty's happiness and prosperity."

Lord North, in his reply, showed that he sympathized with Lord George at least on one point: desire for resignation. He too, ageing, fighting against odds, abused, attacked, obstructed, shared the wish that underlies that phrase: "When I cease to be in his Majesty's Council." "I have long been of opinion," he told Lord George, "and have often represented that a change in my department would strengthen rather than weaken his Majesty's Government." But "this is not his Majesty's opinion."

Lord George was advised by this letter that the King would neither allow him to keep both of the two offices that he held nor to relinquish them both. The King had ordered Lord North to say that he did not consider the separation of these offices in the least degrading, and that he would not wish it if he did. Lord Carlisle must have the Board of Trade, and Lord George must keep the American Secretaryship. Lord Carlisle is to be promoted "without removing the principal direction of the American affairs from those hands where it now is and where he [the King] is most desirous that it should continue."

But, writes Lord George in reply, did the King read your letter to me, and mine to you? And did he, "upon that state of the business," approve of the proposed arrangement? Lord George will submit if he must, but he wants to make quite sure. Once again it is clear that he did not really trust Lord North, that he suspected him of being capable of intriguing behind his back. Lord North replied that the King had read both letters before giving his commands: and Lord George then reconciled himself as best he could to being supplanted in one office, and, equally against his will, continuing in the other. After a month or so Lord Carlisle kissed hands.

Since the opening of this correspondence between Lord North and Lord George the general situation had become still more "embarrassed" and "depressed." News had come of the loss of the islands of St. Vincent and Grenada. Lord

George's load, "that would have sunk the great Lord Chatham," increased in weight. Not only did reverses to British arms increase it, but the more and more formidable force of opposition to the Government in the Commons, and the disheartenment and discontent that were steadily growing worse in England. Wraxall, who was then in London, declares that "never did a deeper political gloom overspread England than in the autumn of 1779." Throughout the kingdom there was "despondency, consternation, and general dissatisfaction." The past years had humiliated Great Britain, and that not only in America. 1778 had been bad enough: 1779 was still worse. The French and the Spaniards were masters of the Channel; fear of invasion was continual and it had real grounds. Devon and Cornwall were threatened, and were ill defended. If the enemy had been better informed, invasion would have happened. In America, there had been one unsuccessful campaign after another; neither by land nor sea did any hope appear, and the country was sick of it. The Ministers grew more and more unpopular, and so did the King, who was known to influence them unduly.

By the spring of 1780 opposition in the House of Commons to the American War was stronger than ever. It was not thought possible that Lord North could continue to face it. But though the attacks were every session more harassing, more menacing, and more hurtful, Lord North kept his place, and so did Lord George Germain. The great abilities of Charles James Fox, Wilkes, Burke, Sheridan, and the younger Pitt were used to their utmost to discredit, to confound, and to destroy the Administration. Minden, as has been already noted, was a weapon not overlooked. In November, 1780 Fox added point to his attack upon the nomination of Sir Hugh Palliser as Governor of Greenwich Hospital by reminding the House of Lord George's disgrace twenty-one years ago. After declaring that it was "characteristic of the present reign to hunt down, to defame, and to vilify great or popular public men, while the infamous were upheld, employed, and rewarded," he stared across at Lord George, and, so that there should be no mistake, he added:

"The recent promotion of Sir Hugh Palliser is dictated by the same spirit which has produced the promotion of a man to one of the greatest *civil* employments who has been publicly degraded and declared to be incapable of serving again in any *military* capacity." Lord George rose instantly; and his rebuke to Fox was one of admirable dignity and restraint. "The aspersion," he said, "which the honourable member has thought proper to throw out in the course of his speech, being obviously directed at myself, the House may naturally expect I should notice it. I rise, therefore, once for all, simply to declare that whenever gentlemen descend to the meanness of personal invectives instead of argument, and shall think proper to make me their object, I am prepared to treat both the invectives and their author with the contempt that they deserve."

1780 was appallingly black: it was a desperately baffling and disturbing and dangerous year for those in high office. As if the pressure of calamities abroad were not enough, there was added the fear and the reality of insurrection at home. The Gordon Riots against Catholic Emancipation, during which nearly three hundred were killed and the corpses of most of them thrown into the Thames, raged in London between the third and the seventh of June. Nothing worse, says Wraxall, happened during the French Revolution, and he hated the French Revolution as much as anyone could. The Gordon Riots were worse because the mob attacked public and private buildings. Wraxall reflected, as Mr. Bernard Shaw has since, that human beings can be only too easily replaced, but not buildings.

It may have afforded some solace to Ministers and their supporters that the rioters did not discriminate between them and the Opposition. They especially marked down Burke. They threatened, beseiged, attacked, or burnt houses of men prominent on either side. Theirs was not a merely Protestant zeal: to most of them Catholic Emancipation was an excuse for a violence which liberated their own raging and vindictive and justifiable discontents. Wraxall, on the night of the seventh of June, the worst night, saw the burning of Lord

Mansfield's house in Bloomsbury Square. The doors were burst open, the house was in a moment filled with rioters who threw everything they could lay hands on out into the street, where a bonfire was made. ("I have not consulted my books," said Lord Mansfield a few days later. "Indeed I have no books to consult.") Soldiers had been summoned and had arrived, but they could do nothing against so many: they attempted nothing, they stood by the bonfire and stayed there. In Holborn, warehouses and the house of their Catholic owner were ablaze. In that house, whilst it was on fire, the ringleaders could be seen tearing down the furniture and throwing it into the street. Most of the crowd were sight-seers, and a good many of them were women, holding their babies in their arms. There was considerable looting of liquor, many of the spectators were drunk; brandy, rum, and wines were pouring down the street-kennels.

Some horse guards arrived and the crowd began to scatter. Wraxall and his friends went on to Fleet Market, where the other magazines and the other house of the same Catholic tradesman, "threw up into the air a pinnacle of flame resembling a volcano." It was a beautiful effect and the house was much improved by it; for it looked like a tower, not like a mere private dwelling. "It would," says Wraxall, "have inspired the beholder with a sentiment of admiration allied to pleasure, if it had been possible to separate the object from its causes and its consequences." He noted that the figures on St. Andrew's Church clock were as clear as they would have been at noon. There was no wind, so destruction did not spread. In Fleet Market the crowd was more disorderly, and there were no soldiers. But the police were about. A watchman, English to the core, passed with his lanthorn in his hand, "calling the hour as if in a time of profound tranquillity."

The Fleet Prison was afire. Wraxall and his party approached Blackfriars Bridge: they had heard that many rioters had been killed there. They saw the King's Bench Prison in flames: "a sublime sight." London, "on every side, offered the picture of a city sacked and abandoned to a ferocious enemy."

Remembering the shouts of the populace, the cries of women, the crackling of the fires, the blaze reflected in the stream of the Thames, and the irregular firing on this side and that, Wraxall observes that " all these sounds and images . . . left scarcely anything for the imagination to supply." They evoked, however, historical memories, of Troy and Rome, which he had " so little expected to see exemplified in the capital of Great Britain."

Wraxall wanted to see more. He and his friends went on through St. Paul's Churchyard to the Bank on hearing that soldiers and rioters were fighting there. They got as far as the Poultry, and were close to the Mansion House when a sentinel stopped them. He told them that the mob had been driven from the Bank, and that he had orders to let no one pass. Dawn was begining to break. Cheapside was silent and empty, but rioting continued all around. Wraxall's party, having had almost enough of it, " satiated in some measure," and tired by their long walk, went back west. Hackney coaches were still about, they took one, and got home at about four in the morning.

Other houses were attacked and plundered, but not Lord George Germain's nor Lord North's. Lord George barricaded his house in Pall Mall and waited for something to happen, but nothing did. Lord North also had had warning; he and his dinner-party at Downing Street were, that night, well defended. His brother, Colonel North, had posted some twenty grenadiers above stairs, ready to fire from the windows as soon as they were told. Dinner was only just over when a threatening crowd poured into Downing Square. Lord North was much at his ease and as humorous as ever. " Here is much confusion," he said. " Who commands the upper tier ?" One of the guests held a pistol. " I'm not half as much afraid of the mob as I am of Jack St. John's pistol," observed Lord North. There was a good deal of noise outside, but no attempt was made to force the door. A politic and eminently English procedure was suggested : that two or three persons—servants, presumably, but perhaps Beau Brummel's father, North's secretary, was to be one of them—

should be sent out to mix with the populace and to tell them that troops were in the house and would fire on them without any reading of the Riot Act as soon as any outrage was done; urging them at the same time to get away out of danger as soon as they could. Sir John Macpherson, who was one of the guests and has told the story, does not say whether this plan was carried out. But the effect was the same as though it had been. People got to know that soldiers were at Lord North's, and they dispersed gradually. No harm had been done. Host and guests sat down again at table and finished their wine. Then they all went to the top of the house to get a good view of London blazing in seven places. Firing could be heard all the time from one part and another.

The rioters, after these three days, were almost completely suppressed. They had no leaders of ability: it was thought at the time that, if they had had, a real revolution would have happened in London and might have spread beyond. Lord George Gordon himself, with his pale thin cunning face, his gentle manners and pleasant way of talking, was obviously a fanatic, more than a little deranged. He wanted to make a name for himself as a leader: his great moment must have been when, on the day before the riots began, he harangued the populace from the House of Commons, urging them to force the Commons to refuse Catholic Emancipation. He might have paid the penalty then and been killed in the House. Many members told him that, if the mob got into the House, they would kill him at once. "I see many lives will be lost," said Colonel Murray, "but, by God, yours shall be one of them." The Duke of Atholl, too, had his sword ready.

As it was, Gordon paid no penalty at all. He was not even arrested until two or three days after the riots. Then he was sent to the Tower, tried and acquitted. Probably he did not mean the riots to happen, at any rate not on that scale. "He had put in motion a machine of which he could not regulate or restrain the movements." Admiral Rodney's son found him in the City on the night of the seventh of June trying to persuade the crowd to disperse. He offered his help to young Rodney, who mistrusted him and would have nothing to do with him. It was natural to mistrust such a man, whose vanity and exhibitionism went to the lengths of inducing him, after he became a Jew, to keep and guard so carefully, as a religious relic, the proof that he had been circumcised. Seven years after the riots these same controlling characteristics expressed themselves when Gordon libelled Marie Antoinette and the French Ambassador. He did not get off so lightly this time. He was imprisoned in Newgate and died of gaol-fever there after six years.

The Gordon Riots brought the Ministry and the Opposition together, but only for the moment. So strong was Lord North's sense of the bitterness and depth of the Opposition leaders' feeling against him that he did not think it possible to open any communication with them, even for the protection of the country. "It is not practicable," he said. But, a day or two after the riots, he and his secretary Brummel did meet Fox and Sheridan ; at the Haymarket Opera House, behind the scenes, both in a literal and in a figurative sense. This meeting certainly had no influence upon the future course of hostilities in the House of Commons. Lord North and Lord George Germain continued to be ruthlessly attacked, while the state of Great Britain in face of her enemies, who were at the end of 1780 joined by Holland, grew more and more alarming.

Fox and Burke, with the utmost severity and violence, blamed the Ministry for the breach with Holland. It is indeed, in our day, almost impossible to imagine a Parliamentary Opposition as condemnatory or as able as it was then. Fox and his friends unremittingly attacked the Ministry, and Lord North in particular, as responsible for all the existing calamities and dangers. They had done so before, they did so now, and so they continued. Material for invective was never wanting, and there was more and more of it as the months passed. By 1781 there were worse troubles everywhere. Not only abroad; faction abounded in all Government departments, the Navy especially suffered from it, and it was advertised by every debate in the Commons and in the Lords. The people were still more greatly discontented, dejected, and apprehensive, in Scotland as well as in England; while the Irish were agitating for both political and commercial independence. British credit was failing, and British commerce grievously suffered. Our East Indian empire seemed likely to collapse at any moment. As to the war with America, it was, of course, long before the surrender of Yorktown, desperately unpopular, generally regarded as sure to be lost. How often, to Lord George Germain, must have recurred that reflection which, in 1770, he expressed in a letter to General Irwin: "The difficulty with us is making peace. Every fool can pick a quarrel, but I do not remember any minister wise enough to end a war without forfeiting his own credit with the bulk of the people."

Operations in America, over a long and dreary period, had moved southwards: from Boston to New York, from New York to the Chesapeake and the Delaware, and then to the Carolinas and Virginia. But, whatever the scene-shiftings, they were of no avail, Successes for British arms occurred from time to time; seemed to promise well; were made the most of: but nothing lastingly fortunate ever happened, nothing that could really offset the successes of the enemies of England. George the Third, almost alone in his kingdom, remained blindly calm, hopeful, and determined.

"I may be got the better of by the American rebels," said King George; "but I will not by the English rebels." Lord George Germain, in the Commons, had more opportunity for gauging the strength of these English rebels than was available for his sheltered sovereign. He was one of the chief objects of their attacks; his "unwary frankness," as Fox called it, was often helpful to them. They goaded him with a purpose: that they might "force from his irritability the secret or the fact which they had vainly attempted to extort from the apathy and tranquillity of Lord North." Thus, in a session of 1781, Burke accused the Government of neglect in supplying the Gibraltar garrison with gunpowder: Admiral Darby had had to strip his fleet of powder to remedy this neglect. In reply to this charge members of the Board of Ordnance adopted the usual House of Commons method of stating that they had "no information." When a better answer was demanded, Lord George rose and, with his usual honesty and directness, said that, though he had no official information, he believed the report was founded in truth; and he added that Admiral Darby had behaved very well in leaving all the gunpowder he could spare. Lord North remained conspicuously silent under this embarrassing display of his colleague's moral courage.

Lord North was a good, easy, humorous, delightful man. Versed in a dissimulation that was never odious or mean, he was shifty or disingenuous in his own lazy, attractive way. He must often have irritated Lord George, who can be imagined as reading, if not writing, the attack of Junius upon him with considerable satisfaction. Few political contrasts of that time can have been more incisive than that between the First Minister and the Secretary for America: Lord North, equable, soft-spoken, myopic, plump, rather pulpy in face and figure, and Lord George, with his tall erect form, muscular and massive, his "quick and piercing,"[1] and sometimes irascible eye, his strong voice, the clear definition of his features with their sardonic and saturnine and intellectual implications.

In the House Lord George spoke easily, in an impromptu style, often neglecting form; he was vivid, often, and ardent; sometimes less cool and self-contained than was politic. Knowing that he was not by nature a politician, he had not intended to become one. But, by resolve of will, he learnt the technique. "No man better understood the management of Parliament, the prolongation or acceleration of a debate, according to the temper or the number of the members present, and every detail of official dexterity or address requisite in conducting affairs submitted to a popular assembly."[2]

[1] "The keenness of his sight gave him a prodigious advantage over Lord North in the House of Commons. Lord George Germain had no sooner taken his place on the Treasury Bench than he pervaded with a glance of his eye the Opposition benches, saw who attended as well as who were absent, and formed his conclusions accordingly on the business of the day. He used to say that for those who were enabled to exercise this faculty, everything was to be *seen* in the House, where, on the contrary, nothing except declamation was to be gained by the *ear*."—Wraxall's *Memoirs:* Vol. 1.

[2] From the same volume of Wraxall's *Memoirs*.

Lord North, on the other hand, had by nature all the political gifts, and none of the gifts of higher statecraft. In character, in general ability, and in force, Lord George, as was generally acknowledged, surpassed him. But most people would certainly have found Lord North the more agreeable companion. It is hard to imagine anyone more agreeable or less difficult; more amusing, and more responsive to other people's jokes, especially, it often seemed, when they were against himself. If George the Third and he were half-brothers, their having different mothers must have determined the marked differences in character between them. King George's father, Frederick, Prince of Wales, once jocularly remarked, *ápropos* the striking physical likeness between his son and Lord North, that either his wife or Lord Guildford's must have played false. If this was so, it is a pity that whichever way it happened was not the other one. Eighteenth-century history might then have made much pleasanter reading for Britons. The latter part of Lord George Germain's life might have been much pleasanter, too.

From 1778 the difficulties of the Administration in the House and out of it had been increasing. In the summer of 1781 the efforts of the Opposition to end the American War, and so to make the resignation of the Government inevitable, notably gained force, and gained more and more of it until they achieved their end.

Fox and the younger Pitt were at that time working together. In June, 1781 Fox, with Pitt's strong support, tried unsuccessfully to force peace with America. Pitt, the month before, in the second speech that he had made in the Commons, had attacked the Government on a financial question and had failed: Burke had failed, too, earlier in the same month, in an attack made especially upon Lord George Germain on account of the orders under which British commanders had acted after their capture of St. Eustasia. Now, in June, the Government still held its ground. Fox's motion was rejected by a majority of seventy-three. Lord North, who would probably have liked the motion to have been carried, did not speak on it. Lord George did, ably and eloquently, but as a man knowing what the end might be. Now was the beginning of an end that must be near. There were continual defections by Government supporters. The country gentlemen were restive. Some who opposed Fox's motion, such as Rigby and the Lord Advocate of Scotland, did not conceal their conviction that independence would have to be given to America. Lord Cornwallis's and Lord Rawdon's successes were giving great help then to the Ministry, but they did not give any real hope. Fox, after stating that the only objection made to his motion was that it must lead to American independence, boldly prophesied that "within six months of the present day Ministers will come forward to Parliament with some proposition of a similar nature." "I know that such is their intention," he asserted. "I announce it to the House."

Supporters of the Opposition, at the end of that session, were urged by George Byng, their "Muster Master-General," not to slacken their attendance when the House met again, so that they might "terminate the wicked and fruitless contest with America." On the 18th July Parliament was prorogued until the 27th November. News of the surrender of Yorktown reached the Ministers and the King on the 25th. When Parliament met, Fox and Burke, with invective and irony more incensed, virulent, and contemptuous than even they had used before, renewed hostilities. Fox declared that Ministers were in the pay of France, and that the vengeance of an undone people would soon compel them to expiate their crimes on the public scaffold. Lord Dundas smiled at this. "Does not the learned lord think the time yet ripe for punishment?" asked Fox, raging. "The British nation," said Burke in one of his most famous flights, "as an animal, is dead, but the vermin that feed on the carcass are still alive. A day of reckoning will, however, arrive. Whenever it comes, I shall be ready to impeach and signally to punish the authors of these calamities." Taxing America, he said, was now like shearing the wolf. Pitt, that prudent prizewinner, spoke with more restraint, and less excitingly.

Lord North could do no more than say, once again, that the maintenance of constitutional authority, not tyranny, over America, was, as it always had been, the object of the war. The war had been unfortunate, but not unjust. And, if he had to mount the scaffold, he would still say that the war was founded in right, and dictated by necessity.

Lord George Germain spoke in his usual straightforward way. He accepted full responsibility for all he had done: he was ready, whenever this should be demanded, to resign his office: "but I will neither be browbeat nor clamoured out of it."

The debate was on the address to the King, which was carried by eighty-nine votes; and when Fox, later, tried to stop supplies, the Government majority was nearly a hundred. Loyalty to the Ministry had been strengthened by the Yorktown disaster. But the American War was, no less, virtually ended. Many Government supporters declared against any further prosecution of it. Lord North, two days after the address to the King had been carried, told the House that supporters of Government were not bound by their votes on that occasion to vote for continuance of the war. But a "defensive war" was now the professed aim of both Lord North and of Lord George Germain. Events had forced Lord George from the conviction expressed by him in September, 1779 that "a tame defensive war" would be fatal. But his understanding of defensive war did not agree with Lord North's, as was soon to become apparent in the House of Commons; and he was still as sure as he always had been that American independence would destroy his country. He did not believe that the war could be so ended without the Ministry deservedly "forfeiting their credit with the bulk of the people." Acknowledgment of American independence would mean, he thought, acknowledgment of complete and literally ruinous failure. That might yet be avoided. The war was ended, in the sense that victory could not now be gained by force of British arms, but the colonists might, if time could be gained by a policy more or less defensive, come round of their own accord. However remote the chance of this, it must be waited for and counted on, the alternative being certain disaster.

Lord North felt differently. He had a clearer "political sense of the possible"; he was better at knowing when he was beaten, and the whole trend of his nature encouraged him to think that the beating might not turn out so badly, after all. But he could not at that time acknowledge American independence. How could he, with the King's shadow across him? After that stubborn affirmation of his Majesty's resolve upon the news of Yorktown, he had to move towards the inevitable conclusion by such degrees as he could devise.

The King's influence was, of course, generally understood. Fox, in the House, almost openly attacked him. Pitt, as usual, was warier; Pitt, indeed, was sly. He professed to believe that the King was deluded by his ministers, and he rarely lost an opportunity of declaring or parading his loyalty, impeccable and exemplary, to the person of his sovereign.

Government majorities might still be contrived, but the Opposition knew they had not long to wait. They had only to go on striking. On the 12th December they struck heavily through Sir James Lowther, who brought on a motion that "all further attempts to reduce the Americans to obedience by force would be ineffectual and contrary to the true interests of the kingdom." Lord George Germain spoke on this occasion for the last time in self-defence as Secretary for America: his resignation was, and now appeared, imminent. Burgoyne had made a pointed and personal attack upon him, and he attacked the King too, by implication. In reply, and in reply to Burke, Lord George declared himself in agreement with Lord North and with all the King's confidential servants that the war must now be defensive, but he would not agree to the evacuation of New York or of Charlestown and other coast towns still held by Britain. He spoke strongly and frankly: it was not at all the same kind of speech as the cautious equivocal one which the House had just heard from Lord North. For the first time disagreement between the two was obvious. If Sir James Lowther's motion were carried, said Lord George, "I shall instantly retire, as I consider it to include a resolution of altogether abandoning the American war."

He made it as clear as he possibly could that his mind had not changed. " Let the consequence be what it may," he went on, " I never will put my hand to an instrument conceding independence to the colonies. My opinion is that the British Empire must be ruined, and that we can never continue to exist as a great or as a powerful nation after we have lost or renounced the sovereignty over America. By this opinion I will abide, because I am resolved to leave the people their country."

" You will not leave us any country!" George Byng shouted at him across the House. Lord George retorted in anger that if Byng wanted to impeach him, " let him do it ! " " But let him do it in the way warranted by the constitution. Let him not convoke the people without doors, and address *them* to change the Administration! It is the province of this House, with the dignity becoming its character, to adopt a constitutional measure. Let the House address the Throne if they think proper. If Ministers have merited it, let them be dismissed, impeached, and brought to punishment. But do not from party violence injure the constitution and risk the subversion of the country."

Byng replied that Lord George had only to look round him to see why he was not impeached, for there was here " a phalanx of hired supporters ready to protect him against the effects of the American war. Give us only an honest Parliament, and we shall then see if security and impunity will result from impeachment." Byng was not answered. Lord North, prudently fearing defection to the Opposition, did not dare to oppose Sir James Lowther's motion. Instead, he moved the order of the day, and this was carried by only forty-one votes.

Two days later everyone could be sure of Lord George Germain's resignation. The difference of opinion between him and Lord North was made a matter of debate. Lord North was asked to tell the House about it. He did not tell them: he denied nothing, he admitted nothing, but evaded the issue by general remarks about his desire for peace and his sense of the American War as the heaviest calamity of his life. Then he did a very odd and remarkable thing; he quitted the Treasury bench and sat down behind it. By this symbolic act Lord George was left alone, unsupported, to face the Opposition.

He said little. There was little for him to say, since he had been so explicit two days before. To Townshend's specific statement that he and Lord North disagreed about the " system of warfare " that was to be carried on in America he replied that " the King's servants are unanimous on one point, namely, that it is inexpedient and would be injurious to the country to withdraw the forces from America." Fox did his best to get Lord North to say something definite, but he could get nothing out of him at all. With great skill the First Minister, though closely cross-examined, continued to evade. Pitt, the twenty-two years old prodigy, choosing the moment as well as he always did, clarified the charge of disagreement between the two ministers. " One asserts that the object of the contest is not to be abandoned, the other gives a more qualified interpretation to those words. The first maintains that the conquest of the colonies is still to be attempted; no, says the second, not to be prosecuted by force. Is it possible that men, thus ignorant of or unacquainted with each other's intentions, can act in concert or be unanimous?" Seeing that Welbore Ellis was whispering to Lord North and Lord George, Pitt stopped short. " I shall wait," he said, " till the unanimity is better settled, and until the sage Nestor of the Treasury bench has brought to an agreement the Agamemnon and the Achilles of the American War."

But Lord North was not seeking for unanimity or agreement. He wanted to have done with the war. He wanted Lord George to retire; then with a freer hand, and with more probability of holding support in the House, he could save the King's face and make the best of a bad job at home and abroad.

Rigby, who with Dundas had that day raised the question of lack of accord between Lord North and Lord George, aimed at disembarrassing Lord North both of the American War and of the American Secretary, for he believed this to be the only way of avoiding the fall of the Administration, which meant so much to him as sole Paymaster. Dundas, Lord Advocate of Scotland, was whole-heartedly on Rigby's side, being as anxious as Rigby was to keep the office which he would lose if North fell. Dundas was urgent for Lord George's resignation. "If there is any one of his Majesty's Cabinet base enough to remain in office and to conduct measures that he disapproves or condemns, be he who he will, he is unfit for society." There could be no doubt that he meant Lord George.

"These are curious times," Lord George wrote to General Irwin just before Christmas of that year, when the Parliamentary recess was beginning; and he adds, with characteristic detachment, that "it is a pity you should not be witness to the extraordinary scenes which pass in the House of Commons." Once again his wish, and his endeavour, to resign are apparent. "I was in hopes some arrangement would have taken place, and that I should have been releas'd from the very unpleasant situation in which I find myself. I have said all that was possible to the King upon this subject, but hitherto it has produced no effect. It would be highly unbecoming to fly from any attack that may be made, so that I must hold on till H.M. can see it for his interest to change hands. If the Admiralty[1] and my department were held to some parts of Opposition, I should think the hands of Government might be strengthened. I begin to fear the adjournment will pass off without doing any thing. However, I shall have nothing to reproach myself with, for I have spoke with a freedom which few masters but ours would approve of."[2]

It was now only a matter of waiting until a new American Secretary could be appointed. Lord George saw Lord North and gave him practical advice: that he should come to an understanding with some of the Opposition. He also advised Lord North not to consider him personally in any way; this advice being a matter of form, for he must have known that it was unnecessary. He told the First Minister that he made no stipulations and asked no favours, and that he would go

[1] Lord Sandwich was at this time, no less than Lord George, the object of violent opposition attack.

[2] He was still a "King George's man." Why, has been explained.

down to Drayton for two or three weeks. During this time his successor could be chosen, and then he would return at the shortest notice to deliver up his seal of office. To Drayton he then went.

But he was still Secretary for America when the House met again on the 20th January, 1782. Lord Sandwich now drew the fire from Lord George, and was accused by Fox and Pitt of gross mismanagement of the Admiralty. Lord North, in a conciliatory manner, defended him, and he was attacked too. Lord George, on the verge of his resignation, stayed in the background.

At the end of January the King at last consented to accept the resignation, and Welbore Ellis, a dull, able old man—"little Manikin Ellis" Junius called him— was put in Lord George's place. Lord George was now no longer a member of the House of Commons; on his resignation he went to the Lords as Viscount Sackville of Drayton.

Lord George Germain was gone; but the Administration did not profit by that. In February Government majorities in the House sank lower; with four hundred voting on Fox's motion against Lord Sandwich the majority against the motion was nineteen. General Conway's motion, two days later, for addressing His Majesty to renounce any further attempts to reduce America by force was lost by only one vote. On this occasion Welbore Ellis spoke ably but could not stand up against Burke who compared him to a caterpillar that had burst the silken folds of his former lucrative employment and was now fluttering forth as the Secretary of the hour; and said he had been brought up at Lord Sackville's feet and had obediently adopted all his master's political ideas. "I may assert that the late Colonial Secretary, though called up by patent to another House, still occupies in effigy his ancient seat. There we behold him with all his plans for reducing America thick upon him. He is the universal legatee of the noble Lord, who has bequeathed to him all his own projects, nay, his very language and ideas, his *ipsissima verba*. He still lives and speaks among us, only transformed into the appearance and form of the right honourable gentleman." There was, however, one important difference between the present and the former Colonial Secretary. Welbore Ellis did not embarrass Lord North.

Fox aimed his shafts higher than Burke did. He attacked the King, and attacked him as specifically as he could without actually naming him. He indicated him as " that evil spirit which produces all our calamities. It is an individual higher than the noble Lord in the blue ribband [North], for that noble person is only his puppet and acts under his direction . . . Those ostensible Ministers who occupy seats on the same bench near him are merely secondary and subordinate agents." George the Third was " that infernal spirit, which really governs and has so nearly overturned this country, a spirit which, though not so visible as Ministers, is far greater than them."

No other man would have dared to go so far as this. Burke, Sheridan, and of course Pitt, were much more politic. Pitt, knowing exactly where to stop, adept at timing, and keeping his ambition perfectly regulated, was always a real politician; while in Opposition he laid the foundations of his career, whereas Fox,[1] though he made himself a great deal more interesting to his contemporaries and to posterity than Pitt did, destroyed his own prospects.

Lord North, in spite of his majority of one, did not resign. Having no wish at all to continue the American War, he was not sorry that General Conway had brought on that motion. The Opposition were now realizing that it was quite possible for the American War to be voted against and ended and for Lord North none the less to remain First Minister. This had already been realized by Lord George, when he advised Lord North to come to an understanding with some of the Opposition. It was quite possible, but it was not what North wanted.

At the end of February General Conway again brought a motion about the American War, with the result that the Government had no majority at all, but a minority of nineteen. Lord North met the motion by declaring, in stronger terms

[1] " Je suis charmée de vous voir, *et de vous avoir vu,*" said Marie Antoinette to Pitt as he took leave of her. She would not have said that to Fox.

than before, now that Lord George was not there, that the Ministry did not propose to wage offensive war in America. If the Opposition did not believe what he said, they should address the Crown for the removal of himself and his Ministers. The Attorney-General spoke of the difficulties in the way of making peace at once with the colonists, but added that a truce might be made, and that he had a motion ready for introducing a bill with this end in view, so would move for a fortnight's adjournment. This way of escape for the Government infuriated the Opposition. The suggested truce was stigmatized as " the wretched stratagem of an expiring party." Some members of the House were influenced in favour of the Government by the prospect of a truce, but abhorrence of the American War, an abhorrence now at its height, had a stronger opposite influence, especially as the Sheriff of the City of London, before the debate, had presented at the bar a petition from the Lord Mayor, Aldermen, and Common Council that the House should do their utmost to stop the war. As soon as the Government minority was known there was a riot of applause. News of his Ministers' defeat was sent at once to the King. Then Conway carried without a division an address to the King, that he should " stop the prosecution of any further hostilities against the revolted colonies for the purpose of reducing them to obedience by force."

The responsibility was now shifted to George the Third, who refused to grant the request ordered to be presented to him at St. James's " by the whole House." He would adopt, he said, " such measures as seem to *me* most conducive to restore harmony between Great Britain and her colonies." He pronounced emphatically the word " me "; and he gave no sort of promise to stop the war.

While the King made this autocratic reply, the American traitor, Benedict Arnold, stood by his chair: " a wanton and indecent insult," so Lord Surrey termed it, "to the representatives of the people." It was an insult that roused great indignation, anger, and alarm, but Lord Surrey was the only member of the House of Commons to refer to it. General Conway now, on March 4th, moved to declare as " enemies to his Majesty and to their country all those who should advise or attempt to prosecute offensive war on the continent of North America.'' Fox, supporting the motion, did not, this time, attack the King, but said that the Ministers were criminal for advising the King not to do as the House told him. Lord North, he said, " stands in a predicament unprecedented since the Revolution. He remains in office when the Commons have condemned his system.'' He then referred to the news just received of the loss of Minorca and of the reported loss of St. Kitt's. After such news no Minister could presume to retain his office. Rigby argued in reply that there was precedent for not resigning upon loss of a majority in the House, and, following Lord North's example of a few days before, he urged the Opposition to show their lack of confidence by moving the dismissal of Ministers. Rigby knew, as North did, that they would not do this, because North was too well and too generally liked, in spite of everything, for such a motion to have any chance of being carried. Rigby did not ask for a division on Conway's motion which passed without one.

The Opposition siege, so protracted and often so spectacular, was now in its very last phase. Next day the Attorney-General moved to bring in the bill of which he had told the House a week before, for " a truce or peace with the revolted American colonies.'' Fox said that the only proper way to treat such a proposition coming from such a quarter was to burst into laughter and leave the House at once. He was willing to serve Ministers in any way that might secure peace, but, he hastily added, he would not come to terms with any one of them, he would be infamous if he did. He would not think for a moment of coalition with them; he would not trust his honour in their hands for a single minute. Lord North replied to this admirably. Fox, he said, had given " good and substantial reasons for not trusting his honour in my hands. Better reasons cannot be assigned, and as they are such, they shall serve me against the honourable member. I will never employ a person who publicly declares that he can repose no confidence in me . . . He seems in a great hurry to get possession of our places.'' Lord North then said that the Opposition had no settled system of action, and that he must remain in office to prevent confusion, until the King dismissed him or until the House unequivocally demanded his resignation. The bill for a truce or peace passed without a division.

As they could not drive Lord North out by motions on the American War, the Opposition had now to consider the possibility of making a more personal attack. Well aware of North's popularity, they went warily. They felt their way, they tried the temper of the House; and it was on March 15th that Sir John Rous moved that "the House has no further confidence in Ministers." The result was hardly an Opposition failure; the Government had a majority of nine.

During this debate members were again to be reminded of Lord George Germain, now Viscount Sackville. They were this time more remarkably reminded of him, and it was Lord North who did it. Defending himself against the motion, he spoke extraordinarily well. He did not only defend: he vigorously attacked. Expressing a view that Sackville had always held, he laid reponsibility for the ill success of the American War upon the Opposition because of the encouragement they had given to the rebels. Then he referred to the charge against him of misrepresenting facts so as to induce Parliament to go on with the war. At this point he was evidently embarrassed: he did not like doing what he felt he had to do, which was to throw the blame from himself to Lord Sackville. He was conscious, perhaps, that Sackville would have been too honourable and too proud to have done anything of the kind to him. After naming a particular misrepresentation, that of the strength of the American loyalists, he told the House that this was not his fault. Once again, after so many years, Sackville, charged as culpable, was not named. "The declaration in question," said Lord North, "came not from me, but from another Minister." He hastened to excuse Sackville, while continuing to dissociate himself from him. "I am convinced that the Minister who made the assertion spoke from good authority. I believe we not only had, but that we still retain, numerous friends throughout the colonies. I confess, at the same time, that I never thought those friends sufficient in point of numbers, nor in any point of view whatever, either to justify our commencing or our continuing the war solely on their account." The sentence is carefully and skilfully worded: Lord North implies, but does not say, that he had always regarded American loyalism as of little practical value. If he had said so, he would not have been telling the truth.

Fox did not let this pass. Not, of course, that he wished to defend Sackville, but the chance of accusing North of lack of generosity was not to be missed. "He throws the responsibility and the blame on another Minister for having deceived us . . . He has, however, himself deluded and deceived Parliament in a variety of instances."

In spite of the Government majority, and Lord North's assurance, once more repeated, that he would stay on until the House turned him out, the end was much nearer than anyone thought. Lord North, like Lord George, had repeatedly begged the King to release him; it was only because the King would not do so, not because of his own stubbornness, that he had for so long held on, for so long devised and practised plans to withstand so heavy a pressure against him. No wonder that, when he was at last released, he could quote, "with the utmost good-humour and complacency," to sympathizing friends, the tragic passage:

"What, amazed
At my misfortune? Can thy spirit wonder
A great man should decline ?"

Only Lord North could have made such a quotation at such a time in such a manner. Urbanity and the comic sense could never desert this admirably level man. He was capable of relieving, with his own amenity, with his own kind of easy pleasant jest, any calamity or misadventure that might come to him. He would have joked about his "fall," however hard it had hit him. As it was, the joke that he played on the House when he surprised them by his resignation was in harmony with his own sense of relief: it did not redress chagrin, dejection, or humiliation, for he felt none. It is, indeed, doubtful if any tragic emotion could have pierced him deeply. He had none of the tragic susceptibilities of Lord George, none of Lord George's bitterness of sardonic irony. He was not passionate, as Sackville, under all his proud reserve, unquestionably was. North could not suffer, nor resent, nor hate, nor excite hatred, as Sackville could. That he should have rather disliked Sackville and held aloof from him with some sort of ill defined mistrust and misgiving was as natural as it was that Sackville should have disliked, mistrusted, and rather despised him. A superficial similarity between the two men is that each of them had humour and was capable of satire, that each of them could entertain a joke against himself; but how different the satire and the humour, how different was Sackville's saturnine dangerous savour from the suave companionable relish of Lord North.

By the middle of March it was evident that the Opposition could not count on the same majority for dislodging the Government as they had for ending the American War, and everyone felt, with reason, sure that Ministers would not resign. When, on the 20th March, Lord North, in a full dressed suit, with his blue ribband over it, came into the House straight from St. James's where he had been seeing the King, no one had the least idea of what was going to happen. He rose to speak: Lord Surrey, who had given notice of a motion against the Government, rose at the same time. There was at once great disorder, Lord Surrey had the right to speak first: Pitt, Fox, and others clamoured above the tumult that he must be heard. The Speaker tried to restore calm, but he could not. Fox moved that Surrey should speak, and in the lull that followed North began to address the House. He had come down that day, he told them, "to announce from authority his Majesty's determination to change his Ministers." Lord Surrey's motion was therefore unnecessary. He moved the adjournment of the House.

Lord North's carriage was waiting. Nobody else had one, because it was so early. "Good night, gentlemen," said North as he stepped in. "You see what it is to be in the secret."

Another brief Rockingham Ministry, with powerful former members of Opposition in office, was to follow. George the Third, forced to capitulate, agreed to Lord Rockingham's stipulation that there should be no veto on a recognition of American Independence, and that no former Minister, except Lord Thurlow, should have place. "I have often been accused of lying," Lord North observed, "but never have I lied like the *Gazette,* which says that the King has been *pleased* to appoint Mr. Fox and the rest." George the Third's mind continued in the same stay. In December, 1782 he, in his speech from the Throne, offered up a prayer to God for the new United States. He deprecated, in their interests, the natural wrath of Heaven, and asked God as a special favour not to punish them as they deserved for being independent and for having deprived themselves of the benefits of monarchy.

What passed between Lord North and his Sovereign at that private interview which ended in acceptance of his resignation, is not known. That the King still did not want his First Minister to resign is certain. He received the letter of resignation at Windsor, when he was just going to hunt: he read it, put it in his pocket, said nothing, mounted his horse. A page ran after him to say that the messenger had been told to bring a reply. "I shall be in town tomorrow morning," said the King. "I will give Lord North an answer then." Lord Sackville's nephew, the Duke of Dorset, and another nobleman were with him. To them he said: "Lord North has sent me in his resignation, but I shall not accept it." When he met North early the next afternoon they were together for about an hour and a half, alone. Both of them, no doubt, went over well worn ground, Lord North indicating the now proved impossibility of any such compromise as coalition, and the danger to the King himself of things as they were. George would have persuaded against a decision which held firm until even he could not help but see that his First Minister was determined to resign whether he liked it or not.

It has been thought that Lord North's determination was

due to his fears of Lord Surrey's motion being carried that evening; but the general opinion was that there would have been a majority against it, if a small one. What is more likely is that he insisted now on resigning because he wished more strongly that ever to do so, and that his wish would have been unchanged even if he could have foreseen Rodney's impending victory[1] over de Grasse which would have saved his Ministry if it had held till then. Like Sackville, who got off a little sooner, he had had enough of it.

Sackville, his difficult, tedious, invidious American Secretaryship ended, had, while North was extricating himself from office, been engaged in his final self-defence as a newly made Viscount against the attacks of peers who were still determined not to forget Minden. When they were silenced, he could, after twenty-two years, feel that the Minden ghost was laid at last. And, six months later, the American War was over; without the ruin of England visibly impending. Lord North was still a notable figure in the Commons, first as an independent arbiter, and then, surprisingly to others, but no doubt amusingly to himself, and to Sackville, as a colleague of Fox. Sackville, from his distance, viewed public affairs with an interest that could now be detached with less effort of will. His letters from above the mêlée show naturally a remoter irony, an observation aloof, though no less keen. "I do not see how the Ministers can change for the better, as nobody seems inclined to obstruct their measures, and if they can agree among themselves they will not want unanimity in Parlt."[2] "Such strange resolutions have lately happened among the Ministers that it is impossible to speak with certainty about any event. A new First Lord of the Treasury and two new Secretarys of State must have surpriz'd you as much as it did me."[3] "We swarm with abusive pamphlets, and Lord Shelburne is the principal object of their invectives. He must now submit to that correction which formerly he bestow'd

[1] On 12th April, 1782, Sackville writes of it that "it was as well timed as it was compleat, and if it tends to peace it will be a happy event indeed." He adds that Rodney "has retrieved the affairs of this country by his able and spirited conduct."

[2] June 22nd, 1782.

[3] July 17th, 1782.

on others. Lord North is courted by all parties, but I do not hear that he has promised his support to either."[1] "The King . . . has by perseverance and firmness regained his authority and is no longer under control . . . The P. of Wales seems to delight in faction and to forget that he may one day be King. Indeed he takes great pains to prevent that event happening, for he ruins his constitution by all sorts of irregularities, particularly in eating and drinking."[2] Political comment is interspersed with family news. "The boys are well and at school." "Mrs. Herbert is arrived at Muckross after many distresses but without accident." "Poor George had a most dangerous fever . . . I hope the boy will soon recover his strength."

The three and a half remaining years of Lord Sackville's life were, by comparison, years of privacy, freedom, and peace.

Chapter XI

LAST YEARS

GEORGE COVENTRY, in his *Memoirs of Lord Viscount Sackville,* writes that from 1782, when Lord George was created Viscount, he "appears to have lived in a retired manner, occasionally at Drayton in Northamptonshire, or at Bolebrook, near Tunbridge Wells; but principally at his beautiful mansion, Stoneland Park[3] . . . Here, away from the bustle of public life, the cavils of party, and the rancorous spirit of his enemies, he passed the remainder of his days in retirement."

But he was not really retired: though "he had withdrawn in some degree from politics," he did not lead the life of a

[1] November 26th, 1782.

[2] June 12th, 1784.

[3] Stoneland Lodge, afterwards called Buckhurst. Wraxall, too, refers to "Stoneland Park," and to "Stonelands."

Lord George, aged sixty-three, *by Romney*.

country gentleman except at intervals. It will already have been seen that he often wrote, during those last years, from Pall Mall. In the summer before his death he revisited Ireland.[1] He spoke in the House of Lords; most notably when opposing the "Irish Propositions" little more than a month before his death. There is much evidence of his continued interest and participation in public affairs. From Drayton in January, 1784 he wrote to Wraxall anticipating that the younger Pitt would finally prevail in the political conflict of that date: and Wraxall, referring to that "quickness of perception which seemed at times to partake of prescience and intuition," and which was "among the peculiar features of Lord Sackville's intellectual formation," gives an example afforded during the following month:

> Being likewise destitute of all reserve where secrecy was not demanded, he rarely declined answering any question put to him, and he was a stranger to circumlocution or evasion. In February, 1784, when Pitt's eventual stability in office began to be evident, and his final triumph over the Coalition almost certain, Lord Walsingham and I asked Lord Sackville, "How long will Pitt remain First Minister?" He looked up for two or three seconds, and then replied, "Five years." The accomplishment of this prediction proved ridiculously accurate.

Lord Sackville continued active, also, in patronage, as when he tried to get Mr. Lindsay, late serjeant in the 20th regiment, placed upon the list of Chelsea Hospital. In this, after nearly two years, he thought he had succeeded; and when, in June, 1785, he found he had not, he wrote, from Pall Mall, a letter very like himself:

> Mr. Lindsay, I am sorry that I should have sent you an account of the assurances I had received of your being placed upon the list, but upon enquiry finding there was a mistake in that business by having placed a person of your

[1] In June, 1784, he writes of his intention to travel to Ardfert and the Lake of Killarney. "Such young, frisky fellows as I am make nothing of a journey of that sort."

name upon it, I cannot permit you to suffer by such an accident, and therefore I enclose to you an order for ten guineas which I desire you to accept as a mark of my regard, and you may depend upon my sending you the like sum every year as long as I live . . . I am your friend and well wisher, Sackville.

Of greater interest is Sackville's patronage of Richard Cumberland,[1] the dramatist. It was not a patronage of the mere figure-head kind: the patron had lively and critical concern, especially during those later years of his comparative leisure, with his protegé's work. Towards the end of 1782 he wrote from Drayton to Wraxall a letter which ends with an expression already cited:

> Cumberland is writing a new sort of tragedy in familiar dialogue instead of blank verse, for which, I conclude, he will be abused till he has a severe fit of the bile. Four acts are finished. The ladies have attended the reading of them, and say they are very moving. I declined the pleasure, because I fear I never can commend any performance equal to the expectation of the author. Such prose as you write I admire, because I understand it; but I have not genius sufficient for works of mere imagination.

About two years later he wrote to Wraxall:

> Cumberland is writing, and indeed has finished, a new comedy, and I have seen it, and the dialogue is remarkably well. There was something in the characters, in the moral part of them, that I disliked, and I was in doubt whether I might venture to declare it. But as I cannot forbear speaking truth, out it came; and instead of being offended, he adopted the idea, and it is all to be altered according to my plan. Was I not a bold man to attack an author ?"

He wrote again about Cumberland early in 1785, and, in the same letter, on another literary subject, *The Rolliad,* showing unqualified appreciation here. Admirably detached,

[1] Sir Fretful Plagiary, in Sheridan's *The Critic,* is a caricature of Cumberland.

he has nothing but praise for this satirical poem, in which himself was an object of satire.[1] "The 'Rolliad,'" he writes, "is indeed highly entertaining. We all admire it, and there is more wit, elegance, and humour in the composition than I could have conceived it possible even for Mr. Sheridan and his friends to have produced." Of Cumberland's comedy he is more critical: "When Cumberland read his comedy here, the character of Dumps, which you commend, struck me as the least to be admired; but we said so much upon that subject that he promised to alter it . . . As I see 'The Natural Son' advertised for the remainder of the week, I am in hopes that the managers expect it will answer."

The Natural Son did not answer well, for it was played, at Drury Lane, only some ten times. One of the characters, Lady Paragon, was, so Genest c' erves, "acted by Miss Farren in an exquisite style." Wraxall's editor says that Cumberland condensed this play into four acts two years later, "but he could not make it a stock piece." His fortunes as a dramatist declined after the early 1780's.

It was in 1775, soon after Lord George's appointment to the American Secretaryship, that Cumberland first met him. Fifteen years before, he had attended the court-martial, "through the whole of its progress," but, apart from that, "I had never been in a room with him in my life." He was taken by Colonel Cunningham to Lord George's house in Pall Mall, with the prospect, owed to the then Duke of Dorset's influence, of becoming his under-secretary. His almost instant appreciation of those essential qualities of Lord George, directness and truth, appears in his *Memoirs* :

> There was at once an end to all our circumlocutory reports and inefficient forms, that had only impeded business, and substituted ambiguity for precision ; there was, as William Gerard Hamilton, speaking of Lord George, truly observed to me, no trash in his mind; he studied

[1] "Say, is not WALSINGHAM himself a host ?
His grateful countrymen, with joyful eyes,
From SACKVILLE'S ashes see this Phœnix rise :
Perhaps with all his master's talents blest,
To save the East as he subdu'd the West."

no choice phrases, no superfluous words, nor ever suffered the clearness of his conceptions to be clouded by the obscurity of his expressions, for these were the simplest and most unequivocal that could be made use of for explaining his opinions, or dictating his instructions.

But, like many others, Cumberland was embarrassed and disappointed by the cold reserve with which Lord George first met him. He writes that " the ceremony of paying my respects was soon dismissed. I confess, I thought my new chief was quite as cold in his manner, as a minister need be, and rather more so than my intermediate friend had given me reason to expect."

To Cumberland's great surprise, as he had not been " flattered with the share of any notices from him, but such as I might reasonably expect," and therefore " built no hopes upon his favour," he was suddenly invited by Lord George to stay at Stoneland :

> One day, as Lord George was leaving the office, he stopt me on the outside of the door, at the head of the stairs, and invited me to pass some days with him and his family . . . It was on my part so unexpected, that I doubted if I had rightly understood him, as he had spoken in a low and submitted voice, as his manner was, and I consulted his confidential secretary, Mr. D'Oyley, whether he would advise me to the journey. He told me, that he knew the house was filled from top to bottom with a large party, that he was sure there would be no room for me, and dissuaded me from the undertaking. I did not quite follow his advice by neglecting to present myself, but I resolved to secure my retreat to Tunbridge Wells, and kept my chaise in waiting to make good my quarters.

He soon found that Lord George was very different from those demonstrative persons, those sympathetic, winning, popular good companions who " pay you by feeling " and by talking and smiling, but that his payment, to those whom he liked and valued, was made in true coin :

When I arrived at Stoneland, I was met at the door by Lord George, who soon discovered the precaution I had taken, and himself conducting me to my bed-chamber, told me it had been reserved for me, and ever after would be set apart as mine, where he hoped I would consent to find myself at home. This was the man I had esteemed so cold; and thus was I at once introduced to the commencement of a friendship, which day by day improved, and which no one word or action of his life to come, ever for an instant interrupted or diminished.

A little later Cumberland became Lord George's secretary, succeeding Mr. Pownall: before, he had been "clerk to the reports" at the Board of Trade. If it were not for the *Memoirs* in which with such whole-hearted loyalty and affection he defended his friend and patron, Lord Sackville's last years, and especially his last days, would be much less clear. It is impossible to write of this chapter of Sackville's life without drawing largely from Cumberland. He was not a great dramatist, nor is his admirably well-intentioned account of Sackville a masterpiece, but he had the dramatist's objectivity in observation and in sense of character, and he was, of all Sackville's intimates, perhaps the nearest to his friend's real qualities of nature, and certainly the most expressive of his sympathy with them. His letters to Lord George from Lisbon and Madrid in 1780 and 1781 have sometimes a vivid descriptive flair; they are in livelier and more familiar style than his *Memoirs*:

I saw seven zebras in the Queen's stables, of exquisite shape and beauty, and in her gardens . . . She has an aviary of Brazil small birds, of incomparable plumage; the gardens are disposed in straight walks between hedges of myrtle, Portugal laurel, and yellow jasmine overarched, and centering in stars; the quarters being planted with limes, citron, and orange, now in high season.

My daughters enjoy themselves, Sophie the best. They have been to a bull fight, but suffered more than words can relate . . . From what has this evening passed between

Mr. Hartford and my daughter I have every reason to conclude upon their certain though not speedy agreement . . . Wherever the girls go, they are sure of a fight and a good prize.

In a letter to Lord George from St. Alban's Street, later in 1781, he writes about his plays :

. . . the Carmelite was triumphantly received, and I am now sitting in a little dirty lodging (*not Mr. Lackington's*) over a chimney by myself under the shade of my laurels. Mrs. Siddons was divine, and crown'd with unceasing peals of applause; Mr. Palmer and Mr. Kemble excellent, Mr. Smith execrable; if anything could have tempted you to sacrilege, you would have crack't his shaven crown for being such a bellowing Carmelite. I found Sir Charles Thompson with Mrs. Siddons this morning and was vastly flatter'd by him, posted between author and actress he scarce knew which way to turn; Lord Loughborough was there and all the fine people in town; poets, painters, printers, writers, devils, and demireps from all quarters.

The Drayton comedy comes out in three weeks, for we strike whilst the iron is hot. I saw Wraxall in the morning, but neither he nor *My Lord* were with Mrs. Siddons at night. Father Hussey was with me in the manager's box, and wept streams, but he anathematis'd his brother monk, and said he acted like an atheist preaching Christianity. I took Henderson into the Green Room, where he was the life and soul of the party, adoring Mrs. Siddons, and cheering every body around him; her brother Kemble was applauded thro' the house, and his likeness to Mrs. Siddons, whose son he is in the play, was greatly felt.

I am excessively happy to hear Mr. and Mrs. Herbert are with you at Drayton, and beg my best remembrances to them. I daresay Mrs. Herbert found her little ones much grown and improved, and that so many good peaches and pears have not been bestow'd upon Bessy for nothing. If I saw her, I could tell her that *William Harry Edward Cavendish Bentinck,* tho' he does not own many more months than names, begins to sing *Malbroock* most divinely, so that I am thinking of sending him my prologue and epilogue, hoping they will go pretty well to that tune, therefore I take it to be high time for a young lady of her standing to cry something else besides peaches and pears.

I beg to be most respectfully remember'd to Miss Sackville, and the ladies. I was sorry for Miss Leighton's sake to find Lord Derby with Lady Paragon, when I came with my book under my arm to read her part; we are great friends, however, tho' rivals, and I was afraid he would have jump'd out of a three-pair-of-stairs slip last night for joy of the Carmelite, and I really doubt if he would not, had not the spikes of the orchestra been in his way; he made it up with screaming. Sheridan behav'd like an angel both to me and the performers, and even Will Woodfall grinn'd a ghastly smile.

What nonsense I have been chattering to you. If I read it over I shall not venture to send it. My only consolation is that it will arrive in a December evening, and as Miss Jane has nothing to do of a Sunday night, she perhaps will read it, if nobody else will . . .

It was three and a half years before his death when Lord George, on resigning his American Secretaryship, was given a peerage by George the Third. Wraxall heard of it, on the same day, from Lord George himself, and notes that the circumstances are " too curious, as well as characteristic, to be omitted."

The separation [he writes] between the sovereign and the secretary, was by no means unaccompanied with emotion on both sides; which became probably augmented by the dark cloud overhanging the throne, together with the circumstances that produced the necessity for Lord George's resignation . . . After . . . thanking Lord George for his services, his Majesty added, " Is there any thing I can do, to express my sense of them, which would be agreeable to you ? " " Sir," answered he, " if your Majesty is pleased to raise me to the dignity of the Peerage, it will form at once the best reward to which I can aspire, and the best proof of your approbation of my past exertions in your affairs." "By all means," said the King, "I think it very proper and shall do it with pleasure." "Then, sir," rejoined Lord George, "if you agree to my first request, I hope you will not think it unbecoming, or unreasonable in me, to ask another favour. It is to create me a *Viscount,* as, should I be only raised to the dignity of a *Baron,* my own secretary, my lawyer, and my father's page, will all take rank of me." The King expressing a wish to know the names of the persons to whom he alluded, "The first," replied Lord George, "is Lord Walsingham, who, as your Majesty knows, was long under-secretary of State in my office, when Mr. de Grey. The second is Lord Loughborough, who has always been my legal adviser. Lord Amherst is the third, who when page to my father, has often sat on the braces of the state-coach that conveyed him, as Lord-Lieutenant of Ireland, to the Parliament House at Dublin." The King smiled, adding, "What you say, is very reasonable; it shall be so; and now let me know the title that you choose." "I have already, sir," answered Lord George, "in the possible anticipation of your Majesty's gracious disposition towards me, spoken to the Duke of Dorset, and obtained his permission, as the head of my family, to take the title of *Sackville*; having been compelled to renounce my own name, in order to avail myself of the bequest of the estate of Drayton in Northamptonshire, made me by Lady Betty Germain in her will. I shall therefore, in some degree, recover it by this means." "I quite approve of that idea," replied his Majesty, "and if you will state to me your title, I will write it down myself before we part and send it directly to the Chancellor."

The King immediately placed himself at a table, took the pen and ink lying upon it, and having committed the *Viscounty* to paper, asked him what *Barony* he chose? Lord George answered, "that of Bolebrook in Sussex, being one of the most antient estates belonging to the family, and contiguous to Buckhurst, the original Peerage conferred by Queen Elizabeth on his ancestor, the first Earl of Dorset." When the King had copied it, he rose up, and with the most condescending expressions of concern as well as satisfaction, allowed Lord George to withdraw from the closet.

The dialogue reads rather as though it had been written by some careful Victorian novelist; but Wraxall was surely right in thinking that the account should not be omitted. He adds a comment on the fact that this was "one of the few Peerages, which in the course of half a century, George the Third has been allowed to confer, wholly independent of ministerial intervention or recommendation, from the impulse of his own inclinations." The hostile fury that it roused in the House of Lords has already been recorded.

During those last three or four years of his life Lord Sackville was occupied not only by political interests, by family concerns, and by the affairs incidental to his position and estate, but by entertainment on a scale that might well have taken up the greater part of his time and energies. Wraxall says that "There was not, probably, a nobleman in England who combined a more liberal economy with a hospitable and splendid establishment." He had, indeed, three establishments, his town house in Pall Mall, Stoneland Lodge, his favourite, which he rented from his nephew the Duke; and Drayton House. Wraxall writes of his "admirably served table," and of the many guests who nearly always surrounded it; and comments on the lavishness of his hospitality in relation to his income of nine or ten thousand pounds a year, and on the generosity which prevented him from making any reduction in his household when he went out of office. He did not "dismiss a single domestic."

"All the world visits him," wrote the poet Gray at the time of the Minden court-martial. Lord George, especially in his later years, when an increased host of memories had gathered, was always well pleased to entertain chosen friends, to drink "a pint of claret" with them, and to talk with them of the many things and the many people that had crowded the life of one who had been set so high, and had been with such violence abased, and then set high again. As a host, as a companion, he rewarded fully and in his own separate way those who could perceive and value his qualities, those who could recognize, as Cumberland did, that " sincerity was his nature," and that " reserve . . . was the result of his misfortunes." Reserve, however, may rather be said to have been confirmed by his misfortunes than engendered by them. " He talked little," says Cumberland, " and his opinions, being expressed without circumlocution, or hesitation, stamped an air of forethought and reflection upon what he said . . . His manners and deportment had not the easy freedom of the present fashion." But without " verbosity or rhetoric, or air of pomp or mystery," he would draw from his " fertile stock " of memories of " illustrious persons, interesting anecdotes and events," " with singular perfection of facts and dates . . . Of many considerable affairs within his own time he had personal knowledge, many others (with several of a curious secret nature) he had collected . . . " " —When he entered on the Events of those Times he might be said to raise the Curtain that concealed from Vulgar Eyes the Palaces of Whitehall, of St. James's, of Kensington, and of Hampton Court."—After any interruption, he would, " with perfect manners and very good grace, take up his discourse where he had left it . . . If anyone spoke with heat in dispute, or raised his voice above its natural pitch, or if more than one speaker talked at a time, it gave him great pain." He stands remote indeed from the *Encyclopaedia Britannica* figure, sullen and haughty and domineering, this man who was " an adept in that art which tends to put others in humour with themselves, and which I take to be of the true species of politeness not laying out for admiration or display."

It was Richard Cumberland who first compared the ageing Sackville with Sir Roger de Coverley, in his description of him on Sundays in church:

On the Sunday morning he appeared in gala, as if he

were dressed for a drawing-room; he marched out his whole family in grand cavalcade to his parish church, leaving only a centinel to watch the fires at home, and mount guard upon the spits . . . He had a way of standing up in sermon time, for the purpose of reviewing the congregation and awing the idlers into decorum, that never failed to remind me of Sir Roger de Coverley at church. Sometimes, when he had been struck with passages in the discourse, which he wished to point out to the audience as rules for moral practice worthy to be noticed, he would mark his approbation of them, with such cheering nods and signals of assent to the preacher, as were often more than my muscles could withstand.

He had nursed up with no small care and cost, in each of his parish churches, a corps of rustic psalm-singers, to whose performance he paid the greatest attention, rising up, and with his eyes directed to the singing gallery, marking time, which was not always rigidly adhered to; and once, when his ear, which was very correct, had been tortured by a tone most glaringly discordant, he set his mark upon the culprit by calling out to him by name, and loudly saying, "Out of tune, Tom Baker!" Now this faulty musician, Tom Baker, happened to be his Lordship's butcher; but then in order to set names and trades upon a par, Tom Butcher was his Lordship's baker . . . I relate these little anecdotes of a man, whose character had nothing little in it, that I may shew him to my readers in his private scene, and be as far as I am able the intimate and true transcriber of his heart.

Cumberland refers to Lord Sackville's "habitual punctuality," which had already impressed him when he served under Lord George Germain, whom he found "so momentarily punctual to his time, so religiously observant of his engagements." Writing now of his friend in a later phase and as the head of a household, he says that Sackville was "never moved from" this punctuality, even by attacks of the stone "that would have confined most people to their beds." He calls such punctuality "curious," and adds that

> Probably, in some men's eyes it would, from its extreme precision, have appeared ridiculously minute and formal; yet in the movements of a domestic establishment so large as his, it had its uses and comforts, which his guests and family could not fail to partake of. As sure as the hand of the clock pointed to the half-hour after nine, did the good lord of the castle step into his breakfast room . . . He allowed an hour and a half for breakfast, and regularly at eleven took his morning's circuit on horseback at a foot's-pace, for his infirmity would not allow of strong gestation. He had an old groom, who had grown grey in his service, who was his constant pilot on these excursions, and his general custom was to make the tour of his cottages, to reconnoitre the condition they were in, whether their roofs were in repair; their windows whole, and the gardens well cropt, and neatly kept. All this it was their interest to be attentive to, for he bought the produce of their fruit trees; and I have heard him say with great satisfaction, that he has paid thirty shillings in a season for strawberries only, to a poor cottager, who paid him one shilling annual rent for his tenement and garden; this was the constant rate at which he let them to his labourers, and he made them pay it to his steward at his yearly audit, that they might feel themselves in the class of regula tenants, and sit down at table to the good cheer provided for them on the audit day. He never rode out without preparing himself with a store of six-pences in his waistcoat pocket for the children of the poor, who opened gates and drew out sliding bars for him in his passage through the enclosures: these barriers were well watched; and there was rarely any employment for a servant: but these six-pences were not indiscriminately bestowed, for as he kept a charity-school upon his own endowment, he knew to whom he gave them, and generally held a short parley with the gate-opener as he paid his toll for passing. Upon the very first report of illness or accident, relief was instantly sent, and they were

put upon the sick list, regularly visited, and constantly supplied with the best medicines, administered upon the best advice. If the poor man lost his cow, or his pig, or his poultry, the loss was never made up in money, but in stock. It was his custom to buy the cast-off liveries of his own servants as constantly as the day of clothing came about, and these he distributed to the old and worn-out labourers, who turned out daily on the lawn in the Sackville livery, to pick up boughs and sweep up leaves, and, in short, do just as much work as served to keep them wholesome and alive.

This is the measured, timed, economical, punctilious generosity which alone can work effectively in regular and continued practice.

The devoted author of the *Memoirs* is perhaps most memorable when he writes of his friend's illness and death. Shortly before Lord Sackville went from Stoneland to London to speak against the Irish Propositions, Richard Cumberland was gravely anxious about him. He records his premonition with that odd and, to us, almost comical stiffness which accompanies the rectitude of manner of so many later eighteenth and earlier nineteenth century writers:

I now foresaw the coming on of an event, that must inevitably deprive me of one of the greatest comforts, which still adhered to me in my decline of fortune. It was too evident that the constitution of Lord Sackville, long harassed by the painful visitation of that dreadful malady, the stone, was decidedly giving way. There was in him so generous a repugnance against troubling his friends with any complaints, that it was from external evidence only, never from confession, that his sufferings could be guessed at . . . It was in the year 1785, whilst I was at Stoneland, that these symptoms first appeared, which gradually disclosed such evidences of debility, as could not be concealed, and shewed to demonstration that the hand of death was even then upon him. He had prepared himself with an opinion deliberately formed upon the matter of the Irish propositions, and when that great question was appointed to come on for discussion in the House of Lords, he thought himself bound in honour and duty to attend in his place. He then for the first time confessed himself to be unfit for the attempt, and plainly declared he believed it would be his death. He paused for a few moments, as if in hesitation how to decide, and the air of his countenance was impressed with melancholy; we were standing under the great spreading tree that shelters the back entrance to the house: the day was hot; he had dismounted heavily from his horse; we were alone, and it was plain that exercise, though gentle, had increased his languor; he was oppressed both in body and spirit; he did not attempt to disguise it, for he could no longer counterfeit; he sat down upon the bench at the tree-foot, and composing his countenance, as if he wished to have forced a smile upon it, had his suffering given him leave, "I know," said he, "as well as you can tell me, what you think of me just now, and that you are convinced if I go to town, upon this Irish business, I go to my death; but I also know you are at heart not against my undertaking it, for I have one convincing proof ever present to me, how much more you consult my honour than my safety; and after all, what do I sacrifice, if, with the sentence of inevitable death in my hand, I only lop off a few restless hours, and in the execution of my duty meet the stroke? In one word, I tell you I shall go, we will not have another syllable upon the subject; don't advise it, lest you should repent of it when it has killed me; and do not oppose it, because it would not be your true opinion, and if it were, I would not follow it."

Written in almost whatever manner, the account would be affecting, and would stir admiration for such sureness, such courage, such calm, and such consideration, humane and delicate, for his friend. As it is, the report of Sackville's words reads as though it were *verbatim*. The change of style from Cumberland's own is striking; and the last sentence in particular, in its decision, its clarity, its logic, its unparading fortitude, its reasonable command, is wholly Sackville. When Cumberland tells us that he " scorns the paltry trick of writing speeches for any man whose name is in these memoirs," —a " trick " lately how popular! — we may believe him. Not only his will, but his dramatic faculty, no doubt helped him to keep intact the words of others.

Sackville did " go to town, upon this Irish business," and he did " go to his death," as he was sure he would; for he did not say, " if it kills me," but " when it has killed me." He spoke on the Irish Propositions with astonishing animation and vigour; he gave the impression of a man in his prime. It was on the eighteenth of July, five or six weeks before his death, that he addressed the House of Lords with what Wraxall describes as " extraordinary energy," " in language of force but of moderation." In place of the commercial union between England and Ireland at which the Propositions aimed, Sackville urged that a political union, involving " one and the same Legislature," would permanently extinguish every source of suspicion, distrust and jealousy. Wraxall observes that it was Sackville who, " in his seventieth year, laid the first stone . . . of the union between Great Britain and Ireland." Many will not think the better of him for that; but it is impossible to read his speech without the certainty that he believed every word he said, and that his words were indeed, as Wraxall called them, " prophetic." He was championing a policy soon to be adopted by the younger Pitt, " in preference to his own rash and ill-digested system:" the Unionist policy which lasted for more than a hundred and twenty years. To the " happy consummation " of Irish union Sackville looked forward, as he told the Lords, with " the utmost anxiety ":

> It will probably not take place in my time. Nevertheless, I hope that the period when it shall be effected is not very distant. Happen whenever it may, the event will ensure to both kingdoms inestimable and lasting benefits . . . I trust the present measure may still be suspended, and that we may be impelled to direct our whole attention to that union, so desirable by the wise of each country. And if

the resolutions before us could only be withdrawn, should no other peer in this assembly be found to undertake it, old as I am, I will move for an address to the King, praying that steps may be taken for accomplishing that union, on which depends the prosperity, not only of England and of Ireland, but of the whole empire.

Another passage has the character of a "farewell speech":

The matter is trivial to myself, in comparison with many of your Lordships. I can only be interested for posterity. Whatever may be the issue of our deliberations, my own personal concern is small. I am arrived at that period of life when it would ill become me to be deeply affected by any decision of this House. But I see before me many peers to whom the system may be productive of most important consequences. They, I make no doubt, will live to curse the day that gave it birth. I perceive in its aspect incurable jealousies and endless discord. Should a rupture take place between the two countries, though it is not difficult to see which would prevail, yet the result will be alike fatal to both. I implore your Lordships to act with caution, and not lightly to come to a vote which admits of no recall.

Lord Sackville's speech brought forward his motion to postpone for four months the consideration of the Irish Propositions. The motion was lost by a majority of more than fifty, and the Propositions were carried through both Houses in spite of the strong opposition of Fox and Sheridan. Fox declared that Ireland did not want this commercial arrangement and that " if by the operation of influence and corruption the resolutions can be forced through the Irish Parliament, yet so violent is the detestation of the Irish people towards them, that the nation will unquestionably effect their repeal within a short time." "That the resolutions are unpopular here," said Sheridan, "daily experience must convince. That they are still more unpopular in Ireland I can assert from indisputable authority. The whole transaction throughout every stage of its progress has been a trick and a fallacy." In the Irish House of Commons Grattan and Curran opposed, with all their eloquence, the proposed system for "finally regulating" commerce between the two Kingdoms. The Government had a majority of only nineteen, and every division made it less, so that the spokesman for Pitt's measure was forced to move an adjournment, and Propositions, Resolutions, the Chancellor's Bill, the whole "system," crashed to pieces. Dublin celebrated, with grand illuminations, the Ministerial defeat.

Irish opposition had of course a motive very different from that of Lord Sackville. The Irish hated the measure because of its threat to their legislative independence; whereas Sackville's motive was rooted in pure Unionism. It was unmixed, although many chose to believe that he acted factiously, to spite the Government, and this notwithstanding his unqualified support, the year before, of the young Prime Minister, Pitt, his friendship with members of the Cabinet, and his evident lack of sympathy with the Coalition. He fought the Irish Propositions because he thought them bad for England and for Ireland. But this last of his public actions instantly exposed him to the kind of attacks that had so often been made on him: he died, as he had lived, libelled and lampooned. Caricatures were at once on sale in shop-windows ridiculing him as a creature of Lord Stormont's and Lord Derby's; the base personal motives of a disappointed and vindictive man were imputed. It is not probable that this disturbed him; he had grown used to it by that time, he knew what it was worth. Cumberland is most likely right when he says that Sackville, being so little used to receive justice, no longer expected it; and that "praise, if by chance he ever met it, seemed to take his senses by surprise." And he was, now, hardly vulnerable by dispraise or injustice: he was a dying man. Wraxall, who remarks on his "undiminished energies of mind," his "vivacity of temper unsubdued by age," notes also that "during the course of the debate he was so much indisposed as to be compelled more than once to leave the House." He continues:

I breakfasted with him on the following morning in

> Pall Mall, previous to his return to Stonelands, which was my last interview with him . . . Nor had I then any suspicion of apprehension of his approaching dissolution, though I remarked that his voice was feeble, and that he did not hold himself so upright as was his custom. There was something more serious and kind than ordinary in his manner of parting with me. Possibly he thought, though I made no such reflection, that we might not meet again. He had declined in strength for several weeks, owing to the effects of a medicine which he was habituated to take with a view of alleviating the pain occasioned by the disease of the stone. This medicine, a species of lixivium, unquestionably produced the effect intended; but by corroding the coats of the stomach it abbreviated, or rather terminated, his life.

In this diseased state, aggravated by effort and exertion, Lord Sackville went back to Stoneland Lodge; and there followed that remarkable interview which, for reasons never adequately explained, he was so anxious to have with Lord Mansfield. Cumberland, after Sackville had asked him "if Lord Mansfield was then at the Wells," went there and brought Lord Mansfield back:

> I was present [he writes] at their interview: Lord Sackville, just dismounted from his horse, came into the room where Lord Mansfield had waited a very few minutes: he staggered as he advanced to reach his hand to his respectable visitor; he drew his breath with palpitating quickness, and, if I remember rightly, never rode again. There was a death-like character in his countenance, that visibly affected and disturbed Lord Mansfield, in a manner that I did not quite expect, for *it had more of horror in it*[1] than a firm man ought to have shown, and less, perhaps, of other feelings, than a friend, invited to a meeting of that nature, must have discovered, had he not been frightened from his propriety.

[1] By the words put between asterisks Cumberland obviously means, "Lord Mansfield showed more horror."

> As soon as Lord Sackville had recovered his breath, his visitor remaining silent, he began by apologising for the trouble he had given him, and for the unpleasant spectacle he was conscious of exhibiting to him, in the condition he was now reduced to, "but my good Lord," he said, "though I ought not to have imposed upon you the painful ceremony of paying a last visit to a dying man, yet so great was my anxiety to return you my unfeigned thanks for all your goodness to me, all the kind protection you have shewn me through the course of my unprosperous life, that I could not know you were so near me, and not wish to assure you of the invariable respec[illegible]ve entertained for your character, and now, in the most serious manner, to solicit your forgiveness, if ever, in the fluctuations of politics, or the heats of party, I have appeared in your eyes, at any moment of my life, unjust to your great merits, or forgetful of your many favours."

Mansfield's protection of Sackville, his favours to him, were certainly never conspicuous. It would seem that Sackville, in this strange intense remorse, exaggerated or invented so as to make the *amende* for that ironical and deadly bitterness of his speech[1] against Mansfield as complete as it could be.

Cumberland continues:

> When I record this speech, I give it to the reader as correct: I do not trust to memory at this distance: I transcribe it . . . these memorials shall go forth respectable at least for their veracity; for I certainly cannot wish to present myself to the world in two such opposite and incoherent characters, as the writer of my own history and the hero of a fiction.
>
> Lord Mansfield made a reply perfectly becoming and highly satisfactory; he was far on in years, and not in sanguine health or in a strong state of nerves: there was no immediate reason to continue the discourse; Lord Sackville did not press for it: his visitor departed, and I staid with him. He made no other observation upon what

[1] Appendix, pp. 288-290.

had passed, than that it was extremely obliging in Lord Mansfield, and then turned to other subjects.

In the days that followed this interview, Sackville grew gradually weaker. Sir Francis Millman was called in, but could do no good. "The saponaceous medicines that had given him intervals of ease, and probably many years of existence, had now lost their efficacy, or by their efficacy, worn their conductors out." But this tall "muscular" man, capable of so much "bodily as well as mental endurance," could not die easily.

In him the vital principle was strong, and nature, which resisted dissolution, maintained at every outpost that defended life, a lingering agonising struggle. Through every stage of varied misery, "extremes by change more fierce," his fortitude remained unshaken, his senses perfect, and his mind never died till the last pulse was spent, and his heart stopped for ever.

In this period, intelligence arrived of the propositions being withdrawn in the Irish House of Commons; he had letters on the subject from several correspondents . . . none of which we thought fit to give him. I told him in as few words, and as clearly as I could, how the business passed, but requested he would simply hear it, and not argue upon it. "I am not sorry," he said, "that it has so happened; something might now be set on foot for the benefit of both countries. I wish I could live long enough to give my opinions in my place; I have formed my thoughts upon it, but it is too late for me to do any good; I hope it will fall into abler hands, and you forbid me to argue. I see you are angry with me for talking, and indeed it gives me pain. I have nothing to do in this life, but to obey and be silent."

From that moment he never spoke a word upon the subject.

There is, as in the Mansfield interview, a note of mystery when Cumberland, after saying that Sackville had "declared himself ready to receive the sacrament," adds that "in one instance only, he confessed it cost him a hard struggle. What that instance was, he needed not to explain to me, nor am I careful to explain to any. I trust, according to the infirmity of man's nature, he is rather to be honoured for having finally extinguished his resentment, than condemned for having fostered it too long. A Christian saint would have done it sooner; how many men would not have done it ever!" That Sackville told Cumberland some secrets, during these last weeks, about Minden and other matters, and that Cumberland never revealed them, appears clearly in the *Memoirs*.

He received the sacrament, the parish clergyman reading at his request the prayers for a communicant at the point of death. He wanted air and space—it was the twenty-sixth of August—and had "ordered all his bed curtains to be opened and the sashes thrown up." The clergyman and Cumberland were the only others present when he took communion.

Soon before his death, he asked for Cumberland, and, when Cumberland came, he took his hand and pressed it between his own. There may then have been in his mind remembrance of the Minden disaster, of the angry, contemptuous words of Colonel Sloper: "For God's sake repeat your orders to that man, that he may not pretend not to understand them—but you see the condition he is in!" "You see the situation in which I am," said Sackville, dying, "and I charge you to mind what I now say to you. I have seen much of life, and I have experienced its vicissitudes, but at no momentous period of my life," he added, veraciously, therefore paradoxically, "was my mind less collected than it is at present."

"I have done with this world," he said, "and what I have done in it, I have done for the best: I hope and trust I am prepared for the next. Tell me not of all that passes in health and pride of heart. These are the moments in which a man must be searched.

"You see me now in those moments, when no disguise will serve, and when the spirit of a man must be proved."

They are the words of a lover of truth, leaving a world of pretence and intrigue.

He was buried in the family vault at Withyham, near Stoneland.

APPENDIX

Chapter II, p. 14.

Letters from Queen Mary the Second of England to Lady Mary Forester. No date of year.

April the 15, Loo.

. . . I was extreamely delighted with all the news you write me, but as every thing is but nine days wonder so I hope strange marriages will now be laid asside to make room for some new . . . therefore I dare say not spake of such old things for fear of seaming as old fashioned as thay, yet the Bp of Oxford's death has not hapend so long ago but that I may say I hope he has seen his epitaph, or known himself to repent & disapoint the joy of the divin.

I don't love the wedings of people I am not aquainted with, yet I shall wish my self to see how you would behave yourself, I phansie that imployment will not become you unlesse you would put on a forehead cloath to which if you will ad a good large mufler so as to hide your face you might pass for an old lady & then you may give instructions with authority. I have bin but once in the litle wood where we played at hide and seek since I came hithere, the ill wethere will not sufer much walking, but I never go there without remembring how you ventured your great belly, big enough for you to brag of as long as you live, I believe there's anothere a comeing by this time, I expect if he be so you should be grown impudent enough to let me know it in your next leter for I never knew any body ashamed after one child, I am sory there are no wedings heer, when my maids marry I intend to act Lady —— exactly I warante they shall know the matrimony by heart & anssere to all with an audible voice, but for want of some such mater I must end my leter, do me the justice to belive I shall ever have all the esteem for you that you can desire.

Marie.

October the 29, Loo.

. . . Your grave Leter makes me think I am writing to that sober Lady M. Forester I once knew at the Hague, if you had allways bin seen at ye basset table makeing *al pios* and wanting an interpreter to ask for what you won you might have gone away allmost without being mist, but since you have been at Loo working walking and romping, you must not wonder if I should have bin very glad to have found you still at the Hague for all you deceived me so much as you really did when we play'd at hide and seek in ye litle wood, if I had then known your condition you had never got the reputation of as good a walker as myself, at least we had never pased ditches as we did togethere, but I am very glad it has suxceeded so well & hope you will get well into England & have a good deliverence wch I think is the best wish can be made you now & that I do very seriously, if there be anything in this leter that is not so 'tis because I think I know you so good humored & so litle formal yt you will bear with it, & I hope you have learnt to know me enough to belive tho' I can make no compliments that no body can wish you beter or will be more glad of an ocatione of shewing the esteem I have for you by actions as well as words then I.

February the 13, Hague.

By the leter I received I was overjoyed to find you the same Lady Mary Forester I knew at Loo, and before I say any more must assure you such leters will be allways very welcome to me for I am not changed in my humour tho' I am in my shape, but yt not by so good a reasson as you had when I saw you last, but meer fatt. I like this subject so litle I shall say no more upon it but wish you joy of your daughter. I was extreamly glad to hear you wear well brought to bed and hope before this you are well up, I own 'tis a shame for me to come so long after, but good wishes never come to late and that you will never want from me. The death of Mr. Wharton is indeed a sad tragedy, I wish poets had more witt then to fight, 'tis a cruel thing to hazard both body and soull for a jest. I find we women have the beter of ye men for that since railiery dos not cost us so deer. The charitable Scotch lady you spake of has mist of her amie since Lady —— to ye nessessity of endevoring a rape to satisfy his heroick passion, I belived his pride to have bin to great to stoop to such beast like inclinations, I thought his love had bin more refined and could not have gone beyond ogleing, tho' now I think on't his great eys may goggle about for fashion's sake, but he is to purblind to see at a distance or els his friends belye him. I find Lady —— adventure as plesant as 'tis extraordinary, if ever any on's fortune wear told ym yt thay should marry twice, 'twoud to some be a disapointment to find the prophecy so fullfiled. 'Twas well 'twas a cold seasson and the Lady's blood not very warme at this age, or else certainly too wedings at once might have put her honor into a feavor, but my Ld Cliford and his Lady are of an age that I belive may be left abed togethere so yt half her troble is saved there, and if the Lady be as fruitfull as her sister, tis likely Mr. Boyl who has bin heer lately won't be long ye youngest brothere. I am so far from finding faut with your leter that I shoud be very glad of many such, and I belive you write them so eassyly that thay will not give you much troble, if I may judg by myself I phansie much lesse than a formall leter, I am sure there is nothing I haet like that and you see I don't write one, neithere is it for fashion's sake but really that I desire you to belive I am treully your afectionat friend.

p. 18.

To his Grace the Lord Lieut. of Ireland &c., &c:
The humbe Petition of Margt. Woffington Spinster.

May it please your Grace, with all Submission
I humbly offer my Petition;
Let others, with as small pretentions,
Teize you for Places and for Pensions:
I scorn a Pension or a Place,
My sole design's upon your Grace;
The sum of my Petition's this,

I claim, my Lord, an anual kiss;
A Kiss, by Sacred Custom due
To me, and to be pay'd by You:
But, least you entertain a doubt,
I'll make my Title clearly out.

It was as near as I can fix,
the fourth of April forty six;
(With joy I recollect the Day)
As I was dressing for the Play,
In stept your Grace, and at your back,
Appear'd my trusty Guardian Mac.
A sudden Tremor shook my Frame,
Lord, how my colour went and came!
At length, to cut my Story short,
You kiss'd me, Sir, Heav'n bless you for't.

The majick touch my Spirits drew
Up to my Lips, and out they flew,
Such pain and pleasure mix'd, I vow,
I felt all o'er, I don't know how.
The Secret, when your Grace withdrew,
Like Lightning to the Green Room flew,
And plung'd the Women in the Spleen,
The men receiv'd me for their Queen,
And from that moment swore allegiance,
Nay, Rich himself was all obedience.

Since that, your Grace has never yet
Refus'd to pay the Annual Debt;
To prove these Facts, if you will have it,
Old Mac will make an Affidavit,
If Mac's rejected as a Fibber,
I must appeal to Colley Cibber.

By good Advice I hither came
To keep up my continual Claim;
The Duty's not confin'd to place,
But ev'ry where affects your Grace:
Which being Personal on you,

No Deputy, my Lord, can do.
But hold, say some, his Situation
Is chang'd, consider his high Station.

Can Station, or can Titles add
To Dorset, more that Dorset had?
Let others void of native Grace,
Derive faint honour from a Place,
His greatness to himself he owes,
Nor borrows Lustre, but bestows.

That's true, but still you answer wide,
How can he lay his State aside?
Then think betimes, can your weak Sight
Support that sudden Burst of Light?
Will you not sicken as you gaze,
Nay, haply perish in the blaze?
Remember Semele, who died
A fatal victim to her pride.

Glorious Example! how it fires me!
I burn, and the whole God inspires me!
My Bosom is to fear a Stranger
The Prize is more enhanc'd by Danger.
I'll bless the wound, when given by you,
And hug the Bolt, tho' Death ensue.

Chapter III, pp. 42 and 43.

Letters from Dean Swift to the Duke of Dorset: and other letters from and to Dean Swift.

Deanery-house,
Ap. 20th, 1732.

My Lord,

I return my most humble acknowledgments to your grace and my Lady Dutchess for your great condescention in inquiring after me at a time when you are so much taken up in crowds and ceremony. I can make no wishes for either of you but a good voyage without sickness or accidents. For your honor, fortune, favor, and the like I can onely pray for the continuance of them. That I so seldom troubled to say grace I am sure you will approve as a matter of conscience in me, not to disturb your hours which in the business of some months left so few for your own leisure and diversions.

I am with the truest respect, my Lord, your grace's most obedient, most obliged, and most humble servant,

Jonath. Swift.

Dublin,
Jan. 14th, 1734.

I am well assured that your Grace will soon receive severall representations of our affair relating to the University here from some very considerable persons. However, I could not refuse the application made to me by a very worthy gentleman who is a Fellow of the College and commissioned by some principal members of the Body to desire my poor good offices to your Grace because they believed you thought me an honest man and because they heard I had the honour to be known to you from your early youth. The matter of their request related wholly to a dreadful apprehension they lye under of Doctr Whitcomb's endeavour to procure a Dispensation for holding his Fellowship together with that Church preferment bestowed on him by your Grace. The person sent to me on this message gave me a written paper containing reasons why they hope your Grace will not be prevayled upon to grant such a Dispensation. I presume to send you as short an extract as I can of those reasons, because I may boldly assure your Grace that party or faction have not the least concern in the whole affair. And, as to myself, I am an entire stranger to the Doctor.

It is asserted that this preferment given to the Doctor consists of a very large parish in a very fine country, thirty miles from Dublin; that it abounds very much with papists and is consequently a most important cure requiring the Rector's residence, and perhaps that of some assistant which it can well afford, being worth near six hundred pounds a year.

That, as to such dispensations, they find in their college books but three or four instances since the Revolution, and these in cases very different from the present. Now, those few livings which obtained dispensations to be held with a Fellowship were sinecures of small value, not sufficient to induce a Fellow to leave his college, and in the body of those dispensations it is inserted as a reason for granting them, that they were such livings as could be no hindrance in the discharge of their duty as a Fellow.

That dispensations are very hurtful to such a Society, because they put a stop to the succession of Fellowships, and thereby give a check to that emulation, industry, and desire of improvement in learning which the hope of obtaining a Fellowship will probably incite men to.

That if the Dispensation now attempted should take place, it may be used as a precedent for the like practice hereafter, which will be very injurious to the Society by encouraging Fellows to apply for such Dispensations when they have interest to get preferment, by which the Senior Fellows will be settled in the College for life. And thus for want of succession by any other way than Death or Marriage all encouragements to the young and most deserving students will be wholly lost.

That a Junior Fellowship is of very small value and to obtain it requires long and close study, to which young students are onely encouraged by hopes of succeeding in a reasonable time to be one of the seven seniors, which hopes will be quite cut off when those seniors are perpetuated by Dispensations.

That the Fellows at their admittance into their Fellowships take a solemn oath never to accept of any Church preferment above a certain value and distance from Dublin as long as they continue Fellows, to which oath the accepting a Dispensation by Doctor Whitcomb is directly contrary in both particulars of value and distance.

That, at this time, there is a set of very hopefull young men who have been in long and close study to stand for the first vacant Fellowship who will be altogether discouraged and drop their endeavours in pursuit of learning by being disappointed in their hopes of Doctor Whitcomb's leaving the college, and opening a way for one of them to succeed in a Fellowship.

I shall onely trouble your Grace with a few remarks of my own upon this subject.

(Here follow the references, quoted in chapter III, to the material differences between Dublin Fellowships and those of Oxford and Cambridge, and to Lord George Sackville's education at " Dublin Colledge.")

This University is patron of some Church preferments which are offered to the severall Fellows according to their seniority, and so downwards to the lowest of them in holy orders.

I desire your Grace further to consider that by the want of Trade here, there is no encouragement for gentlemen to breed their sons to merchandise; thus not many great emoluments in Church and Law or the revenue fall to the share of persons born in Ireland; and consequently that the last resource of younger brothers is to the Church, where, if well befriended, they may possibly rise to some reasonable maintenance.

Your Grace will not want opportunityse during your continuance in this Government or afterwards by the favor you have with his Majesty to make Dr Whitcomb easyer in his prefermt by some addition and in such a manner that no person or Society can have the least pretence to complain of. And therefore I humbly beg your Grace, out of the high veneration I bear your person and virtues, that you will please to let Dr Whitcomb content himself a while with that rich preferment (one of the best in the kingdom) till it shall lye in your way further to promote him to his own content. If upon admittance to his fellowship he took the usuall oath never to accept a church living but with the two usuall limitations of distance and value to hold with his Fellowship, it will be thought hardly reconcileable to accept a Dispensation when the case is so vastly different . . .

I desire to present my most humble respects to my Lady Dutchess. Being loth to give your Grace further trouble I desire you will command my Lady E. Germain to let me know that you do not disapprove of this letter.

Dublin.

Mar. 22, 1734.

Your Grace must please to remember that I carryed you to see a Comedy of Terence acted by the scholars of Doctor Sheridan with which performance you were very well pleased. The Doctor is the most learned person I know in this kingdom, and the best school-master here in the memory of man, having an excellent tast in all parts of Literature. I prevayled on my Lord Carteret to make him one of his chaplains and to bestow him a good living, which the Doctor afterwards exchanged for another about seven miles from Dublin. But his health impairing by the air of this town, and being invited by the gentlemen of the County of Cavan, to accept the Free School of Cavan, which is endowed equal to his living, and he being born in the country, the present school-master, one Mr Knowles, is desirous to change his school for the Doctrs living of much the same value, called Dunboyn, in your Grace's gift. This affair hath been so long managing that it was in agitation before you left us, and I begged your consent for the change which, as a very reasonable request, not crossing any measures of your Grace, you were pleased to grant. All things have been long agreed, the Bp of Kilmore hath writ to you upon it. So your Lords Justices have done for some months past, but being a thing of no great consequence to the public state of the kingdom your secretaryes have forgot it.

In the meantime the poor Doctor hath given up his school in town to his great loss and hath parted with his house, continuing in uneasyness and suspense till your letter comes. Therefore I humbly beg you will please to order one of your secretaryes immediately to send the letter that will impower the Doctr and Knowles the schoolmaster to exchange stations. My letter is the worst part of the matter, because it will cost you three minutes to read, but the request is short and reasonable. I writ some days ago to my Lady E. Germain on the same purpose, but it is possible her ladyship might forget, which your Grace to my knowledge is not capable of.

Deanery House,

Dec. 30th, 1735.

Your Grace fairly owes me 110l. a year in the Church, which I thus prove. I desired you would bestow a preferment of 150l. per ann. on a certain Clergyman. Your answer was that I asked modestly; that you would not promise but would grant my request. However, that Clergyman, for want of good intelligence, or (as the cant word is here) being not an expert King-fisher, was forced to take up 40l. a year, and I shall never trouble your Grace any more in his behalf. But, however, by plain arithmetic it appears that 110l. remain. And this arrear I have assigned to one Mr. John Jackson, no less than a Cousin German of the GRATTANS. He is Vicar of Santry, hath a small estate near it, with two sons and as many daughters, all grown up. This gentleman hath layn severall years as a weight upon me, which I voluntarily took up on account of his virtue, piety, good sense, good nature, and modesty almost to a fault. Your Grace is now disposing the *débris* of two bishopricks, among which is the Deanery of Ferns with between 80l. and 100l. a year, which will make Mr. Jackson easyer, who besides his other good qualityes is as loyal as you could wish . . .

My Lord, I will, as a Divine, quote Scripture. Although the children's meat must not be given to dogs, yet the dogs eat the scraps that fall from the children's table. This is the second request I ever directly made to your Grace. Mr. Jackson is under a necessity of living on his small estate, part whereof is in his parish about four miles from hence, where he hath built a family house more expensive than he intended. He is a clergyman of long standing and of most unblemished character. But the misfortune is that he hath not one enemy, and consequently I have none to appeal to for the truth of what I say.

Pray, my Lord, be not allarmed at the word *Deanry*, nor imagine it a dignity like those we have in England, for, except three or four, the rest have neither Power nor Land as Deans and Chapters. It is usually a living made up of one or more parishes, some very poor, others better endowed, but all in tythes. Mr. Jackson cannot leave his present scituation and onely desires some very moderate addition, consistent with what he holds.

My Lord, I do not deceive your Grace when I say you will oblige great numbers of those who are most in your esteem here by conferring this favour or any other that will answer the same end.

Multa . . . veniet manus auxilio quae
Sit mihi, (nam multo plures sumus) ac veluti te
Judaei cogemus in hanc decedere turbam.

Deanry-House,
May 5th, 1736.

Although your Grace be very soon to leave us, and that considering my years and infirmityes, I cannot reasonably expect ever to see you again, yet since you have many preferments in the Church to dispose of, which it is understood will be done before your departure, I cannot but insist that you will please to think on Mr. Marmaduke Philips, who is the son of a considerable gentleman some years deceased, of a good estate, part whereof he made over in his life time to this son, but being an easy negligent man, careless in his expences, prevailed upon Mr. Marmaduke to restore this bit of an estate to pay some urgent debt, promising to give him a better, which he was never able to do, by which failure Mr. Philips, who was a younger son, was left wholly unprovided for. He is a loyal subject to K. George, perfectly well educated and an ornament to his profession. In his travels he had the good fortune to be known to an eminent commander, my Lady Dutchess's father, [General Colyear] on which account I cannot but think he hath some title to your Grace's favour, having been recommended by the same commander, the effects whereof he hath not yet found, which was neither your Grace's fault nor his own, but by the miserable condition of this unfortunate kingdom . . .

Mr. Phillips is at present in circumstances unworthy of his birth, his virtues and his learning. His last request to me was the meer result of his long despondency. It was to desire that your Grace would please to put him out of suspense by letting him know whether you had any favourable intentions towards him in the distribution of those Church preferments now in your gift, because he is much more uneasy under his present uncertainty than he could be by any determination.

I have not the least intention of putting your Grace to the trouble of answer to this letter, but leave the affair entirely in your own breast.

Deanery House,
Dublin.

Oct. 14th, 1736.

In a former letter to your Grace I taxed you with a debt of 110l. a year in Church livings, being by arithmetick an arrear of 150l. a year which your Grace was pleased to promise me for a friend, and of which I onely received 40l. a year. I often did myself the honor of being so bold (which is no great honor) of telling you that a very worthy clergyman had been so long a weight upon my shoulders to get him some addition, and that his circumstances were such that the addition I desired must consist with the small preferment he hath already. There is now a prebedary vacant which will answer my wish. One Mr. Williamson dyed about 36 hours ago. He was Treasurer of Christ-Church in Dublin. The place is worth between ninety and a hundred pounds a year and no more. The person whom I desire may have it is Mr. John Jackson, minister of Santry, three miles from Dublin, and a relation of the Grattans. He hath been often and earnestly recommended by me to your Grace, and your answers have been favorable. I have added severall times that you would by such a favor oblige this whole city and the most honest gentleman in the kingdom, and I hope such a consideration will have weight with you.

I do therefore hope and expect that your Grace will by the next post send an order to have a patent made out for Mr. John Jackson, Vicar of Santry, or Rector (which ever he be) to confer on him the Treasurership of Christ-Church, Dublin; and at the same time (which is now near the twentyth) this my chief regard is to your Grace's honor that you will reward a most deserving gentleman of this kingdom who had the misfortune to be born in it, with one mark of your favor. Otherwise I shall think it very hard that, as I am of some station and perhaps of some little distinction, besides the honor of being so long known to your Grace and family, I could never have the least power of prevayling on you to reward merit for which no party will repine.

To the reader of these letters it is not surprising that Dean Swift should have expressed himself about the Duke of Dorset as he did in writing to Lady Betty Germain:[1]

Jan. 29, 1736.

Madam,

I owe your ladyship the acknowledgment of a letter I have long received, relating to a request I made to my lord duke. I now dismiss you, madam, for ever from your office of being a go-between upon any affair I might have with his grace. I will never more trouble him, either with my visits or application. His business in this kingdom is to make himself easy: his lessons are all prescribed him from court; and he is sure, at a very cheap rate, to have a majority of most corrupt slaves and idiots at his devotion.

[1] See also pp. 269–278.

The happiness of this kingdom is of no more consequence to him, than it would be to the great Mogul; while the very few honest or moderate men of the Whig party, lament the choice he makes of persons for civil employments, or church preferments.

I will now repeat, for the last time, that I never made him a request out of any views of my own; but intirely after consulting his own honour, and the desires of all good men, who were as loyal as his grace could wish and had no other fault than that of modestly standing up for preserving some poor remainder in the constitution of church and state.

I had long experience, while I was in the world, of the difficulties that great men lay under, in the point of promises and employments: but a plain honest English farmer, when he invited his neighbours to a christening, if a friend happen to come late, will take care to lock up a scrap for him in the cupboard.

Henceforth I shall only grieve in silence, when I hear of employments disposed of to the discontent of his grace's best friends in this kingdom; and the rather, because I do not know a more agreeable person in conversation, one more easy, or of a better taste, with a greater variety of knowledge, than the duke of Dorset . . .

I am, with the truest respect,

Madam, your, &c.

Rather more than four years earlier, Lady Betty Germain had written to Dean Swift about the Duke:

Drayton,
Sept. 7, 1731.

. . . I hope I shall soon hear of the duke and duchess of Dorset's safe landing; and I do not question the people of Ireland's liking them as well as they deserve. I desire no better for them; for if you don't spoil him there, which I think he has too good sense to let happen, he is the most worthy, honest, good-natured, great-soul'd man that ever was born. As to the duchess, she is so reserved, that perhaps she may not be at first so much admired; but, upon knowledge, I will defy any body upon earth, with sense, judgment, and good nature, not only not to admire her, but must love and esteem her as much as I do, and every one else does, that is really acquainted with her. You know him a little; so, for his own sake, you must like him: and, till you are better acquainted with them both, I hope you will like them for mine . . . And I am, as I ever was, and hope I ever shall be, your most sincere friend, and faithful humble servant,

Betty Germain.

To William Pulteney Swift expressed much the same appreciation of and dissatisfaction with Dorset as he did to Lady Betty:

Dublin,
May 12, 1735.

Sir,

. . . I love the Duke of Dorset very well, having known him from his youth, and he hath treated me with great civility since he came into this government. It is true, his original principles, as well as his instructions, from your side the water, make him act the usual part in managing this nation, for which he must be excused: yet I wish he would a little more consider, that people here might have some small share in employments civil and ecclesiastic, wherein my lord Carteret acted a more popular part . . .

Pulteney, writing to Swift at the end of 1736, says that he is " inclined to believe " that the Duke " will go once more amongst you, and the rather since I am told he gave great satisfaction the last time he was with you." Lord Castledurrow, in a letter to Swift of January, 1736, sums up Dorset's qualities and defects fairly enough :

. . . Not any lord lieutenant has done us more honour in magnificence than our present viceroy . . . I have joy in hearing his virtues celebrated. I wish that he had gratified you in your request. Those he has done most for,

I dare affirm, love him least. It is pity there is any allay in so beneficent a temper; but, if a friend can be viewed with an impartial eye, faults he has none; and if any failings, they are grafted in a pusillanimity, which sinks him into complaisance for men who neither love nor esteem him, and has prevented him buoying up against their important threats, in raising his friends. He is a most amiable man, has many good qualities, and wants but one more to make him really a great man.

Chapter IV, p. 61.

From other letters of Diana, Countess of Glandore, to Mr. Gladwell.

1785; asking him to buy her two guineas' worth of foil,

> . . . for as work is my great amusement in the country I hate to be out of materials, you will get them at a little shop the corner of Leicester fields . . . the colours I want are 2 shades of red, a fine bright Lilac and some Gold, they are sold in sheets at 16 pence pr. sheet, get as many as you can for the money and have them pasted with paper at the back as that makes them better for the work, and then send them in covers to me as soon as you can.

Addressed to "Mr Gladwell at Lord George Germain's, Pall Mall, London," and dated merely " Thursday":

> I am quite provoked Gladwell at my frame being broke all to pieces, so that my beautiful work is stopped till I can get another. I should be much obliged to you if you would procure me one; I do not know whether the large frames I mean, for it must be of the kind that stands on the ground, the hand frames not being large enough, are to be had at Willerton's toy shop in Bond St. or of the Embroideress's, but wherever they are to be procured, I wish you would immediately get me one, made of common wood, as the Mahogany ones are too dear, and get it conveyed to Stoneland immediately, if you cannot pack it up and tie it behind the Chaise you must send it by the Stage, but do not lose any time about it.

From Killarney, 1787:

I see by the Papers that Charles is in England, if you behold him pray scold him for not writing to me or answering the long Letter I sent him by Genl Cunninghame, & tell him I take it seriously ill of him. He promised to send Ld Glandore one of the composition Busts of my poor Father & another of the King, pray remind him of it, as Ld G: wishes for them very much & would be flattered by his recollecting his promise.

1788:

. . . I am obliged therefore to enclose a Letter to you which I request you would send him [Lackington, whose address she had forgotten] by the very next Post; add a line also from yourself requesting him to be particularly careful about getting the best toned, best finished, and best looking Flute he can procure, which is what I wrote to him about, and as it is for a present I am anxious to have it superior to any that has been seen in this Country for you know of old that I am a *generous Princess*. I hope you got my last Letter apprizing you of my having drawn on you for fifty Pounds from Limerick.

From Nassau Street, 1789:

. . . Pray let me know what Lackington has done as my brother charges me never to employ him, if I do not wish to be cheated, as he is the greatest rogue alive. I was very sorry to get such an account of a man I have so long been used to think honest faithful & obliging, & it has also greatly excited my curiosity which I beg you would gratify—I wish Charles could be prevailed upon to make me a visit in Dublin which is so much an easier journey than a Kerry one, I long to see him & should be too happy if I could prevail on him to come over.

1792:

. . . My brother and I are again on the best terms possible, which contributes much to my happiness as I always loved him dearly . . .

Undated, from Ardfert:

. . . Mr. Herbert by dint of all sorts of roguery practised by the opposite party has lost his Election after a contest of 30 days, by three votes . . . I am very cross at this failure, as it has cost us no small sum supporting his Interest.

1800, from Dublin:

We arrived here for the meeting of Parlt. but as, notwithstanding the strongest Opposition that ever was known, I do believe the Union will at last be carried, I hope to see you in my native land next year.

From the Earl of Glandore to Mr. Gladwell. In a letter thanking him for sending venison; 1791, from St. James's Street, London:

But you forgot to send me the shoulder, which I told you, I liked the best of any part of the Doe.—I know it is the Keeper's perquisite, & when next you send any, be so good as to buy it from him, & place it to Lady G.'s account.

I am, with great regard, &c.

From the Earl of Glandore to Mr. Gladwell, 1807, from London:

Dear Gladwell

Allow me to put you in mind of your friends at Ardfert Abbey, to whom, a cask of your strong beer is always a most acceptable present . . .

. . . I had great pleasure in finding Lord Sackville so well—Indeed I had no expectation from the state of his health, the last time I was in England, to find him so much recovered . . .

I am, dear Gladwell, yours with great regard,

p. 73.

To Mr Pope,

Occasioned by reading Mr Addison's account of the greatest English Poets.

by Charles Earl of Middlesex at the age of eighteen.

If all who have invok'd the tuneful nine,
In Addison's majestic strains should shine,
Why then does Pope, ye bards, ye critics, tell,
Remain unsung, who sings himself so well?

Attend, great Bard, who canst alike inspire
With Waller's softness, or with Milton's fire,
Whilst I, the meanest of the muses' throng,
To thy just praises tune th'adventurous song.

Spenser ne'er sung so sweet a roundelay.
Sure once again Eliza glads our isle,
That thus propitiously the muses smile.

But cease, my Muse, thy awkward verse betrays
Thy want of skill, nor shows the poet's praise:
Cease then, & leave some abler bard to tell
How Pope in every strain can write, in every strain excel!

p. 75.

Copie exacte de la prière que Milord Jean Sackville fit en sortant de sa melancholie le 26 juillet 1759.

Grand Dieu depuis ma tendre jeunesse tu m'as visité d'une maladie terrible, ta sagesse est profonde, et ceux qui ont eu soin de mon education m'ont appris que tu châtie ceux que vous aimez, faites moi la grace de me faire sentir dans toute son étendue cet amour Paternel et comment je dois tourner à profit les avertissements que j'éprouve sans cesse, je suis plongé périodiquement dans une tristesse accablante, je suis rempli de crainte et de frayeur, je vois un Dieu irrité et tout puissant prêt à m'écraser de sa foudre pour la juste punition des folies sans nombre que je commets continuellement, les sombres nuages de la melancholie disparoissent, et je ne vois dans le Souverain Maître de l'Univers qu'un Dieu rempli de miséricorde et de bonté ; c'est alors qu'un mouvement vif des esprits animaux me font commetre mille désordres et folies qui ruinent ma santé et ternissent ma reputation, et me font passer bien amèrement les jours de tristesse qui ne manquent jamais d'arriver, aidez moi grand Dieu Père de miséricorde par votre grace speciale de modérer ce feu qui m'entraine et me devore, donnez moi le tems de reflection murement avant que j'agisse, que je ne viole pas vos saints commandements, adoucissez aussi, ces violentes attaques qui me jettent presque dans le désespoir le plus affreux, temperez les deux accez afin que je devienne un Etre raisonnable, que je me convertisse totallement, que je devienne un bon exemple aux autres, que je rétablisse entièrement ma reputation, que je raporte le tout à votre gloire et à l'édification de mon prochain, affermissez ma foi, inspirez moi ce que je dois croire, si quelques doutes s'élèvent dans mon esprit dissipez ces doutes par votre grace, douez moi d'une intelligence necessaire pour comprendre les mistères de la Religion, et faites moi agir toujours en honnette homme. Amen.

Five years earlier he had written to Lord George : " You enquire very kindly after my health. It is much as it was. I think if there be any difference the low fit does not last quite so long as it used to do, the good spirits two or three days longer ; but whilst it does last, the low fit is more violent and the high fit less so." About three months after, he writes of a " melancholy fit " which " has been a pretty severe one and lasted a long time."

p. 81.

From Lady Betty Germain's letters to Dean Swift.

Drayton,
Sept. 7, 1731.

To shew how strictly I obey your orders, I came from the duchess of Dorset's country-house to my own, where I have rid and walked as often as the weather permitted me. Nor am I very nice in that; for, if you remember, I was not bred up very tenderly, nor a fine lady; for which I acknowledge myself exceedingly obliged to my parents:

for had I that sort of education, I should not have been so easy and happy, as I thank God, I now am. As to the gout, indeed, I do derive it from my ancestors; but I may forgive even that, since it waited upon me no sooner; and especially since I see my elder and two younger brothers so terribly plagued with it; so that I am now the only wine-drinker in my family; and, upon my word, I am not increased in that since you first knew me.

I am sorry you are involved in law-suits; it is the thing on earth I most fear. I wish you had met with as complaisant an adversary as I did; for my lord Peterborow plagued Sir John all his life-time; but declared, if ever he gave the estate to me, he would have done with it; and accordingly has kept his word, like an honourable man.

. . . Your friend Biddy is just the same as she was; laughs sedately, and makes a joke slily. . . .

Feb. 23, 1730–1.

Now were you in vast hopes you should hear no more from me, I being slow in my motions; but don't flatter yourself; you began the correspondence, set my pen a going, and God knows when it will end; for I had it by inheritance from my father, ever to please myself when I could; and though I don't just take the turn my mother did of fasting and praying; yet to be sure that was her pleasure too, or else she would not have been so greedy of it. I don't care to deliver your message this great while to lieutenant Head, he having been dead these two years. And although he had, as you say, a head, I loved him very well; but however . . . I have ever had a natural antipathy to spirits.

I have not acquaintance enough with Mr. Pope, which I am sorry for, and expect you should come to England, in order to improve it. If it was the queen, and not the duke of Grafton, that picked out such a laureat, [Colley Cibber], she deserves his poetry in her praise.

. . . Mrs. Floyd is much yours; but dumber than ever, having a violent cold.

June 5, 1731.

I fancy you have comforted yourself a long time with the hopes of hearing no more; but you may return your thanks to a downright fit of the gout in my foot, and as painful a rheumatism that followed immediately after in my arm, which bound me to my good behaviour. So you may perceive I should make a sad nurse to Mr. Pope, who finds the effects of age, and a crazy carcase already. However, if it is true what I am informed, that you are coming here soon, I expect you should bring us together; and if he will bear me with patience, I shall hear him with pleasure . . .

Nov. 4, 1731.

. . . Since I came out of the country, my riding days are over; for I never was for your Hyde-Park courses, although my courage serves me very well at a hand-gallop in the country for six or seven miles, with one horseman, and a ragged lad, a labourer's boy, that is to be cloathed when he can run fast enough to keep up with my horse, who has yet only proved his dexterity by escaping from school. But my courage fails me for riding in town, where I should have the happiness to meet with plenty of your very pretty fellows, that manage their own horses to shew their art; or that think a postillion's cap, with a white frock, the most becoming dress. These and their grooms I am most bitterly afraid of; because, you must know, if my complaisant friend, your presbyterian house-keeper, can remember any thing like such days with me, that is a very good reason for me to remember that time is past; and your toupees would rejoice to see a horse throw an ancient gentlewoman.[1]

. . . I mightily approve of my duchess's [the Duchess of Dorset] being dressed in your manufacture; if your ladies will follow her example in all things, they cannot do amiss . . .

Why do you tantalize me? Let me see you in England again, if you dare; and choose your residence, summer or

[1] She was then fifty-one.

winter, St. James's-Square, or Drayton. I defy you in all shapes; be it dean of St. Patrick's governing England or Ireland, or politician Drapier. But my choice should be the parson in lady Betty's chamber. Make haste then, if you have a mind to oblige your ever sincere and hearty old friend.

Jan. 11, 1731–2.

It is well for Mr. Pope your letter came as it did, or else I had called for my coach, and was going to make a thorough search at his house; for that I was most positively assured that you were there in private, the duke of Dorset can tell you. *Non Credo* is all the Latin I know, and the most useful word upon all occasions to me. . . .

I met with your friend Mr. Pope the other day. He complains of not being well, and indeed looked ill. I fear that neither his wit or sense do arm him enough against being hurt by malice; and that he is too sensible of what fools say . . .

London,
May 13, 1732.

I am sorry my writing should inconvenience your eyes; but I fear, it is rather my stile, than my ink, that is so hard to be read: however, if I do not forget myself, I will enlarge my hand to give you the less trouble. Their graces [of Dorset] are at last arrived in perfect health, in spight of all their perils and dangers, though I must own, they were so long in their voyage, that they gave me an exceeding heart-ach; and, if that would be any hindrance, they shall never have my consent to go back to Ireland, but remain here, and be only king of Knowle and Drayton; and I do not think it would be worse for him, either in person or pocket. I dare say, he won't need a remembrancer's office for any thing you have spoke to him about; but however, I will not fail in the part you have set me.

I find you want a strict account of me, how I pass my time. But first I thank you for the nine hours out of the twenty-four you allowed me for sleeping; one or two of them I do willingly present you back again. As to quadrille, though I am, generally speaking, a constant attendant on it every day, yet I will most thankfully submit to your allowance of time; for when complaisance draws me on farther, it is with great yawnings, and a vast expence of my breath, in asking, Who plays? Who's called? and, What's trumps? If you can recollect any thing of my former way of life, such as it was, so it is. I never loved to have my hands idle; they were either full of work, or had a book; but as neither sort was the best, or most useful, so you will find forty years have done no more good to my head, than they have to my face . . . The duke and duchess are just come in, who both present their service to you, and will take it as a favour, if you will bestow any of your time that you can upon lord George.

Adieu, for the duchess, the countess of Suffolk, Mr. Charden, and I, are going to quadrille.

Drayton,
July 19, 1732.

. . . I am such a dunderhead, that I really do not know, what my sister Pen's age was . . . She was the next to me, but whether two or three years younger I have forgot; and what is more ridiculous, I do not know exactly my own, for my mother and nurse used to differ upon that notable point. And I am willing to be a young lady still, so will not allow myself to be more than forty-eight next birth-day; but if I make my letter any longer, perhaps you will wish I never had been born. So adieu, dear Dean.

London,
Nov. 7, 1732.

. . . But you say, you will say no more of courts for fear of growing angry; and indeed, I think you are so already, since you level all without knowing them, and seem to think, that none who belongs to a court can act right. I am sure this cannot be really and truly your sense, because it is unjust: and if it is, I shall suspect there is something of your old maxim in it, (which I ever admitted and found true) that you must have offended them, because you don't forgive. I have been about a fortnight from Knowle, and shall next Thursday go there again for about three weeks, where I shall be ready and willing to receive your commands, who am most faithfully and sincerely yours.

Feb. 8, 1732–3.

. . . As to your creed in politics, I will heartily and sincerely subscribe to it.——That I detest avarice in courts; corruption in ministers; schisms in religion; illiterate fawning betrayers of the church in mitres. But at the same time, I prodigiously want an infallible judge, to determine when it is really so: for as I have lived longer in the world, and seen many changes, I know those out of power and place always see the faults of those in, with dreadful large spectacles; and, I dare say, you know many instances of it in lord Orford's time. But the strongest in my memory is, Sir Robert Walpole being first pulled to pieces in the year 1720, because the South-Sea did not rise high enough; and since that, he has been to the full as well banged about, because it did rise too high. So experience has taught me, how wrong, unjust, and senseless party-factions are; therefore, I am determined never wholly to believe any side or party against the other; and to shew that I will not, as my friends are in and out of all sides, so my house receives them altogether; and those people meet here, that have, and would fight in any other place . . .

May 1, 1733.

. . . His grace of Dorset bids me present his humble service to you, and says, the rectory of Church-town is at Mr. Stafford Lightburn's service. As to the countess of Suffolk's affair in dispute, I cannot possibly (according to your own just rule) be angry, because I am in the right. It is you ought to be angry, and never forgive her, because you have been so much in the wrong, as to condemn her, without the shew of justice; and I wish with all my heart, as a judgment upon you, that you had seen her, as I did, when the news of your friend's [Gay's] death came ; for though you are a proud person, yet (give you, devil, your due) you are a sincere, good-natured, honest one . . . The excise you mention has caused great changes here . . . But if you did dislike it, why did you bestow such a costly funeral upon it, as to burn its bones on a sumptuous pile, like a Roman emperor ?

Adieu, my ever-honoured old friend, and do not let me see any more respects or ladyships from you.

Knowle,
July 9, 1733.

Now, says parson Swift ! What the devil makes this woman write to me with this filthy white ink ? I cannot read a word of it, without more trouble than her silly scribble is worth. Why, say I again: Ay, it is the women are always accused of having bad writing implements; but to my comfort be it spoke, this is his grace my lord lieutenant's ink. My bureau at London is so well furnished, that his grace and his secretary make so much use of it, that they are often obliged to give me half a crown, that I may not run out my estate in paper. It is very happy when a go-between pleases both sides, and I am very well pleased with my office; for his grace is delighted, that it was in his power to oblige you . . .

Feb. 13, 1734–5.

You are a fine gentleman indeed, to teach his grace of Dorset such saucy words; and we have quarrelled so much about it, that I don't know but I shall oblige him to meet me behind Montague-house [where duels were fought]. He says, it is some time ago that he commanded me to write to you, to assure you, he thought himself very much obliged to you for your letter, and that he takes it as a proof of your friendship and good-will to him. So far I own is true; he did humbly beg the favour of me to write you this a great while ago; but I understand he had something else more to say, so I cannot but own I have seen him pretty often since; but yet (at the times I could speak to him) my addle head constantly forgot to ask him what he had to say? So now he says he will do his own business, and write to you soon himself . . .

May 27, 1735.

. . . I did not know lady Kerry had the honour of being your mistress and favourite: however, I approve of your taste . . .

Now . . . I must recommend to you an affair, which has given me some small palpitations of the heart, which is, that you should not wrap up old shoes, or neglected sermons, in my letters; but that what of them have been spared from going towards making gin for the ladies, may henceforth be committed instantly to the flames[1]: for you being stigmatized with the name of a wit, Mr. Curll will rake to the dunghill for your correspondence . . .

London,
July 12, 1735.

I have not answered yours of the 15th of June so soon as I should; but the duke of Dorset had answered all yours ere your letter came to my hands. So I hope all causes of complaint are at an end, and that he has shewed himself, as he is, much your friend and humble servant, though he wears a garter, and had his original from Normandy, if heralds don't lie, or his granums did not play false; and whilst he is lord lieutenant, (which I heartily wish may not be much longer) I dare say, he will be very glad of any opportunity to do what you recommend to him . . . And now to the addition of writing the brave large hand you make me do for you, I have bruised my fingers prodigiously, and can say no more but adieu.

Feb. 10, 1735–6.

I am sorry to hear your complaints still of giddiness; as I was in hopes you would have mended like my purblind eyes, with old age. According to the custom of all old

[1] Swift replied: "When I was leaving England upon the queen's death, I burnt all the letters I could find, that I had received from ministers, for several years before. But, as to the letters I receive from your ladyship, I neither ever did, or ever will, burn any of them, take it as you please: for I never burn a letter that is entertaining, and consequently will give me new pleasure, when it is forgotten.

women, I must recommend to you a medicine, which is certainly a very innocent one, and they say does great good to that distemper, which is only wearing oil-cloath the breadth of your feet, and next to your skin. I have often found it do me good for the head-ach.

I don't know what offences the duke of Dorset's club, as you call them, commit in your eyes; but, to my apprehension, the parliament cannot but behave well, since they let him have such a quiet session. And as to all sorts of politics, they are now my utter aversion, and I will leave them to be discussed by those who have a better skill in them . . .

Nov. 2, 1736.

I am sorry to be so unlucky in my late errands between his grace and you; and he also is troubled at it, as the person you recommend is, indeed, what you say, a very worthy person; but Mr. Molloy, who was lord George's second tutor, had the promise of the next preferment, so he cannot put him by for this. I wish I was more fortunate in my undertakings; but I verily believe it is a common calamity to most men in power, that they are often, by necessity, prevented from obliging their friends; and many worthy people go unrewarded. Whether you call this a court answer, or not, I am very positively sure, he is heartily vexed when it is not in his power to oblige you. I have been very much out of order: and I am now literally setting out for Bath.[1] So adieu! dear Dean.

How little she was affected in spirit by ill health or by old age may be seen from a letter she wrote from Drayton House to Lord George Sackville in 1760:

. . . The Miss Coats Lady Temple brought is a mighty

[1] In January of the same year Dean Swift had written to Lady Betty Germain:

I am extremely afflicted to hear that your ladyship's want of health hath driven you to the Bath; the same cause hath hindered me from sooner acknowledging your letter. But, I am at a time of life to expect a great deal worse; for I have neither flesh nor spirits left; while you, madam, I hope, and believe, will enjoy many happy years, in employing those virtues which heaven bestowed on you, for the delight of your friends, the comfort of the distressed, and the universal esteem of all who are wise and virtuous.

pretty woman, well-bred and sensible; sings both French and English, though never learnt either French or to sing; has prodigious fine black eye-brows, and half her eyelashes are white, the other half black . . . she is a parson's daughter and but a small matter of fortune; I fancy Lord Temple makes pure work with his love to her, for that you know, comes of course. Considering what short dabs I have from Stoneland, this is a pretty long Drayton answer. So God bless you all.

Chapter V, p. 95.

Letter from Lord George Sackville to the Duke of Dorset, May 6th, 1748, from the Camp at Hellenrect.

My Lord, we thought to have march'd from hence five days agoe, but the accounts from Aix-la-Chapelle, I suppose made the Duke alter his resolution. As the preliminaries were signed, and a cessation of arms agreed to by the respective ministers at Aix, excepting what related to the siege of Maestricht, his Royal Highness thought proper to honour me with his commands to go to the Comte de Saxe in hopes of settling their affairs, and at the same time to endeavour to obtain an honourable capitulation for the garrison at Maestricht. Upon my arrival there I found M. de Saxe not at all pleased with what Mr. St. Severin had done, and said as he had no orders from his court to agree to a cessation of arms and hostilitys, he must wait the return of a courier before he could give a positive answer to what his Royal Highness propos'd, but at the same time he said that if he should have orders to conform himself to what had been settled at Aix, the scheme laid down by the Duke was void of objection and what he would readily agree to.

He then deliberated about my being admitted into Maestricht, and the granting an honourable capitulation to the garrison. This took a good deal of time, and Mr de Lowendal was sent for and consulted, but I was present. They then call'd in a third person and I retired, and in about half an hour he told me he consented to what His Royal

Highness desired, and I might go and deliver my despatches to the Governor. Dinner was then upon the table, and the Marechal before he sate down sent an aide-de-camp to stop all his batteries from firing, as an English Officer had business with the Governour. This was communicated to the town, but they had not the same politeness, so that it was near five o'clock before I could contrive to get in without the risk of being killed. At my arrival the batteries from the town were all silenc'd, and the Governor made excuses, and said the thing was misunderstood.

I deliver'd my despatches to him, and I never saw a man more perplex'd. He said the preliminarys were sign'd, and that the town must be taken, that honourable terms were offer'd to him, yet as he could still hold out for six or seven days, and that he had no order from the P. of Orange to capitulate, he was afraid he could not consent to it consistent with his honour and reputation. The Generals were then assembled and they all seem'd of opinion that they could not capitulate, and wanted eight or ten days to send to the Hague. I knew that proposal would have been rejected with scorn from the difficulty the Comte de Saxe had made in giving any terms as he was sure of having them prisoners of war in six or seven days. I then said that I thought that it could be no reflection upon their reputation if they capitulated to march out with military honours upon the day the cessation of arms and hostilities was proclaimed at the head of the respective armys. They all joined in with this proposition and desired I would set down and draw up the capitulations, which I did, and they sign'd it, and Major-General Graham was sent with me to the Marechal to see if he would consent to it. But he was far from approving of it, and talk'd of the cessation of arms as if he might not so soon have orders to comply with it. Much conversation follow'd in which the Duke says by my report to him that I did very right; and, when I almost despair'd of any good arising from it the Comte de Saxe consented to a cessation of arms for forty-eight hours, and permitted General Graham to go to the Prince of Orange for instructions. I do not doubt that upon his return the town will surrender even if hostilitys are not to cease, as there are twenty batallions in garrison there, and surely it is more material for us to save twenty batallions than to employ the French five or six days longer, in which time they might probably lose two thousand men. Upon my coming away, the Marechal told me he would not stand for five or six hours, so that I suppose he will wait the return of Graham from the P. of Orange, and indeed I had more expectations from the orders that might be sent in that time from Paris than in the probability of Graham's return.

The rest of this letter—in which Sackville writes of his riding blindfolded in the French camp—is cited in chapter V.

Chapter VI, pp. 102 *and* 121.

Letter from Lord George Sackville to Colonel Fitzroy.

Minden,
August 2, 1759.

Dear Sir,

The orders of yesterday, you may believe, affect me very sensibly. His Serene Highness has been pleased to judge, condemn, and censure me, without hearing me, in the most cruel and unprecedented manner; as he never asked me a single question in explanation of anything he might disapprove: and as he must have formed his opinion upon the report of others, it was still harder he would not give me an opportunity of first speaking to him upon the subject: but you know, even in more trifling matters, that hard blows are sometimes unexpectedly given. If any body has a right to say that I hesitated in obeying orders, it is you. I will relate what I know of that, and then appeal to you for the truth of it.

When you brought me orders to advance with the British cavalry, I was near the village of Halen, I think it is called, I mean that place which the Saxons burnt. I was there advanced by M. Malhorte's order, and no further, when you came to me. Ligonier followed almost instantly; he said, the whole cavalry was to advance. I was puzzled what to do, and begged the favour of you to carry me to the Duke, that I might ask an explanation of his orders: —but that no time might be lost, I sent Smith with orders to bring on the British cavalry, as they had a wood before they could advance, as you directed; and I reckoned, by the time I had seen his Serene Highness, I should find them forming beyond the wood. This proceeding of mine might possibly be wrong; but I am sure the service could not suffer, as no delay was occasioned by it. The duke then ordered me to leave some squadrons upon the right, which I did, and to advance the rest to support the infantry. This I declare I did, as fast as I imagined it was right in cavalry to march in line. I once halted my Lord Granby to complete my forming the whole. Upon his advancing the left before the right I again sent to him to stop:— he said, as the prince had ordered us to advance, he thought we should move forward. I then let him proceed at the rate he liked, and kept my right up with him as regularly as I could, 'till we got to the rear of the infantry and our batteries. We both halted together, and afterwards received no order, 'till that which was brought by Colonel Web and the Duke of Richmond, to extend in one line to the morass. It was accordingly executed; and then, instead of finding the enemy's cavalry to charge, as I expected, the battle was declared to be gained, and we were told to dismount our men.

This, I protest, is all I know of the matter, and I was never so surprised, as when I heard the prince was dissatisfied that the cavalry did not move sooner up to the infantry. It is not my business to ask, what the disposition originally was, or to find fault with anything. All I insist upon is, that I obeyed the orders I received, as punctually as I was able; and if it was to do over again, I do not think I would have executed them ten minutes sooner than I did, now I know the ground, and what was expected; but, indeed, we were above an hour too late, if it was the duke's intention to have made the cavalry pass before our infantry and artillery, and charge the enemy's line. I cannot think that was his meaning, as all the orders ran to sustain our infantry:—and it appears, that both Lord Granby and I understood we were at our posts, by our halting, when we got to the rear of our foot.

I hope I have stated impartially the part of this transaction that comes within your knowledge. If I have, I must beg you would declare it, so as I may make use of it in your absence: for it is impossible to sit silent under such reproach, when I am conscious of having done the best that was in my power.—For God's sake, let me see you, before you go to England.

I am, my dear Sir,
Your faithful humble servant,
George Sackville.

Letter from Colonel Fitzroy to Lord George Sackville.

Minden,
Aug. 3, 1759.

My Lord,

His Serene Highness, upon some report made to him by the Duke of Richmond of the situation of the enemy, sent Captain Ligonier and myself with orders for the British cavalry to advance. His Serene Highness was at this instant one or two brigades beyond the English infantry, towards the left. Upon my arrival on the right of the cavalry, I found Captain Ligonier with your Lordship. Notwithstanding, I declared his Serene Highness's orders to you; upon which you desired I would not be in a hurry: I made answer, that galloping had put me out of breath, which made me speak very quick. I then repeated the orders for the British cavalry to advance toward the left, and at the same time, mentioning the circumstances that occasioned the orders, added, "That it was a glorious opportunity for the English to distinguish themselves, and that your lordship, by leading them on, would gain immortal honour."

You yet expressed your surprise at the orders (*as they*

differed so materially from what Captain Ligonier had just brought), saying, it was impossible the duke could mean to break the line. My answer was, that I delivered his Serene Highness's orders, word for word as he gave them. Upon which you asked which way the cavalry was to march and who was to be their guide. I undertook to lead them towards the left, round the little wood on their left, as they were then drawn up, where they might be little exposed to the enemy's cannonade. Your lordship continued to think my orders neither clear nor exactly delivered; and, expressing your desire to see Prince Ferdinand, ordered me to lead you to him; which order I was obeying, when we met his Serene Highness. During this time I did not see the cavalry advance. Captain Smith, one of your aids-de-camp, once or twice made me repeat the orders I had before delivered to your lordship, and I hope he will do me the justice to say they were clear and exact. He went up to you whilst we were going to find the duke, as I imagine, being sensible of the clearness of my orders and the necessity of their being immediately obeyed. I heard your lordship give him some orders. What they were I cannot say: but he immediately rode back towards the cavalry.

Upon my joining the duke, I repeated to him the orders I had delivered to you; and, appealing to his Serene Highness to know whether they were the same he had honoured me with, I had the satisfaction to hear him declare they were very exact. His Serene Highness immediately asked where the cavalry was; and upon my making answer that Lord George did not understand the orders, but was coming to speak to his Serene Highness, he expressed his surprise strongly.

I hope your lordship will think I did nothing but my duty as aid-de-camp, in mentioning to his Serene Highness my orders being so much questioned by your lordship.

I am, &c., &c., &c.

Fitzroy.

Chapter VIII, p. 160.

One of the "Miscellaneous Letters ascribed to Junius."

To the Printer of the *Public Advertiser*.

July 30, 1768.

Sir,

It is not many months since you gave me an opportunity of demonstrating to the nation, so far as rational inference and probability could extend, that the hopes which some men seemed to entertain, or to profess at least, with regard to America, were without a shadow of foundation. They seemed to flatter themselves that the contest with the colonies, like a disagreeable question in the House of Commons, might be put off to a long day, and provided they could get rid of it for the present, they thought it beneath them to consult either their own reputation, or the true interests of their country . . . The conduct of the King's servants in relation to America, since the alteration in 1765, never had a reasonable argument to defend it, and the chapter of accidents which they implicitly relied on, has not produced a single casualty in their favour. At a crisis like this, Sir, I shall not be very solicitous about those idle forms of respect, which men in office think due to their characters and station; neither will I descend to a language beneath the importance of the subject I write on. When the fate of Great Britain is thrown upon the hazard of a die, by a weak, distracted, worthless ministry, an honest man will always express all the indignation he feels. This is not a moment for preserving forms, and the ministry must know that the language of reproach and contempt is now the universal language of the nation.

We find ourselves at last reduced to the dreadful alternative of either making war upon our colonies, or of suffering them to erect themselves into independent states. It is not that I hesitate now upon the choice we are to make. Everything must be hazarded. But what infamy, what punishment, do those men deserve, whose folly or whose treachery hath reduced us to this state, in which we can neither give up the cause without a certainty of ruin, nor maintain it without such a struggle as must shake the empire? If they had the most distant pretence for saying that the present conjuncture has arisen suddenly, that it was not foreseen and could not be provided for, we should only have reason to lament that our affairs were committed to such ignorance and blindness. But when they have had every notice that it was possible to receive, when the proceedings of the colonies have for a considerable time been not less notorious than alarming, what apology have they left? Upon what principle will they now defend themselves? From the first appearance of that rebellious spirit which has spread itself all over the colonies, the chief members of the present ministry were the declared advocates of America. Every art of palliation, of concealment, and even of justification, was made use of in favour of that country against Great Britain. Some there were who did not even scruple to pledge themselves for the future submission and loyalty of the colonies. Every principle of government was subverted, and such absurdities maintained as common sense should blush for. When all these arguments failed, and when the proceedings of the colonies gave the lie to every declaration made for them by their patrons here, still the ministry thought it not too late for further temporizing and delay. Even after the combination at Boston they would not suffer parliament to be informed of the real state of things in that province. They endeavoured to conceal the most atrocious circumstances, and what they could not conceal they justified . . .

If we look for their motives, we shall find them such as weak and interested men usually act upon. They were weak enough to hope that the crisis of Great Britain and America would be reserved for their successors in office, and they were determined to hazard even the ruin of their country, rather than furnish the man [George Grenville] whom they feared and hated with the melancholy triumph of having truly foretold the consequences of their own misconduct. But this, such as it is, the triumph of a heart that bleeds at every vein, they cannot deprive him of. They dreaded the acknowledgment of his superiority over them, and the loss of their own authority and credit, more than the rebellion of near half the empire against the supreme legislature. On this patriotic principle they exerted their utmost efforts to defer the decision of this great national cause till the last possible moment. The timidity, weakness, and distraction of government at home, gave spirits, strength, and union to the colonies, and the ministry seemed determined to wait for a declaration of war with our natural enemy, before they attempted to suppress the rebellion of our natural subjects. At last, however, they are compelled to take a resolution which ought to have been taken many months ago, and might then have been pursued with honour to themselves, and safety to this country. How they will support it is uncertain. A resolution adopted by a small majority in a divided council can be little depended on. It must want the first strength of union, and what effect can we hope for even from a vigorous measure, when the execution of it is committed, most probably, to one of the persons who have professed themselves the patrons of lenient moderate measures, until the very name of lenity and moderation became ridiculous? They will execute by halves; they will temporize and look out for expedients; they will increase the mischief; they will defer the stroke until we are actually involved in a war with France; and when they have made the game desperate, they will resign their places, to save themselves, if possible, from the resentment of their country.

. . . Yet, Sir, I hope there is still enough blood in our veins to make a noble stand even against these complicated mischiefs. Far from despairing of the republic, I know we have great resources left, if they are not lost or betrayed. A firm united administration, with the uniform direction of one man of wisdom and spirit, may yet preserve the state. It is impossible to conceal from ourselves that we are at this moment on the brink of a dreadful precipice;

the question is, whether we shall still submit to be guided by the hand which hath driven us to it, or whether we shall follow the patriot voice [George Grenville's] which has not ceased to warn us of our dangers, and which would still declare the way to safety and to honour.

Chapter IX, p. 188.

From the Letter of Junius of 9th April, 1771 :

This violent state of things cannot long continue. Either the laws and Constitution must be preserved by a dreadful appeal to the sword; or the people will grow weary of their condition, and surrender every thing into the King's hands, rather than submit to be trampled upon any longer by five hundred of their equals.

From Junius' *Dedication to the English Nation* :

I cannot doubt that you will unanimously assert the freedom of election, and vindicate your exclusive right to choose your representatives . . . The liberty of the press is the *palladium* of all the civil, political, and religious rights of an Englishman . . . I am persuaded you will not leave it to the choice of seven hundred persons, notoriously corrupted by the crown, whether seven millions of their equals shall be freemen or slaves . . . There are instances in the history of other countries, of a formal, deliberate, surrender of the public liberty into the hands of the sovereign.

Lord George Sackville, in the speech quoted from on p. 187, says that the crown may be corrupted by the legislature, not that the legislature is corrupted by the crown, but perhaps he means the same thing. Speaking in the Commons, he put it as he did : "A snare is now laid to involve our sovereign in the gulph of his corrupt administration."

These parallelisms, with others, some of which are less curious, were pointed out by George Coventry in his *Critical Enquiry into the Letters of Junius,* by which he seeks to prove that Junius was Lord George Sackville. The *Enquiry* is often of great interest and of considerable force, although sometimes Coventry is less than convincing; as when he quotes from a Miscellaneous Letter of August, 1768, (xxxiii), signed " Atticus " and of disputed authenticity, to show that Junius was selling Funds to buy landed estate when Lord George was doing the same thing. " Lord George," Coventry writes, " sold property out of the Funds at about this time; by a decree of the Court of Chancery, Bolebrook . . . was at this period ordered to be sold, and Lord George became the purchaser." But the dates do not square: Lord George bought Bolebrook in 1770, about two years after Junius had described himself as " safely landed." The interest of this Miscellaneous Letter of 1768 lies in a certain parallelism with a letter, not quoted by Coventry, from Lord George to General Irwin, of June, 1770. Lord George writes :

> I never mind the alarms of the City or the fluctuations of stocks. It is always the interest of some of the monied men to raise reports which affect the public credit.

Junius, or " Atticus," writes :

> . . . yet I never lay in wait to take advantage of a sudden fluctuation, much less would I make myself a bubble to bulls and bears, or a dupe to the pernicious arts practised in the alley.

Chapter XI, p. 247.

From Lord George Germain's speech upon Lord Mansfield, in the House of Commons, after Serjeant Glynn, on the 6th December, 1770, had moved for a Committee to enquire into the Administration of Criminal Justice :

> Consider, gentlemen, what will be the consequence of refusing this demand, this debt, which you owe to the anxious expectation of the public. The people, seeing his [Lord Mansfield's] avowed defenders so loth to bring him forth on the public stage, and to make him plead his cause before their tribunal, will naturally conclude, that he could not bear the light, because his deeds were evil; and that, therefore, you judged it advisable to screen him behind the curtain of a majority. Though his conduct

was never questioned in Parliament, mark how he is every day, and every hour, pointed out in print and conversation, as a perverter of the law, and an enemy of the constitution. No epithet is too bad for him. Now, he is the subtile Scroggs, now, the arbitrary Jeffries. All the records of our courts of law, and all the monuments of our lawyers, are ransacked, in order to find sufficiently odious names by which he may be christened. The libellous and virulent spirit of the times has overleaped all the barriers of law, order, and decorum. The judges are no longer revered, and the laws have lost all their salutary terrors. Juries will not convict petty delinquents, when they suspect grand criminals go unpunished. Hence libels and lampoons, audacious beyond the example of all other times; libels, in comparison of which, the *North Briton,* once deemed the *ne plus ultra* of sedition, is perfect innocence and simplicity. The sacred number forty-five, formerly the idol of the multitude, is eclipsed by the superior venom of every day's defamation: all its magical and talismanic powers are lost and absorbed in the general deluge of scandals which pours from the press.

When matters are thus circumstanced, when the judges in general, and Lord Mansfield in particular, are there hung out to public scorn and detestation, now that libellers receive no countenance from men high in power, and in the public esteem; what will be the consequence when it is publicly known, that they have been arraigned, and that their friends quashed the enquiry, which it was proposed to make upon their conduct? The consequence is more easily conceived than expressed. I foresee that the imps of the press, the sons of ink, and the printers' devils, will be all in motion, and they will spare you as little as they will the judges.

Like the two thieves in the Gospel, both will be hung up and gibetted, with the law crucified between you, for the entertainment of coffee-house politicians, greasy carmen, and porters, and barbers, in tippling houses and night cellars. I cannot help thinking that it is the wish of Lord

Mansfield himself to have his conduct examined, nay, I collect as much from the language of a gentleman, who may be supposed to know his sentiments. What foundation then is there for obstructing the enquiry? None at all. It is a pleasure to me to see my noble friend discovering such symptoms of conscious innocence. His ideas perfectly coincide with my own. I would never oppose the minutest scrutiny into my behaviour. However much condemned by the envy or malice of enemies, I would at least shew that I stood acquitted in my own mind. *Qui fugit judicium, ipso teste, reus est.*

The hostility to Lord Mansfield, relentless and destructive in its mask of irony, is unmistakable.

BIBLIOGRAPHY

ADAMS, RANDOLPH G. The Papers of Lord George Germain: a brief Description of the Stopford-Sackville Papers now in the William L. Clements Library. Ann Arbor, 1928.

ANDREWS, CHARLES M. Guide to the Materials for American History to 1783, in the Public Record Office of Great Britain. Vol. 1. The State Papers. Vol. 2. Departmental and Miscellaneous Papers. Washington, D.C., 1912-1914.

The Art of Preserving: a poem, humbly inscribed to the Confectioner-in-Chief of the B-t-sh C-v-l-y. London, 1759.

ASGILL, JOHN. An Apologetical Oration on an Extraordinary Occasion. London, 1760.

BARRINGTON, Sir JONAH. The Historic Memoirs of Ireland. 2 vols. London, 1833.

BOBADILL, Captain (pseud.). An Express from Capt. Bobadill, Who beat the French by standing still. London ?, 1759.

BRYMNER, DOUGLAS. Report on Canadian Archives, 1885. Ottawa, 1886. (Letters between Sir Guy Carleton and Lord George Germaine, 1777).

The Cabinet Conference, or Tears of Ministry. Present: The King, . . . Lord George Germaine, etc. London, 1779.

CAMPBELL, THOMAS. A Philosophical Survey of the South of Ireland. London, 1777.

Captain Parolles at Minden. London, 1778.

COKE, Lady MARY. The Letters and Journals of Lady Mary Coke; edited by the Hon. J. A. Horne. 4 vols. Edinburgh, 1889-1896.

A Consolatory Letter to a Noble Lord. London, 1760.

COVENTRY, GEORGE. A Critical Enquiry regarding the real Author of the Letters of Junius, proving them to have been written by the Lord Viscount Sackville: With the Memoirs of Lord Viscount Sackville. London, 1825.

CUMBERLAND, RICHARD. The Character of the late Lord Viscount Sackville. London, 1785.

—— Memoirs of Richard Cumberland. 2 vols. London, 1807.

(DAY, THOMAS). The Devoted Legions: a Poem addressed to Lord George Germain and the Commanders of the Forces against America. London, 1776.

A Dialogue between the Ghost of A—l B—, and the substance of a G—l. London, 1759 ?

DODINGTON, GEORGE BUBB. The Diary of the late George Bubb Dodington, Baron of Melcombe Regis. London, 1784.

(DOUGLAS, JOHN). The Conduct of a noble Lord at the Battle of Minden scrutinized. London, 1759.

—— The Conduct of a late noble Commander candidly considered; with a view to expose the misrepresentations of the anonymous author of the two Letters addressed to his L—p. London, 1760.

ENTICK, JOHN. The General History of the Late War. 5 vols. London, 1763. (Especially Vol. 4 for the Battle of Minden.)

An Epistle to the Right Honourable Lord G... G... London, 1778.

Further Animadversions on the conduct of a late noble commander at the battle of Thonhausen (Minden). By the author of Two Letters to a late noble Commander. London, 1759.

GRAY, THOMAS. The Letters of Thomas Gray; edited by Duncan C. Tovey. 3 vols. London, 1904–1912.

An Heroic Epistle to Viscount Sackville. London, 1783.

HISTORICAL MANUSCRIPTS COMMISSION. Report on the Manuscripts of Mrs. Stopford Sackville of Drayton House, Northamptonshire.

—— Report on the Manuscripts of the Marquess of Lothian preserved at Blickling Hall, Norfolk. London, 1905.

JAQUES, J. The History of Junius and his works: and a review of the controversy respecting the identity of Junius. London, 1843.

JUNIUS. The Letters of Junius. 2 vols. London, 1772.

KNOWLES, Sir LEE. Minden and the Seven Years War. London, 1914.

LENNOX, Lady SARAH. The Life and Letters of Lady Sarah Lennox, 1745-1826; edited by the Countess of Ilchester and Lord Stavordale. 2 vols. London, 1801.

A Letter from a P . . m . . e to a certain Great Man who was out of town on the first of August last. London, 1759.

A Letter to a late noble Commander of the British forces in Germany. London, 1759. 4th edition, revised . . . to which is added a postscript. London, 1759.

An Answer to a Letter to a late noble Commander of the British forces, in which the candor is proved to be affected, the facts untrue, the arguments delusive, and the design iniquitous. London, 1759.

A Second Letter to a late noble Commander of the British forces in Germany: In which the noble Commander's address to the public, his letter to Colonel Fitzroy . . . are considered. By the Author of the first Letter. London, 1759.

A Letter to Lord George Germaine; giving an account of the

Origin of the Dispute between Great Britain and her Colonies. London, 1778.

(MANNING, JOSEPH B.) Junius Unmasked; or Lord George Sackville proved to be Junius. Boston, Mass., 1828.

Matrimonial Overtures from an enamour'd Lady to Lord G— G-rm-ne. London, 1778.

MAXWELL, CONSTANTIA. Dublin under the Georges, 1714-1830. London, 1936.

A Parallel . . . between the Case of the late Honourable Admiral John Byng and that of the Right Honourable Lord George Sackville. By a Captain of a Man of War. London, 1759.

Remarks on a Pamphlet lately published, entitled, the Conduct of a Noble Lord scrutinized. By an Officer. London, 1759.

The Rolliad. London, 1791.

SACKVILLE, Lord GEORGE. Correspondance du Lord George Germain, avec les Generaux Clinton, Cornwallis et les Amiraux dans la station de l'Amérique, avec plusieurs lettres interceptées du General Washington, du Marquis de la Fayette et de M. de Barras. Traduit de l'Anglois sur les originaux publiés par ordre de la Chambre des Pairs. Berne, 1782.

—— His Lordship's Apology. (Together with the Orders issued on the 2nd August by Ferdinand, Duke of Brunswick-Luneburg). London, 1759.

—— Lord George Sackville's Vindication of himself, in a Letter to Colonel Fitzroy . . . with Colonel Fitzroy's answer; and of the declaration of Captain Smith, one of the Aids de Camp to Lord George. Containing a full . . . account of . . . Lord George Sackville's conduct . . . at the battle of Thornhausen. London, 1759.

—— A short Address from Lord George Sackville to the Public. London, 1759.

—— A Parallel between the two Trials of Lord George Sackville, lately published, pointing out their difference . . .: in which the evidence and matter are compared and canvassed. London, 1760.

—— The Proceedings of a Court Martial, appointed to enquire into the Conduct of a certain Great Man, together with their remarkable sentence. London, 1759.

—— The Proceedings of a Court Martial taken on the Spot. London, 1760.

—— The Proceedings of a General Court-Martial held on the 7th–24th March; and 25th March–5th April, 1760 . . . upon the trial of Lord George Sackville. London, 1760.

—— The Sentence of the Court Martial on Lord George Sackville, 1760. (Cuttings from a newspaper . . . with MS. title-page).

—— The Trial of . . . Lord George Sackville, at a Court-Martial, for an enquiry into his Conduct, being charged with disobedience of orders, while he commanded the British horse in Germany. Together with his Lordship's defence. London, 1760.

SACKVILLE, N. V. STOPFORD. Drayton House, Northamptonshire. Privately printed, 1939.

SACKVILLE-WEST, VICTORIA. Knole and the Sackvilles. London, 1922.

A Seasonable Antidote against the Poison of Popular Censure: being the substance of a Letter from a noble Lord to a Member of Parliament relative to the case of a certain Right Honourable General. 1759.

SHELBURNE, Lord. The Life of William, Earl of Shelburne, aft. first Marquess of Lansdowne; with extracts from his Papers and Correspondence. By Lord Edmond Fitzmaurice. 3 vols. London, 1875.

(SLOPER, Colonel ROBERT). Colonel S—r's Letter to the S(ecretar)y at War, with Genuine Affidavits . . . relating to the Evidence given on the Tryal of L—d G—e S—e. Dublin, 1760.

STEVENS, B. F., and BROWN, H. J. A Report on the American Manuscripts in the Royal Institution of Great Britain. 4 vols. London, 1904-1909.

STOCKDALE, PERCIVAL. Memoirs of the Life and Writings of the Rev. Percival Stockdale. 2 vols. London, 1809.

SWIFT, JONATHAN. The Correspondence of Jonathan Swift; edited by F. Elrington Ball. 6 vols. London, 1910-1914.

T——E, J. A Letter to the Marquis of Granby. London, 1759.

THEMISTOCLES. A Reply to Sir H. Clinton's narrative, wherein his numerous errors are pointed out and the conduct of Lord Cornwallis fully vindicated . . . including the whole of the correspondence between Lord George Germain, Sir H. Clinton, etc. London, 1783.

The True Cause of a certain G——l Officer's conduct on the first of August last. London, 1759.

A Vindication of the Right Honourable Lord George Sackville. London, 1759.

Yet one Vindication more of the Conduct of L*** G***** S********. London, 1759.

WALPOLE, HORACE. The Letters of Horace Walpole; edited by P. Toynbee. 16 vols. London, 1903-1905. Supplement to the Letters. 2 vols. London, 1918.

—— The Yale Edition of Horace Walpole's Correspondence; edited by W. S. Lewis. London, 1937–

WHITTON, Lieut.-Col. F. E. Service Trials and Tragedies. London, 1930.

WRAXALL, Sir NATHANIEL. The Historical and the Posthumous Memoirs of Sir Nathaniel Wraxall; edited with notes and additional chapters from the author's unpublished MS. by Henry B. Wheatley. 5 vols. London, 1884.

INDEX